The New Graduate Experience

The New Graduate Experience

Post-MLS Residency Programs and Early Career Librarianship

Megan Zoe Perez and Cindy Ann Gruwell, Editors

LIBRARIES UNLIMITED

AN IMPRINT OF ABC-CLIO, LLC
Santa Barbara, California • Denver, Colorado • Oxford, England

Copyright 2011 by ABC-CLIO, LLC

All rights reserved. No part of this publication may be reproduced, stored in a retrieval system, or transmitted, in any form or by any means, electronic, mechanical, photocopying, recording, or otherwise, except for the inclusion of brief quotations in a review, or reproducibles, which may be copied for classroom and educational programs only, without prior permission in writing from the publisher.

Library of Congress Cataloging-in-Publication Data

The New Graduate Experience : Post-MLS Residency Programs and Early Career Librarianship /
   Megan Zoe Perez and Cindy Ann Gruwell, editors.
     p. cm
  Includes bibliographical references and index.
   ISBN 978-1-59158-886-3 (pbk. : acid-free paper) 1. Academic librarians--In-service training--United States. 2. Academic librarians--Recruiting--United States. 3. Interns (Library science)--United States. 4. Academic librarians--In-service training--Canada. 5. Academic librarians--Recruiting--Canada. 6. Interns (Library science)--Canada. I. Perez, Megan Zoe. II. Gruwell, Cindy A. (Cindy Ann)
  Z682.4.C63N49   2011
  020.71'55--dc22   2010044946

ISBN: 978-1-59158-886-3

15 14 13 12 11   1 2 3 4 5

This book is also available on the World Wide Web as an eBook.
Visit www.abc-clio.com for details.

Libraries Unlimited
An Imprint of ABC-CLIO, LLC

ABC-CLIO, LLC
130 Cremona Drive, P.O. Box 1911
Santa Barbara, California 93116-1911

This book is printed on acid-free paper ∞
Manufactured in the United States of America

Contents

Foreword xi
Acknowledgments xii
Introduction xv

Chapter 1: Early Career Development and Post-Master's Residency Programs 1
Julie Brewer
What Is a Residency Program? 1
What Is the Rationale for Residency Programs? 2
What Do Residency Programs Look Like? 2
    Size 3
    Specialization 3
    Diversity Focus 3
What Is the Role of Diversity in Residency Programs? 4
How Does Recruitment Differ for Residency Programs? 5
How Are Work Assignments Developed? 6
What Types of Professional Development Opportunities Are Most Valuable? 7
How Are Residency Programs Administered, Supported, and Assessed? 8
What Is the Career Impact of Participation in a Residency Experience? 8
How Do Residency Programs Benefit Libraries? 9
Summary 10
References 10

**Chapter 2: Design and Implementation of a New Residency Program
at Towson University** 11
*Carrie Bertling Disclafani, Carissa Tomlinson, Patricia A. MacDonald, and
Deborah A. Nolan*
Background 11
Program Design 13
    Position Description 13
    Departmental Rotations 14
    Mentoring 15
Recruitment 15
    Advertising the Position 15
    Diversity Recruitment 18
    Telephone Interviews 18
    On-Site Interviews 20
Implementation 24
    Supervision 24
    Supportive Environment 25
    ACRL's Support for Residency Programs 26
Conclusion 26
References 27

Chapter 3: Evaluation of Three Canadian Academic Library Internship Programs 31
Kathleen De Long
- Background 32
- Problem Statement 32
- Literature Review...33
- Research Design..34
- Procedures 35
  - Methodology 35
  - Data Quality..36
- Limitations 36
- Findings 37
  - Survey Participant Profiles 37
  - Participation in Program Work and Training Activities and Perceived Importance to Career Development 38
  - Participation in Specialized Program Components: Perceived Importance to Career Path and Development 38
  - Career Path and Development Path of Former Interns 39
  - Recruitment into Permanent Positions in University Libraries.......40
  - Retention in University Libraries 41
  - Perception of Intern Program Experience as a Factor in Career Path and Development 42
- Discussion 43
- Conclusion 44
- Notes 44
- References 45

Chapter 4: The Development of the University of Louisville Libraries' Diversity Residency Program 47
Latisha Reynolds, Caroline Daniels, John Chenault, and Toccara Porter
- Original Internship Program 48
- Library Residency Experience (John Chenault)......................49
- From Internship to Residency 50
- Creating a Formal Residency Program 51
- Initial Design 52
- Seeking and Preparing for the Resident...........................53
- Library Residency Experience (Toccara Porter) 55
- Conclusion 58
- References 59

Chapter 5: Program Management: Challenges and Lessons Learned: Purdue University.....61
Scott Mandernack and Rebecca A. Richardson
- Assessment of Need...62
- Program Design 62
  - Year One 63
  - Year Two 64
- Program Management 65
  - Participant Roles and Expectations 65
  - Program Assessment 65

Program Strengths 66
    Program Flexibility: Rotation Schedules..66
    Professional Development..67
    Mentoring Program 68
Lessons Learned..71
Conclusion 72
References 72

Chapter 6: Come Be a Part of the University of Tennessee Libraries' Diversity Librarian Residency Program 81
Jill Keally
Introduction 81
Program Development 82
    Purpose 82
    Recruitment, Selection, Orientation 82
Program Components...83
    Job Assignments 83
    Professional Development..84
    Mentoring 84
    Creative Accomplishments 84
Program Changes 85
How Is the Program Unique?...86
Lessons Learned..87
Thoughts for the Future 87
    Expectations for the Residents 87
    Expectations for the Library 88
Conclusion 88
References 89

Chapter 7: Nurse Preceptors and the Academic Library: A Model for New Graduate Development 91
Megan Zoe Perez
Introduction 91
Why Study Nursing? 92
Preceptors: Then and Now 94
Preceptor Models 95
    Short-Term or Administrative Approaches 95
    Long-Term or Institutional Approaches 98
Summary and Review 103
Methodology and Research Questions...103
    Results 104
Findings/Discussion..107
Recommendations 108
Summary and Conclusion 110
References 110

Chapter 8: The Residents Report 115
   Megan Zoe Perez, Damon Campbell, and Shantrie Collins
   Introduction 115
   Methodology 116
   Findings and Results 117
      Residents' Demographic Information 118
      Degree Information 119
      Program Information 120
   Significant Findings and Discussion 128
   Limitations 130
   Future Research 131
   Conclusion 131
   References 132

**Chapter 9: Communities of Practice in Residency Programs: The NCSU Libraries
   Fellows Program** 137
   Hyun-Duck Chung and Sandra Littletree
   The Social Context of Learning at Work 137
   At Work in the NCSU Libraries Fellows Program 138
   Social Context of Residency Programs 139
      The Cohort Effect 140
      Second-Year and Former Fellows 141
   Conclusion 142
   References 142

**Chapter 10: An Intern's Path to Academic Library Administration: 10 Years after
   the Open Letter** 145
   Jon E. Cawthorne
   Introduction 145
   Planning and Self-Assessment 147
   Embracing Calculated Risks 148
   Practicing Shared Leadership 150
   Becoming the Mentor 150
   Conclusion 151
   Selected Readings 152
   References 153

**Chapter 11: Fires, Floods, and Residents, Oh My! The Residency Program at the
   University of New Mexico Libraries** 155
   Sarah Stohr
   A Little Background 155
   Getting the Job 156
   Organization of the Residency Program 158
   Orientation 158
   Reference and Instruction 159
   Resident Projects 160
   Unique Support System 161
   Unique Opportunities 161

Conclusion 163
Reference 163

Chapter 12: Meeting the Challenge: My Experience in a Residency Program (and a little advice for others who might be thinking about entering one). 165
Asher Jackson

Chapter 13: A Law Library Residency: My Georgetown University Law Library Experience 171
Yasmin Morais
Introduction 171
My Road to Librarianship 172
The Job Search 172
The Residency 173
Year One: Learning the Ropes 174
    The Reference Rotation 174
    Cataloging Department Rotation 175
    Special Collections 176
Year Two: Toward Proficiency 176
    Collection Services 176
    My Final Project 177
    Professional Development Support 177
    The Residency Search Committee and My Own Job Search 177
Conclusion 178
References 179

Chapter 14: Recollections of a Resident 181
    Patrick José Dawson
References 187

Chapter 15: Welcome to the Ozarks: The Making of Crickets, Mandalas, and Monographs 189
    Megan Zoe Perez
In Pursuit of the Degree 190
After the Degree 192
    The Job Search 193
    The University of Arkansas Librarian-In-Residence Program 194
Summary 201
Conclusion 203
References 204

Conclusion 205
Index 209
About the Editors and Contributors 217

Foreword

Raquel Von Cogell

As coeditor of *Diversity in Libraries: Academic Residency Programs*, published a decade ago, it gives me great pleasure to introduce to you *The New Graduate Experience: Post-MLS Residency Programs and Early Career Librarianship* by Megan Perez and Cindy Gruwell. Although a significant thrust of the work focuses on library residency programs and librarians who participated in them, this is not *Diversity in Libraries: Part II*. It is more. Not only does it continue the conversation about academic residency programs and the role they play in increasing diversity in the academy, it also moves the conversation forward.

Whereas *Diversity in Libraries* focused exclusively on the personal narratives of residency librarians and program managers, *The New Graduate Experience* goes a step further and includes results of several research studies in addition to the narratives presented. One study focuses on residency programs in three Canadian universities. Kathleen De Long answers the question of whether internship programs, as they are known in Canada, have been successful in recruiting new librarians into Canadian academic libraries at the conclusion of the internship. The results of another study are presented in the chapter, "The Residents Report," which focuses on former resident librarians who participated in programs in the United States and Canada from 1983 through 2008.

In Chapter 1 of this valuable work, Julie Brewer, a prolific writer on residency programs, provides an excellent overview for understanding the role of residencies, both historically and at present. She outlines strategies for establishing and developing successful post-MLS opportunities. *The New Graduate Experience* also documents the history and development of residencies at Towson University, the University of Louisville, Purdue University, and the University of Tennessee, the programs of which were all started or significantly revamped in the 2000s.

The resident voices in this text are varied and diverse. They come from a range of backgrounds and discuss, with candor, their residency experience. These poignant stories tell of the rewards, benefits, lessons learned, and challenges of participating in a residency position. They offer perspective on what it means to be a resident librarian and how the opportunity eased their entrée into the profession.

Perhaps one of the most insightful aspects of this book is the chapter, "Nurse Preceptors and the Academic Library: A Model for New Graduate Development." Mr. Perez pens a provocative review of a model in the nursing field (the preceptor model), and how it can inform the design of library residency programs to include principles and practices that have proven successful in developing new nurses. Library leaders and managers of residency programs should take note and consider how this model might enhance the development of new librarians. It is also in this chapter that Mr. Perez shares results of a survey of residency program mangers and offers a comparative analysis of results from an earlier study.

To the library school student reading this book and considering a residency program but is reticent, you need not be. Residency programs are a viable path to a long-lasting library career, as evidenced by the current positions held by Jon E. Cawthorne and Patrick José Dawson, an interim dean and dean, respectively, in academic libraries. They write about their current positions here in *The New Graduate Experience* and were also contributors to *Diversity in Libraries*. Among the other contributors to *Diversity in Libraries*, one is now head of the Social Work Library at Columbia University; another is head of Access Services at the University of Maryland; and still another has a PhD in higher education and is on the faculty at a school of library and information science.

Many others continue to work as reference and government documents librarians, subject specialists, and coordinators for instruction and public services in college and research libraries. *Diversity in Libraries* alums are active professionally, and some are serving at high levels in professional associations. For example, Courtney L. Young is one of the American Library Association's eight executive board members. She is serving a three-year term slated to end in 2012. Seeking a temporary job straight out of library school may seem unconventional or even irrational to some, but be assured that residency programs can be a springboard to a fulfilling career.

What does the future portend for academic residency programs? At this juncture, it remains to be seen, but we can be sure that residency programs should remain an integral part of library recruitment efforts and should continue to serve as a catalyst for developing and cultivating a whole new generation of library professionals. Mr. Perez and Ms. Gruwell are to be commended for compiling and editing a work that will speak to library leaders, residency program managers and advocates, and, most especially, to prospective residency librarians.

Acknowledgments

There are a great many people I would like to recognize for helping bring this work to fruition. Dr. Kathy Wisser, my master's paper advisor and friend always said, "If a work is important to you, it's worth doing." I miss working with you, Kath. To my colleagues at Cornell, Mister Engle and Skipp, who set me on the path; Raquel who first introduced me to Cindy who, in turn, served as mentor and guide for me, and who reeled me in when I spun out of control; my colleagues from SILS (how I miss you); my friends from the different walks of my life; my virtual friends from, believe it or not, Facebook, who tracked our progress and sent encouraging words on a regular basis; the University of Arkansas Libraries for providing me with release time for this project; all the individual contributors of this work (it wasn't easy, but we did it); my role model, Julie Brewer; and Jim Ovitt, who tolerated my shortcomings during stormy times. May you rest in peace.

—Megan Z. Perez

I would like to thank my husband Michael for his never-ending patience and support, my children Kevin and Jada for inspiring me to hang in there, and numerous others who have provided words of encouragement along the way. To our authors, I say kudos! Thank you for taking this adventure with us. A special thank you goes out to my colleagues at St. Cloud State University, several of whom have acted as sounding boards for many of my ideas. And finally Megan Perez, who not only talks the talk, but always walks the walk. In many respects you made this easy . . . thank you.

—Cindy A. Gruwell

Introduction

Megan Z. Perez

In 1980, Margo Trumpeter and Paul Gherman wrote an often overlooked, and almost forgotten, article on library training programs (Trumpeter and Gherman 1980). In it, the authors trace the development of post-MLS training programs all the way back from the 1938 Tennessee Valley Authority libraries to the Orleans Parish Medical Society Library in 1941 and into the post-WWII-era programs of the National Library of Medicine, the Library of Congress, and Ohio State University. Two things of note stand out in that article: 1) the studies undertaken on library training programs recommended the use of a special committee comprised of members of the American Library Association's (ALA) Board of Education for Librarianship, representatives of the library schools, and representatives from the participating institutions to set minimum requirements for a library training program and 2) the authors insistence that a post-master's training program on a national scale would have an impact on new talent in the field, revitalize institutions, and greatly affect the profession as a whole.

In August 2009, nearly three decades later, a group of residents and program coordinators petitioned the Association of College and Research Libraries (ACRL) to form an interest group with the hope of continuing these points: centralizing and coordinating the efforts of national associations, host institutions, and library educators to create industry standards and best-practice guidelines; and developing new graduates into competent professionals who will have an immediate impact on their host institution—and on the future direction of librarianship. In November of that year, their petition was approved, and the first interest group within ACRL was formed: ACRL's Residency Interest Group (ACRL RIG).

According to its website, the ACRL RIG is "an assembly of library residents, residency program coordinators, library deans, administrators, diversity officers, and human resources professionals from over 20 different library systems across the country." It is also a network of individuals who have come together to share their knowledge and expertise with one another and, at the same time, help solve problems across organizational boundaries with those who may face similar challenges. This group was founded to encourage interested parties to share more broadly their experience regarding residency programs and capture their expertise while making it both available and accessible for future residents and coordinators. In addition, the group considers itself a resource for newer members, particularly library school students, who may be considering a residency program upon graduation.

It is assumed that this monograph will appeal to residency program coordinators and future residents. It is our hope, however, that it will have a wider audience and appeal to library and information science practitioners interested in recruitment and retention issues, library and information science faculty who teach courses on diversity and recruitment strategies, and researchers of library diversity history. We also hope human resources managers, personnel officers, residency program coordinators in other professions, and researchers from other industries interested in cross-disciplinary applications of staff development models may all benefit from the contents that lay within.

Diversity in Libraries: Academic Residency Programs (Cogell and Gruwell 2001) was the first major work to highlight and focus on residency programs and residents' experiences in depth. The work in hand is, to some degree, modeled after it in terms of arrangement and content, but it is also designed as an extension of some of the purposes of the ACRL RIG. This book was written to capture the expertise of residency program managers and coordinators. Additionally, it was written to provide students of library and information science with a series of firsthand accounts of the experience of being a resident.

However, it should not be considered an updated or revised edition of *Diversity in Libraries,* and it does not, in any way, supersede it. This book is meant to be a companion to the former so that the two, together, make available a history of library residency programs spanning multiple decades. Scholars, historians, researchers, and other interested parties will do well to consider the breadth of information contained in both texts as a set rather than as individual works.

It is important to note that there are at least two chapters of this work that mark a distinct departure from *Diversity in Libraries*. First, one chapter is dedicated to nurse "preceptors" (see Chapter 7). Loosely speaking, a preceptor is an experienced nurse who is responsible for the training and development of new nurses and recent graduates of nursing school. Although the authors of an ACRL white paper titled "Recruitment, Retention, & Restructuring" (ACRL 2002) incorporated a discussion of nursing shortage and supply issues in its discussion of recruitment and retention in librarianship, the model of the preceptor in the design of library residency programs is currently absent from the library and information science literature. For this reason, an entire chapter describing nurse preceptors as prototypical models is presented here to the academic library community as an example of unique mentorship opportunities. In it, a series of different models are discussed. Survey findings are presented, as are implications for our profession and recommendations for future action.

The other unique chapter is "The Residents Report" (Chapter 8). This chapter is designed to fill a gap in the literature regarding resident demographics as well as data regarding the programs' host institutions. The annual Association of Library and Information Science Education's (ALISE) Statistical Report provides data on "Post-Master's" program participants, but these participants are current students who are working toward a post-master's degree or certificate in library and information science, not recently graduated students who already hold a master's degree in library science (ALISE 2005). The participants are not residents as we understand them here. Other statistical reports issued by the Census Bureau, the National Center for Science Education, the Association of Research Libraries, and the ALA provide information regarding library and information science professionals, but they do not separate out data regarding post-MLS residents from other kinds of degree-holding librarians.

Although some programs may keep demographic data on their residents, both past and present, it is not widely accessible. If it does exist, it is not aggregated between programs nor is it collected for analysis across institutional boundaries. Regarding the alumni of the schools themselves, there are some schools of library and information science—for example, the University of Michigan's School of Information—that annually collect and publish demographic data of their graduates' postdegree employment as a group, but their publication does not contain information regarding residents specifically.

In early 2009, therefore, the authors of "The Residents Report" set out to fill the gap left by these publications and distributed a survey to both current and former residents. Its purpose was threefold: 1) to better inform residency program managers of the design of other residency programs; 2) to assist institutions and administrators who are considering implementing a residency program in the future; and 3) to provide library and information science students who are interested in learning more about residency programs with a centralized source of information. The authors hope this data will prove valuable and that its collection will be a regular occurrence in the future.

The chapter also serves as a point of transition in this book away from discussions of program management and toward the testimonials of the residents themselves. These are the firsthand experiences of librarians who participated in a residency program and agreed to share their experiences. From their testimonials, several themes emerge. First, many of these residents were participants in scholarship and recruitment programs such as the ALA's Spectrum Scholars program and the Association of Research Libraries' Initiative to Recruit a Diverse Workforce (IRDW). A substantial number of these residents were also participants in the Minnesota Institute for Early Career Librarians from Traditionally Underrepresented Groups (Minnesota Institute), a weeklong training institute for librarians from traditionally underrepresented groups with less than three years of postgraduate experience.

Second, in addition to participation in these external programs of support, the residents describe the value of internal support strategies—namely, mentoring, socialization, and an extensive orientation to the host library. Third, significant emotional components are described, such as feelings of isolation and the importance of having a "home" department with regular supervision to help ground and stabilize the residents while they rotate through other departments.

As you navigate the various chapters contained herein and read about the experiences of both program managers and program participants, we would like to encourage you to do two things. Familiarize yourself with the development and administration of these different models of library residency programs. You may ask yourself questions such as: Would this model work for my institution? Would one model work better than another? Can a hybrid be imagined that would fit even better? Can a residency program be repurposed to facilitate the fulfillment of a larger strategic goal, such as planning for diversity and succession? Do we currently have the labor, skill, and knowledge to work with a program of this sort? Where would the resources come from, and who would manage the program?

As you consider these questions, bear in mind specific challenges to recruitment programs that bear considerable attention, particularly with regard to the future of residency programs. Let us not forget that at this point in time there remains the long-awaited specter of baby boomer retirements. Previous retirement prognostications of a looming retirement crisis from the first decade of the twenty-first century proved premature. Baby boomers did not exit the workforce in mass numbers before 2010 as had been anticipated. In fact, after updating its 2002 study of librarian retirements using more currently available Census data, the ALA determined retirements would be delayed and would peak in 2015–2019 rather than 2010–2014 as previously believed (Davis and Hall 2007; Lynch, Tordello, and Godfrey 2005). This delay can be attributed to the following factors outlined by the Bureau of Labor Statistics (Toossi 2007).

First, older individuals are living healthier and longer lives than previous generations of the same respective age. Second, older individuals now have higher levels of formal education than their counterparts in the past had. Third, there has been a shift away from pension plans to contribution plans. Pension plans encourage early retirement, whereas contribution plans are unconcerned with retirement age. Professional librarians, therefore, have an economic incentive to continue to work and contribute to their retirement plans. Fourth, Social Security laws changed in 2000. These new laws delayed the eligibility age for full retirement benefits for certain birth dates and also decreased the benefits for early retirement. Fifth, health insurance costs have increased, and, simultaneously, health benefits have decreased, encouraging seasoned (senior) workers to remain in the workforce after retirement eligibility to maintain their benefits.

These factors are subject to change due to a variety of circumstances, including alterations in legal and corporate policy and economic fluctuations. Social Security laws, for example, can be amended with the election of new legislative representatives. That being said, there is one immutable constant regarding the issue of retirement, and it is critical to understanding the complexity of the problem at hand: the workforce will continue to age.

According to Toossi (2007), the oldest of the boomers will turn 65 in 2011. Although the civilian labor workforce is projected to increase by nearly 13 million by 2016, it will continue to age. Between 2006 and 2016, the population of workers 55 and older is expected to grow by 46.7%, a growth that is more than five times the projected growth for the aggregate labor force (Toossi 2007). At the same time, the pool of workers aged 35 to 44 is expected to shrink almost 10% by 2013 (DeLong 2004), and the number of workers aged 16 to 24 is projected to reduce by 7% by 2016 (Toossi 2007). This is the same pool of workers our profession, among others, is depending on to succeed those librarians who will be retiring.

Retirements will undoubtedly leave the workforce short of personnel, but it will also leave the workforce short of different kinds of knowledge[1] (DeLong 2004) and experience needed to perform effectively in the workplace. The loss of these types of knowledge is therefore another challenge recruiters and recruitment programs will face because of the natural attrition of the workforce. Time is the critical element here. The acquisition and transfer of each of these types of knowledge takes place through instruction, practice, and the guidance of a more experienced, knowledgeable practitioner over an extended period of time. In our profession, independent practice is not given to new librarians with less than two years of post-MLS work experience. Upon graduation, they are expected to move up the ranks slowly from grade to grade or classification to classification as was the case with previous generations.

Historically, many industries have had low rates of voluntary attrition. Employees did not leave for positions elsewhere. Although this is not currently the case in some countries such as Japan, for example, it is of concern for Western, industrialized countries (DeLong 2004). There is a growing acknowledgment that younger employees have qualitatively different values than their baby boomer predecessors (Lancaster and Stillman 2002). This difference in values implicates a gap in generational approaches to work and presents another challenge to recruiters.

This value difference may very well result in increased rates of attrition among younger workers new to their chosen profession. "The culture shift for us is we've got to challenge people more when they come in, and give them more opportunity to grow . . . our culture says 'Wait, your turn will come.' So people leave to apply their skills somewhere else" (DeLong 2004, 37–38). A common refrain DeLong heard during his interviews with executives and staffing directors is: "We don't have 20 years for them to learn from experience" (DeLong 2004, 95).

According to DeLong (2004), the new goal of recruiters, therefore, is to transfer leadership and management skills more quickly to a new generation of workers who will replace those who are retiring, and to accelerate the acquisition of the four types (see note 1, next page) of knowledge that would otherwise be hidden or lost through natural attrition of the workforce. It is prudent to consider that residency programs can be used more efficiently to accomplish precisely this: to shorten the time to competence in anticipation of a loss of knowledge, skill, and expertise.

In addition to the retirement issue that faces the entire workforce population across professional boundaries, there are two other recruitment challenges facing academic libraries in particular. First, academic settings may be less inviting for young professionals, particularly in rural areas. Many young professionals are single, educated, independent, and geographically mobile. Attracting such professionals to these locations, especially new professionals from traditionally underrepresented groups, may prove particularly difficult. In an increasingly diverse, global market, these professionals may be unwilling to join a profession that remains a predominantly white culture in the twenty-first century. A 2008–2009 ARL survey found that 85.9% of professional staff in U.S. ARL libraries are Caucasian/White (Bland 2009).

The second, and perhaps the more important, challenge specific to academic libraries is the tendency of recruitment initiatives to work in isolation and apart from retention and retirement strategies. Residency programs, for example, are useful recruiting tools but are not integrated into a larger approach to resolving human resources challenges. Acquiring new talent is tantamount, but equally critical is the need to keep that talent in house, that is, to retain that talent to sustain current workforce needs and future workforce capabilities.

Retirements, at both high and low volumes, leave behind vacant spaces not only in terms of a human body or a salary line but in terms of skills and knowledge. The loss of one employee due to natural attrition creates the need for an "experienced hire" to replace the expertise lost to retirement. The pool of experienced hires prepared to step into positions of management, supervision, and administration will continue to shrink unless our recruitment efforts are matched and synchronized by our retention efforts—a synchronization necessitated by the inevitable retirement of the baby boomer generation.

What, then, can be done to address the aging of the workforce on one hand, the challenges of recruitment on the other, and the loss of knowledge, skills, and expertise that is somewhere in between the two? How do residency programs help resolve any of these issues, if they do at all? Perhaps these are questions that can be addressed by the ACRL Residency Interest Group in the near future. At the time of this book's publication, it is a small, relatively new group, but as more programs emerge and as more new graduates complete a residency program, it can grow into a larger, more influential group. It can help provide standards for programs and offer solutions to broader problems all of us will face in the near future, including the exodus of the baby boomer generation; the absence of a workforce large enough, young enough, and sufficiently experienced to fill the gap left by this exodus; and the specific cultural issues complicating recruitment initiatives.

NOTES

1. Social knowledge is the set of relationships one has with other individuals or groups. It is the network of other people and other experts that can serve to orient one to a setting or a profession. Organizational knowledge is the awareness of policies, procedures, and formal rules that describe expectations of workplace behavior and performance. This is slightly different from cultural knowledge, which is a set of informal norms, mores, folkways, and customs that guide behavior in the workplace. These are the underlying, unwritten rules that reflect a common understanding of how things are done and how one can comport oneself in a manner that is acceptable to the rest of the members of the organization. The last of these, technical or functional knowledge, is skill based. It is the ability to perform a given task or execute a specific function. Cataloging a book, for example, is an activity that requires a certain amount of technical skill, and to some extent, it can be learned through self-study, training, and education.

REFERENCES

ACRL Ad Hoc Task Force on Recruitment & Retention Issues. 2002. *Recruitment, retention, & restructuring: Human resources in academic libraries.* Chicago: Association of College and Research Libraries.

Association for Library and Information Science Education (ALISE). 2005. *Library and information science education statistical report.* State College: ALISE.

Bland, L. 2009. ARL salary survey highlights. *Research Library Issues* 266:17–20.

Cogell, R. V., and C. A. Gruwell. 2001. *Diversity in libraries: Academic residency programs.* Westport, CT: Greenwood.

Davis, D. M., and T. D. Hall. 2007. Diversity counts! American Library Association. http://www.ala.org/ala/aboutala/offices/diversity/diversitycounts/diversitycounts_rev0.pdf

DeLong, D. 2004. *Lost knowledge: Confronting the threat of an aging workforce.* New York: Oxford University Press.

Lancaster, L. C., and D. Stillman. 2002. *When generations collide.* New York: Harper Business.

Lynch, M. J., Tordello, S., and T. Godfrey. 2005. Retirement & recruitment: A deeper look. *American Libraries* 36:26.

Toossi, M. 2007. Labor force projections to 2016: More workers in their golden years. *Monthly Labor Review* 130:33–52.

Trumpeter, M. C., and P. Gherman. 1980. A post-master's degree internship program. *Library Journal* 105:1366–1369.

Chapter 1

Early Career Development and Post-Master's Residency Programs

Julie Brewer

Post-master's residency programs have served to support and shape the professional development of early career librarians for more than forty years. Since the National Library of Medicine started the first post-master's professional development initiative in 1966, many other academic and research libraries have implemented similar programs. What we've learned over the past several decades as these programs have evolved and adapted to changing needs can help in understanding how best to support early career development for librarians throughout the profession.

WHAT IS A RESIDENCY PROGRAM?

A library residency is a post-master's work experience program that provides entry-level employment and professional development for early career librarians. Residencies are short-term experiences that typically last one to three years. The Association for Library and Information Science Education (ALISE) guidelines for residency programs distinguish post-master's residency programs from pre-professional internships and midcareer fellowship programs (ALISE 1996).

Today there are approximately two dozen active programs employing thirty to thirty-five residents. More than fifty academic and research libraries have hosted residency programs for early-career librarians at one time or another. Although new programs continue to be started and the overall number of programs increases, changes in the economy, institutional leadership, and organizational priorities affect the availability of programs. Although post-master's residency programs have existed for many years, they are not well known beyond the community of large research libraries, in part because inconsistencies in program titles make it difficult to identify programs with similar objectives.

WHAT IS THE RATIONALE FOR RESIDENCY PROGRAMS?

Residency programs are found almost exclusively in academic and research libraries, and predominately in very large institutions where the nature of work is highly specialized, the organizational structure is often complex, and the academic culture favors multiple advanced degrees from prestigious institutions, along with a scholarly record of research, publication, and professional service. Employment opportunities for early-career librarians, especially those with minimal pre-professional experience, are limited in this environment.

The few early-career librarians who find entry-level positions in research libraries face other challenges. New graduates, especially those who complete their master and undergraduate degrees back-to-back, have a significant experience gap to overcome in transitioning from theory to practice. The development needs and support required for new librarians differ from those more advanced in their careers. In organizations that predominately comprise mid- and late-career librarians, the needs and interests of early-career librarians may not be well understood or addressed. Early-career librarians can become isolated in such complex and specialized environments.

Yet new librarians can contribute significantly to large library organizations. Their recent experience as students and ability to connect with the library's primary constituency is valuable. Their enthusiasm, new ideas, and flexibility with emerging technologies are greatly needed. Progressive library managers value the diversity and career-span balance new librarians bring to the organization. Library human resource specialists often challenge search committees to broaden their view of job qualifications to remove unintended, yet traditional institutional and cultural employment barriers. Establishing residency programs is a deliberate strategy to recruit talented new librarians and support their professional development.

Concern for the recruitment and retention of early-career librarians continues to increase, with the perception that younger generations bring different expectations and attributes to the workplace, along with the need to attract and retain talented employees that can advance the strategic changes coming to academic libraries. The Association of College and Research Libraries' Recruitment and Retention wiki includes a section, "Working with and Retaining New Librarians," that features perspectives from new librarians and retention strategies for libraries. Residency programs already incorporate many of the retention strategies proposed on the wiki, such as mentoring and professional development, and have assisted many new librarians launch successful careers in academic and research libraries.

WHAT DO RESIDENCY PROGRAMS LOOK LIKE?

Residency programs are generally categorized by size, degree of specialization, and diversity focus. These dimensions provide a quick way to distinguish programs from each other. However, in reality, these dimensions can be very fluid. The structure of residency programs changes over time to reflect the immediate organizational goals of the host institutions.

Size

Size of a residency program can be the most dynamic characteristic. The number of new librarians hired at one institution in each recruitment cycle can vary year to year. The early residency programs at the University of Illinois—Chicago and the University of Michigan hired multiple new librarians at one time. The University of Illinois—Chicago hired as many as sixteen new residents in 2000. These programs intentionally recruited and developed cohorts of new librarians to learn and work together. The University of Michigan program structured group interviews as part of the selection process to assess how well prospective residents would potentially interact in a cohort experience.

Smaller programs at Ohio State University, Notre Dame, and the University of Minnesota hire one new librarian during each recruitment cycle. Some new graduates feel a smaller residency offers a more personal experience. These solo residencies can simulate some of the benefits of the cohort model by retaining past residents on staff, as well as intentionally hiring early-career librarians in other professional positions.

Most of these programs last for one or two years. Programs such as the Rutgers University Libraries Internship/Residency Program, on the other hand, require a three-year commitment: two to complete the master's degree and one additional year as a resident upon graduation. The program is administered by both the Library and Information Science Department and the Rutgers University Libraries. It is, however, like many of the latter programs listed. It allows for only one participant at a time over the duration of three years. There is not a cohort of interns or residents each year, nor are there overlapping participants as is sometimes the case with other programs.

Specialization

Degree of specialization varies considerably from program to program. Some programs provide work assignments across a number of functional areas in the library. Residents in these programs get a broad exposure to many areas of work. Generalist residency programs are well suited to new librarians with minimal pre-professional experience or who want to explore new areas of librarianship. This exposure provides an excellent foundation for career advancement.

Specialized residency programs focus work assignments in one academic discipline or functional work area. The Eskind Biomedical Library at Vanderbilt University offers a health sciences library residency. The Georgetown University Law Library residency program focuses on early career development in law library librarianship. The Eugene Garfield Residency in Science Librarianship at the University of Pennsylvania supports the growing information literacy program in the School of Engineering and Applied Science. Residency programs at the University of Iowa, University of New Mexico, and Marquette University focus on reference and instructional services. Larger programs, such as the Libraries Fellows Program at North Carolina State University, hire multiple residents at one time, each in a different area of specialization. Residency assignments in these specialized programs resemble more traditional entry-level positions.

Diversity Focus

The University of Delaware and University of California Santa Barbara were the first institutions to implement library residency programs with minority recruitment as a programmatic focus in the mid-1980s (see Chapter 14). Recruiting new librarians from underrepresented groups has since become a priority for most all academic and research libraries. However, how this priority is communicated and achieved in relation to library residency programs varies widely. Programs such as the Mary P. Key Diversity Residency at Ohio State University Libraries and the Pauline A. Young Residency at the University of Delaware Library emphasize the diversity focus of the residency by honoring librarians from underrepresented groups who have made significant contributions to the profession.

WHAT IS THE ROLE OF DIVERSITY IN RESIDENCY PROGRAMS?

Programs vary in the extent to which residents are expected to be a diversity specialist, or "the" diversity specialist. Some programs set no expectations. Others seek residents to coordinate diversity outreach and training (see Chapter 15). Unless residents already have substantial subject expertise and program management skills, expecting a new librarian to coordinate diversity responsibilities may not be realistic. Understanding what the diversity expectations are and how they are communicated is critical to managing the diversity function of a residency program.

When diversity residency programs were first implemented, library leaders from underrepresented groups expressed some concern. They worried that minority recruitment residencies would stigmatize new librarians as underprepared or not full-fledged librarians. Some questioned why academic libraries would not hire new librarians from underrepresented groups into regular, continuing positions.

Residents in some of the first diversity programs also had concerns. Before residency programs began implementing standard terminology, "minority intern" was a common title. Some residents expressed discomfort with the term "minority." Although proud of their racial or ethnic heritage, they felt the term drew more attention to their race or ethnicity than their professional attributes (Brewer 1997). Residents also disliked the term "intern" because it implied they were students, not yet professional. New librarians are proud of their professional credentials and do not like being treated as students. Modifying program names has reduced some of the confusion, as has the success of the many residents who have since advanced in their careers.

Yet race still matters in academic librarianship. In a recent study of African American female leaders in libraries of the Association of Research Libraries (ARL), respondents acknowledged that racial stereotyping continues. When asked what it takes to become a library leader, they noted that in addition to the knowledge, skills, and attributes required of all library leaders, it is also necessary to have the ability to overcome negative stereotypes and navigate hostile work environments (Epps 2008). Leading predominately white organizations as a member of an underrepresented group requires finesse. Residency programs preparing early-career librarians for leadership positions can assist residents in navigating these organizational dynamics with mentoring and effective library diversity programs.

Managing diversity effectively in a large organization requires a sophisticated type of leadership. Simply increasing the number of librarians from underrepresented groups is not enough. It requires a comprehensive diversity plan and staff members who interact effectively with others from diverse backgrounds. A comprehensive diversity plan outlines recruitment and retention strategies, addresses staff diversity training, and provides organizational systems for assessing and addressing concerns of all library staff. A library residency should be one part of the larger library diversity program and should allow residents, like other members of the staff, the opportunity to choose how involved they wish to be in diversity initiatives.

Residencies are most successful in organizations that value diversity. Institutions that design learning opportunities on the basis of cultural competencies and organizational development based on assessment demonstrate a strong commitment to diversity. The new ACRL cultural competency guidelines can be used to help library staff understand specific actions, behaviors, and attitudes that contribute to a positive work environment. The ClimateQual survey instrument developed by ARL, in collaboration with several member libraries, assesses organization climate and diversity. Research data from the ClimateQual assessments demonstrate that climate for diversity improves the way an organization operates (Lowry and Hanges 2008). Prospective employees notice a positive organizational climate and strong diversity program. These organizational characteristics affect the recruitment and retention of librarians from diverse backgrounds in all library positions. Having a residency program is a visible way for a library to communicate its commitment to diversity.

HOW DOES RECRUITMENT DIFFER FOR RESIDENCY PROGRAMS?

Recruitment for residency positions follows the same employment policies and procedures as other professional librarian positions. Yet residency positions differ from traditional entry-level professional library positions in that they are intentionally designed as professional development experiences, often with generalist responsibilities that do not require specialized technical skills and experience. Beyond the required master's degree, application criteria tend to emphasize transferable skills and experiences such as interpersonal relations, communication abilities, initiative, and leadership experience that will support the intensive learning environment of a residency program.

Requiring a written statement of interest is a standard way to assess an applicant's aptitude for professional development and career advancement. Employment references who understand residency programs and are familiar with an applicant's professional development and career aspirations can be a great asset to both the applicant and the search committee. Some residency programs invite nominations from the deans of graduate library education programs to identify talented students with minimal or no previous library work experience.

To attract minority applicants, many residency programs target advertisements to racial and ethnic caucuses in the American Library Association (ALA), as well as to graduate students in minority recruitment initiatives such as Spectrum, Knowledge River, and the ARL Initiative to Recruit a Diverse Workforce.

Successful recruitment requires ongoing marketing strategies. An effective web presence that communicates program design, goals, history, and examples of work assignments attract the most informed applicants. The National Library of Medicine Associate Fellows Program website features a webinar addressing frequently asked questions with short presentations by current fellows, along with descriptions of their various work assignments. Listeners get a good sense of what to expect and the types of learning and practicum experiences that are available.

The University of Tennessee—Knoxville Libraries (see Chapter 6) excels at promoting its program. Residents and program administrators have published numerous articles and reports about the program. The residents are frequently featured as speakers at professional conferences. They are enthusiastic and clearly well supported. As a result, the program is well known.

The support of professional library associations has been a great assistance to recruiting prospective residents, as well. The ALA Office for Diversity has done a lot to share information about residency opportunities. ARL has consistently supported the development of residency programs, as well as organizational development and diversity initiatives in member libraries. The new ACRL Residency Interest Group website serves as an excellent clearinghouse of contacts and information for potential applicants. Continuing communication among these groups, as well as with ALISE, will be important to sustain support for residency programs.

HOW ARE WORK ASSIGNMENTS DEVELOPED?

Designing work assignments that match both the development level and interests of the resident, as well as the needs of the library, is the key to a successful residency experience. This requires an accurate assessment of the resident's knowledge and abilities in specific skill areas, as well as an understanding of the expected outcomes. Instruction librarians and human resource development specialists can provide valuable input when designing work assignments and learning activities, especially for organizations that have minimal experience with early-career librarians.

The planning process is naturally more involved for residency programs that offer multiple first-year experiences, especially if the intent is to sequence learning to achieve an integrated project. An example of an integrated assignment would be the processing and cataloging of a gift collection, in which the work touches on collection development, acquisitions, and bibliographic control. Staff from multiple areas of the library will be involved. Support from library administration helps facilitate these types of cross-functional assignments. Discipline-specific residency programs such as those in the health sciences design work assignments to correlate with a structured curriculum and specific learning outcomes.

Institutions that develop new resident assignments with each recruitment cycle generally put out a call for proposals to team leaders or department heads to identify current institutional needs. Some institutions vary the number of residents hired in a given year on the basis of the number and quality of the proposals submitted. North Carolina State University has a dynamic process for matching current organizational needs with the skills and interests of new residents. The work assignments change with each recruitment cycle.

Supervisory support is an important factor in the success of a residency assignment. Working with early-career librarians requires supervisors to provide more direction, structure, and training than for more experienced librarians or for those who have more technical expertise on a specific task. New librarians want feedback and mentoring. Having just recently completed a graduate education program, they are accustomed to frequent and specific appraisals of their performance (grades). The need for this different style of supervision is easy to overlook when residents display so much confidence, initiative, and strong interpersonal relations. Work assignments with clear expectations and structured deadlines or outcomes accelerate the development of new skills and provide a basis for assessment.

Most residency programs rely on day-to-day feedback among residents, program coordinators, and departmental supervisors to assess performance. Good informal communication is essential. Program coordinators have the additional responsibility of actively monitoring work assignments and responding quickly when problems arise or organizational needs change. More formal assessment measures such as written evaluations, capstone presentations, and exit interviews contribute to the development of future work assignments.

The University of Delaware residency program requires written evaluations at the conclusion of each work assignment to gather feedback from residents and supervisors, as well as exit interviews at the conclusion of the second year, and occasional capstone presentations. The written evaluations ensure that structured feedback takes place and provide immediate assessment of the quality of the work assignment. This documentation also provides a history of the residency program and contributes more broadly to the assessment of the program.

WHAT TYPES OF PROFESSIONAL DEVELOPMENT OPPORTUNITIES ARE MOST VALUABLE?

Early-career librarians want employment experiences that support learning. As intentionally designed professional development experiences, residency programs serve these early career interests well. Travel funding to attend professional meetings and conferences is an essential component of a library residency. Attending professional meetings provides residents with opportunities to learn best practices, explore current issues, and build professional relationships. Additional funding to participate in library diversity conferences and meetings of racial and ethnic caucuses also can be valuable for residents from underrepresented groups.

Other learning opportunities such as mentoring, seminar series, site visits, and committee assignments also accelerate early-career development. Many residency programs provide formal mentoring, along with the opportunities for informal mentoring that naturally occur. Individuals who actively seek mentoring and have previous success in establishing mentoring relationships make ideal residents. The Purdue University Libraries Diversity Fellowship program instituted a networking mentoring model with formal training for mentors, advisors, supervisors, and fellows in 2006 (see Chapter 5). The networking model, based on the work of M. J. Haring, includes multiple participants and is characterized by the expectation that each participant contributes to the others' success (Haring 1999).

Peer mentoring is provided more informally in cohort residency programs that hire multiple residents in each recruitment cycle. Participants in cohort programs find these peer relationships invaluable. Simply being a member of a cohort is developmental. Smaller residency programs can cultivate the benefits of peer mentoring and support by retaining a cohort of past residents on staff and by intentionally hiring early-career librarians in positions throughout the library.

Seminar series and site visits to other area research institutions are common features of larger residency programs, especially those in geographic proximity to other research libraries. Seminars may include meetings with the dean, presentations by key project or service teams, discussions of readings and case studies, or guest lectures. Residents also may be required to present their own work. Site visits allow residents to learn firsthand how new services and professional concerns are handled in other institutions. In the past, the University of Michigan Research Library Residency Program regularly supported travel for groups of residents to visit the national libraries in Washington, D.C.

Institutional members of research library consortia also collaborate to provide development opportunities for early career librarians. The Institute for Museum and Library Services' (IMLS) grant–funded Chesapeake Information and Research Library Alliance (CIRLA) Fellows program hosted a multiyear seminar series and site visits to the national and research libraries in the Washington, D.C., area for early-career librarians. The University of Minnesota's Institute for Early Career Librarians from Traditionally Underrepresented Groups provides a rich one-week intensive learning experience every two years. Collaborative learning opportunities across institutions are especially enriching for small residency programs.

As professional library associations and e-learning services increasingly deliver online learning opportunities, residency programs may find new ways to collaborate. Perez (2008) challenges residents and program coordinators to use e-learning technologies to customize learning opportunities. The ACRL Residency Interest Group is exploring resources such as Internet courseware and virtual meeting and webinar services for residents to interact and share learning across different institutions and geographic areas. Specific learning modules related to mentoring, leadership development, and resumé writing would extend the offerings available in any one residency program.

HOW ARE RESIDENCY PROGRAMS ADMINISTERED, SUPPORTED, AND ASSESSED?

The administration of residency programs varies from institution to institution. Most have a designated program coordinator, but others are coordinated by a team or committee. The director of library human resources is almost always involved in one capacity or another.

The leadership of the library dean is critical to the continuing success of the program. No residency exists without the visible support of the dean. Library administrators who have sustained long-term residency programs through shifting legal and economic landscapes have shown extraordinary leadership. Residency programs that have continued through multiple deans are especially noteworthy and reflect extraordinary staff commitment and broad organizational support.

Residency programs are typically funded with line salaries from the general operating budget at individual institutions supplemented with travel support and office and equipment expenses. Indirect costs include the time of program administrators and departmental supervisors. The Kress Fellowship in Art Librarianship at Yale University is an example of a residency program supported with private funding. The Haas Family Arts Library at Yale received its second five-year grant from the Samuel H. Kress Foundation in the fall of 2008 to fund residents through 2014. Private funding, especially endowments, are ideal for ensuring the future of residency programs, as well as providing flexibility with recruitment processes.

Cultivating support to start or continue a library residency requires administrators to demonstrate that the program targets an organizational priority and adds value to library services. Staffing data is often used to assess diversity impact. Changes in staff relations, organizational productivity, quality of library services, and career development of program participants, although harder to measure, are other factors to consider. The primary factors program coordinators consider in program evaluation are placement in other academic libraries, quality of applicant pool, and completion of the program by residents (Brewer and Winston 2001). Some programs conduct formal surveys of past residents to gather feedback and track career advancement. Vibrant residency programs keep in touch with past residents and take pride in their continuing academic careers.

WHAT IS THE CAREER IMPACT OF PARTICIPATION IN A RESIDENCY EXPERIENCE?

Life after a residency experience varies as widely as the many individuals who have participated in the programs (see Chapter 8). Although it's not easy to measure the impact residencies have on career paths in general, many past residents have written about and made presentations at professional meetings about their experiences. Their accounts provide valuable information about the experiences of early-career librarians and the state of diversity in academic libraries. As E. J. Josey wrote in *Diversity in Libraries,* their voices need to be heard (Josey 2001).

Whether recalling positive or negative experiences, the personal accounts conclude that, overall, residency opportunities are valuable. Many past residents trace their current work or specialization to a professional interest that was sparked by an assignment, a learning opportunity, or the influence of a key person in their residency. Residents in generalist programs often advance into career paths they had never imagined as a result of exposure to multiple areas of work in their first-year programs. Residency programs offer unique opportunities for discovery and career exploration.

Most residents have little difficulty finding a position immediately after, if not before, the conclusion of the residency program. Residents are in high demand. Having two years of professional work experience in and the endorsement of staff from a large research library gives residents a competitive advantage in the employment market. Having already relocated to accept the residency position, most residents are geographically mobile, which continues to be the reality to advance in higher education. Most important, however, residents were initially selected for the initiative, leadership abilities, and commitment to professional development that they had already demonstrated. These characteristics are increasingly weighted as individuals advance in their careers.

Following a residency experience, some residents express surprise at the limitations of more traditional library positions. Former residents begin to encounter some of the organizational limitations that program coordinators and mentors may have eased during the residency. The special attention and latitude given to residents is gone. Residents must actively seek new mentors and keep up professional networks. Byke and Lowe-Wincentsen (2009) encourage new librarians to continue their focus on professional development. They also offer many strategies for early-career and experienced librarians to work together to manage change in library organizations.

HOW DO RESIDENCY PROGRAMS BENEFIT LIBRARIES?

The focus on diversity and professional development that residency programs bring to academic libraries enhances organizational effectiveness and outcomes in many ways. Diversity residencies are primarily intended to increase the number of new librarians from underrepresented groups who in turn enrich the diversity in large research institutions. Career-span diversity allows individuals at different points in their careers to learn from each other. Senior staff have opportunities to mentor and be recognized for their expertise and experience. Newer staff members bring questions, ideas, and energy for change. When early-career residents are paired with more senior librarians to work collaboratively, the professional development interests of both parties are addressed. Employing librarians in all ranges of early, mid, and late careers provides a richness of expertise and talent in an organization.

The consideration given to supporting early career librarians and their professional development creates a culture of learning that benefits library staff in general. Mentoring programs, seminars, and site visits initially created for residents can be readily extended to others. Collaborative learning and networking opportunities across institutions make it feasible to customize learning for individuals and small groups. These efforts are especially valuable at a time when libraries are intentionally moving individuals earlier into leadership positions in their careers and reorganizing organizations to share more leadership.

Library residencies also enhance organizational flexibility. Having a temporary, professional position available every year or two provides staffing flexibility to experiment with the design and delivery of new services. Residents can fulfill short-term staffing needs before committing continuing resources. Residents often assist libraries in exploring and adopting emerging technologies. As a result, flexible, learning organizations are more adept at managing change. They provide the dynamic environments in which future leaders desire to work (Maloney et al. 2010).

SUMMARY

Residency programs have proven to be valuable professional experiences that engage new librarians early in their careers. They expose new librarians to a breadth of professional work, provide early-career development, and break down many of the unintentional employment and cultural barriers that make it difficult for early-career librarians, especially those from underrepresented groups, to obtain employment opportunities in large research institutions. With the number of former residents increasing every year, there is a wealth of information available for institutions aspiring to start new programs. A number of former residents and program coordinators serve as advocates and consultants for the development of residency programs. Several have advanced into leadership positions at other institutions and have started or are exploring similar programs. Many of the best practices of successful residency programs highlighted in this chapter can assist any institution, regardless of size, that hopes to be more intentional about the organizational entry and professional development of early career librarians.

REFERENCES

Association for Library and Information Science Education (ALISE). 1996. Guidelines for practices and principles in the design, operation, and evaluation of post-master's residency programs. *Library Personnel News* 10:1–3.

Brewer, J. 1997. Post-master's residency programs: Enhancing the development of new professionals and minority recruitment in academic and research libraries. *College and Research Libraries* 58:528–537.

Brewer, J., and M. D. Winston. 2001. Program evaluation for internship/residency programs in academic and research libraries. *College and Research Libraries* 62:307–315.

Byke, S., and D. Lowe-Wincentsen. 2009. *A Leadership Primer for New Librarians: Tools for Helping Today's Early-Career Librarians to Become Tomorrow's Library Leaders.* Oxford: Chandos Publishing.

Epps, S. 2008. African American women leaders in academic research libraries. *Portal: Libraries and the Academy* 8:267.

Haring, M. 1999. The case for a conceptual base for minority mentoring programs. *Peabody Journal of Education* 74:5–14.

Josey, E. J. 2001. Foreword. In Cogell, R. V., and C. A. Gruwell. *Diversity in Libraries: Academic Residency Programs.* Westport, CT: Greenwood Press.

Lowry, C., and P. Hanges. 2008. What is the healthy organization? Organization climate and diversity assessment: A research partnership. *Portal: Libraries and the Academy* 8:1–5.

Maloney, K., K. Antelman, K. Altisch, and J. Butler. 2010. Future leaders' views on organizational culture. *College and Research Libraries* 71:322–347.

Perez, M. 2008. Practicing proficiency: The future of library residency programs. Paper presented at the National Diversity in Libraries Conference, October 4, Louisville, Kentucky.

Chapter 2

Design and Implementation of a New Residency Program at Towson University

Carrie Bertling Disclafani, Carissa Tomlinson, Patricia A. MacDonald, and Deborah A. Nolan

BACKGROUND

Towson University launched its library residency program in 2009. The first of its kind in the state of Maryland, the residency program is designed to provide new librarians from underrepresented groups with two years of rich experience in a supportive and innovative academic library environment. This chapter includes a description of the genesis, design, and implementation of the program.

Located in Towson, Maryland, eight miles north of Baltimore, Towson University is a comprehensive university offering more than 100 bachelor's, master's, and doctoral degree programs in the liberal arts and sciences and the applied professional fields. Towson University enrolls more than 21,000 students, is the second largest public institution of higher education in Maryland, and is part of the University System of Maryland (Towson University 2008a). The Albert S. Cook Library supports the university with fifty staff members, eighteen of whom are librarians.

Towson University is a metropolitan university, committed to the educational, economic, and social development of the region. Approximately 80 percent of the undergraduate students are residents of the state of Maryland, and 84 percent of the graduate students are Maryland residents. Fall 2008 enrollment demographics reported total undergraduate and graduate student ethnicity of 67.8 percent Caucasian, 11.6 percent African American, 4 percent Asian, 3.4 percent foreign, 2.4 percent Hispanic, 0.4 percent American Indian, and 10.4 percent other/unknown. Faculty demographics for fall 2008 indicate ethnicity of 84.5 percent Caucasian, 5.8 percent Asian, 5 percent African American, 1.9 percent Hispanic, 0.9 percent foreign, 0.3 percent American Indian, and 1.5 percent other/unknown (Akers, Sellers, and Simone 2008).

According to the university diversity statement, "Towson University values diversity and fosters a climate that is grounded in respect and inclusion, enriches the educational experience of students, supports positive workplace environments, promotes excellence, and cultivates the intellectual and personal growth of the entire university community" (Towson University 2009).

A wide variety of programs advance Towson University's commitment to diversity. "The Reflective Process for Diversity" is a key university initiative that "seeks to engage all campus stakeholders—administrators, faculty, staff, and students—to reflect upon personal and divisional approaches to diversity, develop and assess diversity goals, and maintain an ongoing campus dialogue regarding diversity" (Towson University 2008b). Other notable programs emanate from Towson's center for student diversity, disability support services, diversity action committee, institute for academic diversity and inclusion, and the international student and scholar office. The library residency program enriches Towson's portfolio of diversity initiatives.

In 2006, a new university librarian, Deborah A. Nolan, came on board and introduced the idea of a post-master's degree library residency program for underrepresented minorities. After instituting structural changes to the organization, the university librarian used unfilled vacancies to shape the future of the library. The residency librarian concept was an integral piece in the new vision for the library. The provost gave full support to the residency program, and an existing vacancy was converted to a residency librarian. Organizational changes and redeployment of staff, including the newly created residency librarian position, ensure twenty-first-century library support to the university's expanding programs, student enrollment, and emerging technologies.

The organization was flattened, and departments were consolidated. Reference, instruction, research assistance, circulation, reserves, stacks, interlibrary loan, and document delivery functions were combined into public services under the management of a new position, assistant university librarian for public services. Collection management, acquisitions, cataloging, database management, copyright, and scholarly communications were merged, reporting to a new position, assistant university librarian for content management. Media resources services and library technology were formally joined to become a unified department under a technology manager. Each library vacancy was carefully examined, and new position descriptions were crafted to create an enthusiastic, learning-centered community enriched with technology and committed to the academic and scholarly success of students, faculty, and staff. New positions included a university archivist/digital collections librarian, an associate university librarian for administrative services, and three emerging technology librarians. The residency librarian program became a significant component of the library's organizational development, reflecting the library's commitment to positive change, growth, diversity, and the library profession as a whole.

Several factors contributed to the successful launch of Towson's residency program. The new university librarian developed a broad knowledge base about similar programs through literature reviews and participation in interest groups, discussion groups, and conference programs. The national network of librarians involved with diversity initiatives and residency programs provided invaluable knowledge and insight. The Towson library staff, when presented with the idea and a general outline of the proposed program implementation, expressed strong support, and several librarians volunteered to develop the framework for the program. Towson's university counsel worked with the university librarian and adjusted the standard permanent status track librarian contract to create a full-time, two-year contract carrying full faculty benefits.

In addition, university counsel advised that the job description could state that one of the purposes of the position was to "increase the presence of underrepresented groups in academic librarianship" (see Appendix 2.1). It was made clear, however, that the search committee could not require candidates to be a member of an underrepresented group and that the committee could not eliminate candidates on the basis of race or ethnicity.

PROGRAM DESIGN

Position Description

The position's framework took shape during the proposal stage, and many details required further development before the idea could become reality. To begin with, the program needed an official job description. The description was outlined during a series of design meetings involving the university librarian; Patty MacDonald, the associate university librarian; and Carrie Bertling Disclafani, David Dahl, and Carissa Tomlinson, the university's three newest librarians. The associate university librarian would be the resident's primary supervisor. The new librarians provided valuable input about their first professional job searches as recent graduates. Additionally, one of the new librarians had completed a one-year residency program before coming to Towson University, and the other two had considered residency programs during their job searches.

In preparation for the initial design meeting, each planning group member read several existing residency job and program descriptions. Each considered which aspects of the descriptions were essential to include and which would require modification for Towson University.

First and foremost, Cook Library sought to offer an early-career librarian a broad introduction to academic librarianship in a supportive environment, while providing opportunities for professional exploration and focused specialization. Residency programs frequently offer departmental rotations during the first year, followed by a year in a specific area. The planning group determined that this structure would work well for the Towson program. On the basis of the cycle of the academic year and the structure of Cook Library's main departments, the resident's first year would be spent evenly among three areas. The rotation would include four months in each of three departments: research, reference, and instruction services; technical services; and university archives/digital collections.

Also of utmost importance was the desire to increase the presence of underrepresented groups in academic librarianship. The first paragraph of the job description articulated this goal and described Towson's commitment to diversity. Despite the prominent placement of this statement, the majority of applicants failed to address a commitment to diversity in their application materials. In hindsight, the program's diversity purpose should have been reiterated in the requirements section of the position description.

In addition to providing a new librarian with a wide range of professional experience, the library wanted to offer several opportunities for both formal and informal mentoring. It was clear that the resident would have an abundance of formal mentors: the primary supervisor (the associate university librarian) and the three department heads he or she would work under throughout the first-year rotations. Therefore, the job description specified that the library would also provide an informal mentor to help the resident acclimate to the library, the university, and the greater metropolitan community. Anticipating a national search directed toward recent MLS graduates, the planning group understood that the resident would be new to academic librarianship and would most likely have many nuanced questions ranging from the culture of the institution to the joys and challenges of moving to a new city. The informal mentor would serve as a person to turn to with any question, no matter how big or small.

The group also chose to emphasize the program's commitment to fostering a mutually beneficial experience for both the resident and the library. Everyone agreed that the two-year position should offer the resident more opportunity for growth than one would find in a traditional entry-level job. Nonetheless, the library was not entirely selfless in its goals for the position. As a new graduate, the resident would contribute fresh ideas and new perspectives to the library and the university. A statement reflecting this goal was included in the first line of the job description. Fixed-term, recurring positions guarantee institutions periodic influxes of fresh ideas and revitalized energy with each new hire. This phenomenon is especially true for residency programs that recruit recent graduates. The work invested in establishing the residency librarian position illustrates Cook Library's desire to ensure the exchange of ideas between new and seasoned library professionals.

The second year of the program was designed to include a capstone project based on the resident's career interests while simultaneously addressing the needs of the library. The description of the second year emphasized three distinct yet mutually beneficial goals: provide the resident with specialized experience in an area of their choosing, contribute toward the long-term goals of the library, and culminate in a professional conference presentation or journal article that would shine favorably on both the resident's dossier and the program's merits.

Departmental Rotations

The university librarian and the associate university librarian met with the heads of research, reference, and instruction services; technical services; and university archives/digital collections to discuss the resident's particular responsibilities within the departmental rotations. Unlike an intern, the resident would have full faculty status as an entry-level librarian and would be required to fulfill responsibilities comparable to those of a Towson University Librarian I. Each department would assist the resident in attaining this level of expertise by providing substantial training and meaningful, practical experience pertaining to the area's major functions.

The time required for the resident's initial training at the start of each rotation and the workload cycles of each department were considered when deciding how to schedule the rotation cycle. Early in the discussions, it became clear that the spring semester was the best time for the resident to work in reference, research, and instruction services. During the fall semester, especially September and October, the instruction librarians have heavy teaching loads, leaving them little time to work with a new resident. Conversely, the summer semester's light class schedule would not afford the resident many opportunities to try his or her hand at instruction. Therefore, starting in technical services or archives/digital collections would allow the resident time to observe a variety of instruction sessions, before taking on teaching responsibilities in the spring.

The technical services and archives/digital collections departments afforded flexibility, allowing the library to customize the rotation cycle to the resident's interest. For example, the library's first resident had experience in archives and felt that she might want to focus the second year of her residency in that department. Ending her rotations in archives/digital collections would allow for an easy transition from the first year into the focused second year. Keeping this in mind, it was decided the most practical approach would be for the resident to start in technical services, followed by research, reference, and instruction, and ending in archives/digital collections. This sequence seemed the most logical but may vary for future residents.

Lastly, the planning group discussed committee responsibilities for the resident. At Towson University, like most academic institutions, there are countless committee opportunities, and restraint must be demonstrated to avoid overcommitment. Considering this factor, it was decided that the resident should start small, serving on a single, significant library committee, supplementing this experience by sitting in on various university and consortium committee meetings based on the resident's interests and goals. The intention was to provide the resident with a broad overview of university and library consortium issues and governance.

Mentoring

The library believed that providing an informal mentor was important for a recent graduate new to the profession, the institution, and the greater metropolitan community. Towson University's library had experienced success with a relatively new mentorship program in research, reference, and instruction services that pairs new hires with senior librarians. The pairs meet frequently for one-on-one discussions, and once a semester, all mentors and mentees join together to debrief over lunch. Although a variety of mentoring relationships will form naturally throughout the course of an employee's tenure, it is hoped that offering an informal mentor early on will ensure that new hires feel they have someone to turn to with any questions, both pressing and trivial.

It is essential that discussions between mentors and mentees remain confidential, yet the mentor can serve as an advocate for the new hire. This role seems especially important in the case of a new residency program for two reasons. First, like any newly designed position, the job responsibilities are nebulous, gaining definition incrementally over several months as the employee and the institution negotiate their relationship. Understanding the institution and the resident's broad interests, the mentor can suggest ways in which each can serve one another. Second, although employee satisfaction is a goal for every new hire, it seems especially important for a newly created program that is working to establish itself within the university and the professional job market. The library's role in nurturing and developing a new professional affects the resident's commitment to the profession and future career decisions. Thus, the resident's level of job satisfaction has a wide-ranging impact. It is essential that the program prove productive for both the resident and the library, thus demonstrating its benefit to the institution and future applicants.

RECRUITMENT

Advertising the Position

Recruitment for the residency position followed the standard process used for hiring librarians at Towson University. While the process began later than planned because of the time required for administrative approval of the new position, the search committee hit the ground running in March 2009. The associate university librarian chaired the search committee and a diverse group of staff from library departments relevant to the position served on the committee. The position was advertised on the Towson University and the library's websites; in *American Libraries, C&RL News*, and nineteen library-related, diversity, or library school websites; and on online discussion lists. To expedite the selection process, the job announcement stated that the review of applications would begin immediately rather than providing a deadline (see Appendix 2.1).

The job requirements for the residency were somewhat flexible because of initial concern that the unique nature of the position would result in a shortage of candidates. In years past, residency coordinators at other universities, such as the University of Iowa, noted difficulty in hiring qualified residents because of the short-term nature of the position and the demand for minority applicants (Simmons-Welburn and Dewey 2001). Therefore, although the residency was designed for recent MLS graduates, job qualifications stated that an MLS received during the previous year was preferred but not required. Despite some of the past experiences in residency recruitment, Towson began receiving applications in record numbers. More than 300 applications were received. The chair conducted an initial screening to streamline the review process and selected the candidates who met the basic criteria for the residency. It was evident that many of the applicants had applied for the position not because of its unique residency components but because they sought employment, any employment, in a tough economic time.

Although many of the applicants had excellent qualifications, some failed to demonstrate a commitment to diversity, an essential aspect of this residency, and others submitted their applications after candidates were selected for telephone interviews. The chair selected approximately one hundred candidates who met preferred requirements for consideration, including a recent MLS degree and experience with diversity efforts. The search committee scored these applications on a scale from 0 to 10 in categories based on relevant experience and necessary characteristics, for example, potential for a career in academic librarianship, involvement with diversity initiatives, and enthusiasm for new technology (see Figure 2.1).

RESUME SCREENING
Residency Librarian Candidate
Resume Screening Form

Candidate's name _____ Date_____

____ A ____ B ____ C   (Point range for each group   A = 10-12   B = 6-9   C = 0-5)

Required: ___ Recent MLS (ALA Accredited)   ___ Cover Letter & Resume   ___ References

Rankings – Please rank the candidate in each category and add comments as necessary

    0 = no evidence   1 = meets requirements   2 = exceeds requirements

____ interest and potential for career in academic librarianship

____ underrepresented groups in academic librarianship / involvement with diversity initiatives

____ communication / writing skills

____ commitment to public service

____ enthusiasm for new technology

____ involvement in professional organizations or scholarship activities

Additional comments / qualifications:

Figure 2.1. Resume screening form.

Several immediate lessons were learned for the next recruitment cycle. In particular, future vacancy announcements will provide specific guidelines for the cover letter and request that applicants address both their commitment to diversity initiatives and their qualifications relevant to other requirements of the position. Recruitment will also start earlier to allow sufficient time for all interested, qualified candidates to apply and to be considered. With the position strongly established, the library will be well prepared to make necessary modifications to the residency program and advertise the position well in advance of the start date.

Diversity Recruitment

The announcement was posted on several diversity resources, including the websites or discussion lists of the Black Caucus of the American Library Association, the Chinese American Library Association, the Association of College and Research Libraries' (ACRL) Racial & Ethnic Diversity Committee, and the Library Leadership and Management Association's (LLAMA) Diversity Officers Discussion Group. It is interesting to note that the candidates for this residency position relied heavily on national library career websites, rather than diversity resources such as the online discussion lists or websites of minority library associations.

Of the 115 applicants who indicated the source that prompted their application, 63 percent saw it on the American Library Association's (ALA)-JobLIST.org, LISjobs.com, or Libgig.com. Specifically, thirty-nine applicants (34 percent) viewed it on ALA-JobLIST.org, twenty-seven (23 percent) on LISjobs.com, and seven (6 percent) on Libgig.com. None of the applicants, however, mentioned seeing the job announcement on a diversity online discussion list or website. Library school online discussion lists, in contrast, proved to be important resources for positions targeted to recent graduates of these schools.

These results support findings of a 2008 Harris Interactive study, which found that minority candidates actively use major job recruiting websites rather than those geared to a diversity audience (Monster.com 2009).

Telephone Interviews

Despite the exceedingly large candidate pool, the committee quickly reached agreement on the top contenders. Six applicants were selected for telephone interviews. The position's uniqueness required the search committee to develop interview questions that would reveal both the most qualified candidates and those most interested in a residency experience. As a residency program designed to provide opportunities to gain experience in three distinct library departments, the search committee sought candidates who expressed some interest in each of those functional areas. With this in mind, the committee developed residency-specific questions in addition to the standard interview questions touching on technology, public service, and academic librarianship (see Figure 2.2). Some questions included:

- Why are you particularly interested in a residency experience?

- In your first year, your rotation will be in three different departments. What strengths would you bring to Cook Library in these areas? *(The departments were purposely not mentioned; the search committee wanted the candidate to show that he or she researched the position and was excited about each area.)*

- Describe how you would use an emerging technology to enhance a service or workflow in one of these three departments. *(This provided the candidate a second opportunity to show interest and knowledge in each area of the residency).*

TELEPHONE INTERVIEW

Phone Script and Questions for Residency Librarian

Hello. My name is _____. I am calling from Towson University in reference to the Residency Librarian position. Thank you for agreeing to this telephone interview. I am the Associate University Librarian for Administrative Services and Chair of the Search Committee. Here also are [list names and titles of search committee members]. We will ask you a series of questions and will note your answers. Before we begin, do you have any questions about the interview?

Candidate's name _____ Date_____

Interviewer's name _____

1.) Why are you particularly interested in a residency experience?

2.) In your first year, your rotation will be in three different departments. What strengths would you bring to Cook Library in these areas?

3.) Describe how you would use an emerging technology to enhance a service or workflow in one of these three departments.

4.) Please describe your role in a successful project you've completed in graduate school or your career so far.

5.) Please tell us about an experience with a difficult patron or colleague and how you handled the situation.

6.) What do you think is the leading issue in academic librarianship at this time/

7.) What contributions to academic librarianship do you hope to make in the next five years?

8.) What questions do you have for us?

Figure 2.2. Telephone interview questions.

The telephone interviews took about thirty minutes each. Unlike the initial screening of candidates, the search committee did not use a formal rating system during the phone interview process. Instead, following each phone call, the committee simply discussed the strengths and weaknesses of each candidate in terms of commitment to diversity, public service skills, interest in technology, and dedication to academic librarianship.

While the committee had hoped to narrow the pool from six to three candidates for the on-site interviews, four candidates excelled in the telephone interview. The university librarian decided that bringing in an extra candidate was worth the additional investment of effort and funds to ensure a successful search. Time was also a concern. A failed search would eliminate any chance of having the resident start before the beginning of the fall semester. After contacting references, the four top candidates were invited for campus visits and interviews. Within a short time, one person dropped out after accepting another job offer, further validating the library's decision to invite all four suitable candidates.

On-Site Interviews

As soon as schedules were coordinated, the three remaining candidates came to campus. Although similar to a standard academic library interview, the on-site interview for the resident librarian had significant differences and considerations. An interview for this type of position required more time than a standard librarian position. Towson's program rotates residents through three distinct departments during the first year, making it important for the candidate to meet with a variety of people within a relatively short time period. The candidate met with the search committee, the university librarian, and supervisors from three rotation departments. Additional informal time was scheduled for dinner, lunch, and a staff meet-and-greet.

Because of the instruction component of the position, candidates were asked to give a presentation as part of the interview. All these components, plus a driving tour of the area, required a tightly scheduled day and a half interview. Nonetheless, because the resident would play such an important role in so many parts of the library, it was crucial to have a full understanding of the candidate's strengths and weaknesses in the various areas of librarianship. Just as important, the candidate needed ample time to get to know the library and its staff, the university, and the position that he or she was considering.

The individual meetings with the three department heads were extremely helpful in further revealing each candidate's potential for success while informing the candidates about the rotations. The department supervisors gave feedback on the candidates' skills, knowledge, and perceived interest in that particular department. These meetings helped clarify how the candidate would perform and contribute in each department and in the yearlong placement in one chosen area during the second half of the residency.

The search committee's meeting with the candidates focused on broader topics, such as academic librarianship and technology. The committee interview also revisited the program goals and asked candidates to comment on their commitment to diversity and their interest in the specific components of this unique residency position (see Figure 2.3).

ON-SITE INTERVIEW
Residency Librarian Candidate
Search Committee On-Site Interview Questions

Candidate's name _____ Date_____

Interviewer's name _____

1. What do you hope to gain from this residency experience and what would you contribute to Towson University?

2. Describe the experiences that make you especially qualified for a career in academic libraries.

3. What is your proudest accomplishment over the last year? What could you have done better?

4. One of the main purposes of this residency position is to promote the presence of under-represented groups in academic librarianship. Demonstrate how your background will support diversity efforts in the library field and at Towson.

5. What would be the most challenging about this job and how would you overcome it?

6. Please discuss the role of information literacy in producing university graduates ready to compete in the global marketplace.

7. What is your opinion of the value of academia's use of social networking sites such as Facebook and Twitter?

8. How can the library best serve Millennial (or NextGen) students in their research and scholarship?

9. Have free information resources, such as Google, been a help or a hindrance in promoting an information literate society and how should the library leverage these resources?

10. What are your research interests and ideas for a capstone project during the second year of the residency?

Figure 2.3. Onsite interview questions.

22 \ The New Graduate Experience

For the presentation portion of the day, the candidates were asked to describe a leading issue in academic librarianship and how he or she would apply an emerging technology to address this issue. The hope was that this topic would allow candidates to speak broadly about academic librarianship as well as discuss applications of technology within specific departments. The search committee invited the entire library staff and representatives from the instructional technology department to attend the presentations. Because of the diversity aspect of the position, the university diversity officers were also invited. Attendees were asked to evaluate each presenter on content, delivery, and interaction with the audience (see Figure 2.4).

PRESENTATION EVALUATION
Residency Librarian Candidate
Presentation Evaluation Form

Candidate's name _____ Date_____

Presentation's Topic: Describe a leading issue in academic librarianship and how you would apply an emerging technology to address this issue.

Overall Evaluation: 1   2   3   4   5
(5 being excellent)

Comments:

Content

Presentation / Delivery

Interaction with the audience

Figure 2.4. Presentation evaluation form.

To conclude the formal interviews, each residency candidate met with the university librarian for approximately one hour. The university librarian used this time to elicit the candidate's impressions of the position, the library, and the university. In addition to asking each candidate a set of standard questions, the university librarian provided the candidate with time to ask questions (see Figure 2.5). Through this process, the university librarian was able to gauge the candidate's understanding of, interest in, and readiness for the residency position.

UNIVERSITY LIBRARIAN INTERVIEW
Residency Librarian Candidate
University Librarian Interview Questions

Candidate's name _____ Date_____

1. How has your day been? What are your impressions and thoughts about Cook Library?

2. What were your best or most fulfilling experiences in your MLS program and in your library-related work?

3. Please describe some examples of your role in successful team projects.

4. By now you have a better understanding of the scope of our residency program and the functions of our technical services, archives/digital collections, and reference/instruction units. Tell me what you would hope to learn and do in each of these functional areas.

5. What strengths do you have that you believe would be instrumental in your success in our residency program?

6. In addition to working within the carious units and benefiting from mentors/coaches, what strategies would you use to strengthen your knowledge of the areas in which your experience is limited?

7. Why Towson University?

8. Why are you looking for a residency program rather than a tenure track librarian position?

9. What are your professional goals for the next 5 years?

10. Is there anything else you'd like to tell me that would help us in our decision?

Figure 2.5. University librarian interview questions.

In an attempt to reduce stress during the long interview process, informal social interactions were interspersed throughout the schedule. These informal activities included lunch with a small group of librarians and dinner with the university librarian and two members of the search committee.

In addition to helping library staff and the candidates get to know one another informally, these casual meetings also provided the candidates with better insight into the culture of the library.

Despite the abundance of applicants for the position, the search committee knew it was possible that the strongest contenders may receive other job offers. Therefore, the pressure to impress one another was shared equally between the search committee and the job candidates; the committee wanted the selected candidate to accept the position without hesitation. It was also important to provide each candidate with a sample of life off-campus and with information about possible neighborhoods in which he or she might reside. Candidates were contacted prior to their on-site interviews and asked about the kinds of areas they would be interested in living in (urban, suburban, rural). The neighborhood tours were tailored to the candidate's interest.

The interviews were very successful, providing the search committee with well-rounded views of the candidates, and the candidates with comprehensive information about the residency position, Cook Library, Towson University, and the surrounding area. Once all of the interviews were complete, the search committee met to review the candidates. Feedback from the department heads, presentation evaluations, committee member notes, and discussions with candidate references were all considered. The committee determined whether each candidate was acceptable, compiled a list of his or her strengths and areas of concern, and submitted a recommendation to the university librarian. The university librarian, along with the provost, and the vice president for academic affairs made the official hiring decision.

Following the job offer, the chosen candidate accepted the position and made arrangements to move to the Greater Baltimore area. The new hire received relocation assistance consistent with the package offered to all new Towson faculty. Upon arrival, she quickly settled into her new home and office and prepared to embark on her professional career as Towson's first library resident.

IMPLEMENTATION

Supervision

The residency coordinator, who is the associate university librarian at Towson University, has the critical responsibility of managing the residency program, ensuring that it is a cohesive, challenging, and rewarding experience for the resident as well as a beneficial program for the institution. As Julie Brewer, University of Delaware Personnel and Staff Development Librarian, states, "Balancing the interests of the host organization and the residents is the key challenge of a program coordinator" (Brewer 2001, 7). To help the Towson resident balance responsibilities, the coordinator met frequently with the resident, at first weekly and then at biweekly intervals, to assist with setting priorities and addressing any concerns. It is important to keep in mind that in most positions, a new librarian can focus on the primary responsibilities of that job. In the first year of a residency, however, a resident must learn new skills and assume substantial responsibilities in three distinct departments.

Along with departmental responsibilities, there are ongoing activities associated with the residency, such as committee work and university service. Time can pass quickly, and demands for the resident's attention are many. Thus, the coordinator needs to gauge whether the resident is fully challenged without being overwhelmed by work, that the rotations are progressing smoothly, and that the resident takes advantage of the variety of campus initiatives and opportunities. In addition, the coordinator helps the resident develop annual goals, which include journaling, professional development, scholarship, and service. The weekly journal is written as a narrative outlining the resident's activities and reactions to the program. Other goals may vary, but journaling will be a standard requirement for Towson residents. The journal will provide useful material for the resident's portfolio and for any future publications or presentations he or she may produce about the residency experience. The library will also gain insight into what worked best or what might be improved for future residents.

While the coordinator provides overall supervision for the resident, department heads oversee work in their functional areas during each rotation. As part of the resident's annual performance review, each department head develops goals for the rotation based on the resident's job responsibilities and on current projects within the department.

Supportive Environment

From the institutional standpoint, Towson University has several strengths that contribute to the success of the residency: commitment to diversity; friendly, professional staff; an inclusive, collaborative environment; and enthusiasm for new ideas and technology. First, diversity is a key initiative at Towson, one that is articulated by the president and implemented by the entire university community with leadership from the president's special assistant for diversity and equal opportunity, the director of the institute for academic diversity and inclusion, and the deans, including the university librarian. This campus-wide commitment to diversity opens doors and provides opportunities to the resident.

Although the Towson resident is not intended to be a spokesperson for minorities, he or she may choose to become involved with campus diversity initiatives. Because of her interest, the first resident became a member of the important new university diversity action committee, which is composed of a cross-section of department representatives who initiate and promote campus diversity efforts. The library will continue to have a representative on this committee, and, for interested residents, this committee will provide high-level participation in support of university diversity initiatives.

Another positive factor in the Towson residency program is that the resident librarian has status comparable to a faculty librarian. As such, the resident is fully integrated into orientation activities for new Towson faculty and new library employees. The resident attends new faculty events hosted by the provost including a welcome dinner, a workshop on grant support for faculty research, and monthly faculty information sessions. The university's human resources department provides a session on benefits and a campus tour, and the office of technology services provides workshops on classroom technology and computer software used at the university. In addition, the library hosts a reception to introduce the resident to library staff; and the coordinator meets with the resident to review policies, the job description, and other information included in the library's new employee manual. Consequently, the resident receives a thorough introduction to the university and to the library within the first few weeks on the job.

Towson librarians and staff work in a highly collaborative environment, and the first resident quickly became involved in the library's outreach events, including orientation for new students and a book discussion club. As a result of these outreach activities, the resident continued work on creative, promotional projects alongside reference and instruction librarians, in addition to assignments during the initial rotation in technical services. The resident also joined the library marketing committee.

Although original plans for the residency included only an observational role on university and consortium committees, the Towson University Diversity Action Committee offered a perfect avenue for the current resident to become more fully involved. Many university committees require two-year terms. Future residents, therefore, will be encouraged to apply for membership on a university committee of their choosing during their first few months at Towson. All of these collaborative and cross-departmental projects, groups, and relationships help create a cohesive experience and make the resident an integral part of the library and university.

ACRL's Support for Residency Programs

Beyond the supportive environment at Towson, the Association of College and Research Libraries' Residency Interest Group (ACRL-RIG) has played a key role in the success of this new program. During the planning and implementation stages, the interest group has been an excellent gateway for information and for networking with other residents and coordinators. In designing the Towson program, the ACRL-RIG website provided a central resource for information about academic residencies.

Both the Towson residency coordinator and the resident have made contacts at other institutions through attendance at the ACRL-RIG meetings at professional conferences and through communication on the group's website. This networking has led to invitations to visit nearby institutions, such as the National Library of Medicine, to attend workshops or learn more about their programs. A one-day meeting for residents from four states has also been planned at the University of Delaware, where the Towson resident will be able to meet new colleagues and share her experiences. Active participation in ACRL-RIG will continue to be an important avenue for making personal connections and for keeping up with current trends in academic residencies.

CONCLUSION

The planning and implementation of the residency program have gone relatively smooth, and a process of continuous improvement has been incorporated into the endeavor. The library will make modifications in future cycles based on lessons learned. The recruitment process, for example, will be adjusted as follows:

- Towson librarians will visit area library schools to describe the program and conduct brief on-site interviews.
- The residency application requirements will be stated more clearly. The cover letter must address how the candidate's background demonstrates a commitment to diversity, how the candidate is well suited for work in multiple departments of the library, and how the residency experiences will support the candidate's career goals.
- The position will require, rather than prefer, that applicants receive their MLS degree within a certain time period.

For future residents, the library will explore offering a project-oriented introduction to the major areas of academic librarianship rather than a series of four-month department rotations during the first year. Hands-on experience has been the most instructive and beneficial, as it gives the resident the opportunity to gain skills and actively contribute to meaningful library projects. Assigned duties can also be tailored to the resident's interests, strengths, and skills that need to be developed. For example, some of the resident's major assignments during the initial rotation in technical services involved archival materials, an area of high interest for the resident. This type of interdepartmental, cross-functional work promotes an understanding of the roles of coworkers in support of the program and focuses attention on the key initiatives of the institution. Thus, the resident has an integral role in undertaking new and significant projects that require communication and collaboration with staff throughout the library.

With the support of the university, the leadership of the university librarian, and the cooperative efforts of staff, Towson has launched a new and what promises to be long and fulfilling venture introducing library residents to the world of academic librarianship. Even in the first few months of Towson's initial library residency, the experience has been exciting and rewarding for all partners. The resident has learned new skills and has been fully engaged in a range of professional endeavors. Staff from all library departments have been energized and gained fresh insights from a new librarian, and the university has added a talented new faculty member who enhances the diversity of its community. Although there will be modifications of the Towson program, the initial reaction of the library's first resident early in her appointment testifies to the residency's successful design and implementation. "Since I am encouraged to pursue so many library and academic avenues," she commented to one of the authors, "I know that I'll have a more focused career path when my residency is completed."

REFERENCES

Akers, J., K. Sellers, and N. Simone. Data journal. *Towson University*. http://wwwnew.towson.edu/ir/DJFALL08.pdf

Brewer, J. 2001. Reflections of an academic library residency coordinator. In *Diversity in Libraries: Academic Residency Programs,* edited by R. V. Cogell and C. A. Gruwell, pp. 7–16. Westport, CT: Greenwood Press.

Monster.com. 2009. Back to the future: The rapidly evolving world of diversity recruitment *Monster.com*. http://media.monster.com/a/i/intelligence/pdf/BackToTheFuture_2009.pdf

Simmons-Welburn, J., and B. I. Dewey. 2001. Advocating diversity in research libraries: The University of Iowa Minority Research Library Residency Program. In *Diversity in Libraries: Academic Residency Programs*, edited by R. V. Cogell and C. A. Gruwell, pp. 23–28. Westport, CT: Greenwood Press.

Towson University. 2008a. About TU. *Towson University*. http://www.towson.edu/main/abouttu

Towson University. 2008b. Reflective Process for Diversity. *Towson University*. http://www.towson.edu/reflectiveprocess

Towson University. 2009. Commitment to diversity. *Towson University*. http://www.towson.edu/main/abouttu/comdiv

APPENDIX 2.1

Residency Job Announcement

Towson University

Albert S. Cook Library

Residency Librarian Program

2009-2011

Beginning fall 2009, the Towson University Residency Librarian Program will offer an early-career librarian the opportunity for rapid professional growth in academic librarianship. The two-year program is designed to provide a broad introduction to academic librarianship, a supportive environment for professional exploration, and an opportunity for concentrated experience in an area of specialization. The purpose of the program is to help increase the presence of underrepresented groups in academic librarianship. Towson University values diversity and encourages all qualified individuals to apply.

Position Description:

The Residency Librarian will be provided with a wide range of academic librarian experiences to develop and enhance his or her professional skills and prepare for future career opportunities. Library administrators, faculty, and staff will serve as formal and informal mentors and will help the Resident acclimate to the library, university and Greater Baltimore metro area.

In year one of this two-year residency, the Residency Librarian will gain meaningful work experience within three library departments:

- Research, Reference, and Instructional Services
- Technical Services—Collection Development, Acquisitions, Cataloging, and Serials
- Archives and Digital Collections

The Resident will be involved in library and university committees, develop collegial relationships with faculty outside the library, and participate in professional organizations.

In the second year, the Residency Librarian will work with his or her supervisor and mentor to identify a capstone project that is tailored to his or her professional interests and to the needs of the library. A goal of this project is for the Resident, working independently or with a mentor, to develop, complete, and report research to be presented at a professional conference or in a professional journal.

The Residency Librarian will be appointed for a two-year term with non–tenure track visiting faculty status. Salary is commensurate with that of an entry-level professional librarian. Full benefits package is provided with health insurance and retirement options, relocation allowance, and financial support for professional development. This position is contingent on the availability of funds at the time of hire.

Required:

MLS from an ALA-accredited institution preferably granted between January 2008 and August 2009. Strong interest in developing a career in academic librarianship; demonstrated commitment to public service and user satisfaction; excellent communication and presentation skills; strong, positive interpersonal skills; enthusiasm for learning new technologies; commitment to professional growth; and ability to work independently as well as collaboratively with colleagues and patrons from diverse backgrounds.

Towson University:

The largest comprehensive university in the Baltimore area, Towson University is nationally recognized for its excellent programs in the arts and sciences, communications, business, health professions, education, fine arts, and computer information systems. As the second largest school within the University System of Maryland, TU enrolls over 19,000 students and offers 62 undergraduate majors, 39 master's programs, and 4 doctoral degree programs. The University is located in the suburban community of Towson, Maryland, eight miles north of downtown Baltimore.

With a staff of fifty including twenty faculty librarians, Albert S. Cook Library houses nearly 700,000 volumes, over 9,000 sound recordings, nearly 10,000 video recordings, and provides access to over 55,000 print and electronic journals.

Application Process:

Review of applications will begin immediately and continue until the position is filled. Please submit letter of interest, resumé, and contact information for at least three professional references. Transcripts will be requested of final candidates. Submit application materials to:

Residency Librarian Search

Albert S. Cook Library

Towson University

8000 York Road

Towson, MD 21252-0001

Electronic applications are encouraged and should be submitted to xxxxx@towson.edu.

Towson University is an equal opportunity employer and has a strong institutional commitment to diversity.

Chapter 3

Evaluation of Three Canadian Academic Library Internship Programs

Kathleen De Long

Library internships or residency programs are a fairly new arrival on the Canadian library scene and, as such, have not become well established. Peter Hepburn (2001), a Canadian participant in the University of Illinois at Chicago program, contrasts the number of Canadian programs with those in the United States and suggests that Canadian academic libraries could achieve the same benefits as U.S. counterparts if more programs were to be developed. Although acknowledging some degree of cynicism, he points to advantages, such as having an in-house pool of qualified, already-trained, candidates for tenure-track positions, salary savings from the lower wages of entry level interns, and, ideally, the fresh ideas and practices that interns bring to their institutions.

Hepburn's comments are directed primarily to the short-term benefits, albeit self-interests, which are realized by an institution providing an internship program. There are, however, long-term advantages that can also be identified, such as the opportunity to introduce new professionals to the practice of specific skills and competencies and to launch careers in academic librarianship.

The terms "internship" and "residency" are both used in program descriptions of U.S. academic residency or internship programs. The Association for Library and Information Science Education defines a "residency" as "the post-degree work experience designed as an entry level program for professionals who have received the MLS degree from a program accredited by the American Library Association." In contrast, "internship" is defined as "the structure of pre-professional work experience which takes place during graduate course work or after coursework but preceding the degree, usually for a short amount of time" (Association of Research Libraries 1992, 67). Although these definitions are not uniformly followed, Canadian programs seem to prefer the term "internship" to describe post-MLS programs.

BACKGROUND

In the late 1990s and early 2000s, academic library internship programs[1] were developed at three Canadian institutions: the University of New Brunswick, University of Alberta, and University of Winnipeg. All three were post-MLS programs. Only one program, at the University of Alberta (U of A), is still in operation. In comparison, residency programs have existed at U.S. institutions since the 1940s, and today approximately 20 programs can be identified (Brewer 2007).

Canadian academic library internship programs have not been well documented. Contact with the institutions, however, reveals one common thread. All three institutions had a common goal of attracting the interest of new graduates to careers in academic libraries. The University of New Brunswick advertised the first academic library internship in Canada in 1999. The internship was intended to be ongoing and to attract applicants interested in pursuing a career in academic libraries. In total, six interns participated in the one-year term program, which was discontinued in 2005, and the funding was shifted to tenure-track positions. There is some indication, however, that the program could be restarted, pending funding.[2]

In 2001, the University of Winnipeg announced an internship program that focused on information literacy and was intended to position the library as a leader of innovative information services in the academic environment. However, by 2006, this program was also discontinued. Four interns participated in the program for one- or two-year terms. There is hope that this program may also be revived in the future, assuming that it can be fit into the collective agreement for librarians.[3]

Finally, the U of A Libraries introduced an internship program in 2000 to address a growing need to recruit new academic librarians and to revitalize the professional corps with fresh perspectives and ideas within a climate of tight budgets and hiring restrictions. The U of A Libraries could foresee that the retirement of the "baby boomers," who made up the majority of the professional complement, would occur within the next five to ten years. It was critical that new graduates were attracted and introduced to academic librarianship.

At the same time, it was not possible to recruit new professionals into permanent tenure-track positions. The U of A's program was designed to meet these organizational objectives while providing new graduates with skills and experience in a wide range of academic library activities, mentoring and networking opportunities, professional development, and training that would enhance their employability and competitiveness for positions within academic libraries. Although funding has varied through the years, the program at the U of A continues and employs at least three interns every year.

PROBLEM STATEMENT

As retirements accelerate in Canadian academic libraries and tenure-track positions become available, it is important to know whether internship programs have been successful in promoting recruitment into academic librarianship. As Brewer (1998) points out, post-master's programs offer specialized training and development opportunities that most traditional entry-level positions do not afford the new professional; one measure of success would be how many interns are recruited into academic library positions upon program completion. None of the Canadian programs, however, have been evaluated with respect to the program resources and activities (inputs and outputs), nor with respect to the impact the program had on those who participated.

It is the latter that is the focus of this study, specifically whether former interns have been recruited into and retained in academic libraries. Further, do former interns perceive particular career development experiences or elements of an internship program (e.g., mentorship relationships, professional development and training) as providing them with the opportunity, and informing their decision, to stay in academic libraries?

The findings of this study have relevance to Canadian academic library organizations that are beginning to feel the impact of "boomer" retirements and are considering academic library internships as a recruitment strategy. Former interns have not been followed up and tracked to see whether they have remained in academic librarianship or to explore whether the experiences that they had were relevant to their career development. Furthermore, libraries that have formerly had programs and would like to reemploy this strategy will have information on which to base rationale for budgetary and institutional support.

This study will provide library schools and academic institutions with a solid basis on which to discuss the recruitment needs of academic libraries in Canada and the resources that they are willing to invest in training and development of new professionals. It will also benefit library graduates who are considering internship programs as an avenue for developing a career in academic libraries.

LITERATURE REVIEW

Although library and information science (LIS) researchers have focused minimal attention on residency or internship programs, several key studies have evaluated programs from the perspective of the program/institution or participants.[4] Brewer and Winston (2001) support the importance of knowing whether residency programs have been successful in promoting recruitment into academic librarianship. They surveyed library administrators and program coordinators at twenty-two U.S. institutions that have residency programs and asked them to identify the importance of a number of factors related to the evaluation of programs.

Most of the factors that were identified focused on performance measures such as size and quality of the applicant pool, completion rate, or work performance of the program participants. Two outcomes, however, "placement in other academic libraries" and "placement in host institution," were consistently identified. Placement in academic libraries was identified by 100% of the respondents as being very or somewhat important, and 62% of the respondents identified placement in host institution as being very or somewhat important. This supports the understanding that recruitment into academic librarianship is an important factor in evaluating programs and that it is not just an institutional perspective of short-term benefit or self-interest that is seen as important in evaluation.

Perez's (2007) study for his master's thesis surveyed library administrators and program coordinators at 12 Association of Research Libraries' (ARL) institutions that have active residency programs. He describes the retention of residents in academic libraries as the "ultimate goal" of residency programs in ARL libraries. Although the sample size for his thesis was small ($N = 12$), his results support Brewer and Winston's (2001) findings about the importance of these programs as recruitment tools for academic librarianship and the lesser, but still important, short-term aspect of recruiting residents by the home institutions. In addition, 82% of Perez's survey respondents identified "placement in academic library" as a measure in determining program success and 46% identified "retention of resident upon program completion" as an applicable measure of success.

Perez also explored nursing residency models and the program elements that they have in common with library residencies. One of the major points of comparison between the two was the curricular component of nursing residency programs that was directed to skills development in areas such as critical thinking, interpersonal communication, and time management. He recommends that library residency programs identify necessary skill areas for academic librarianship and develop curricular components to satisfy these skill sets. Perez also makes the link between development of skills and competencies in the residency program and development of competence in practice or future careers.

Two other articles are of particular interest to this study because of the research focus, which includes gathering data about career development (Brewer 1997) and career success (Lanier & Henderson 1999) from the perspectives of former interns or residents. Both studies, however, are also inconclusive about how much the internship or residency experience contributed to developing a career in academic librarianship.

Brewer (1997), on behalf of the American Library Association, Office for Library Personnel Resources, conducted a study from the perspective of 109 former residents in post-master's programs in U.S. academic and research libraries. The study gathered qualitative data from participants about the design and structure of their program as well as career development. Brewer (1997) found that 64% of the respondents were offered positions in their host institutions, with 51% of the respondents accepting their respective offers.

Overall, Brewer (1997) concludes that such programs are very successful in attracting individuals who may not have been interested in academic and research libraries. These programs can also provide positive experiences and developmental opportunities that are important to those beginning their careers. Conclusions cannot, however, be drawn about career development or retention in academic libraries, and the data is not explicit as to whether skills and competencies developed during the program experience were useful in developing a career in academic librarianship.

In a study by Lanier and Henderson (1999), research into residency/internship programs was structured around five outcomes: finding a job, key competency development, leadership development, career success, and program satisfaction. Former program participants in three post-master's degree programs were surveyed: University of Illinois at Chicago, the National Library of Medicine, and the Library of Congress. Although the respondent's recruitment into any specific library sector cannot be identified, it is interesting to note that 68% of the respondents indicated that they felt the internship was a factor in attaining their current position, and 75.5% felt opportunities for advancement or promotion were greater as a result of the program. Most significantly, 90% of the former interns felt the competencies they developed in their programs were still useful in their current positions, although there is no indication of how many years had elapsed since program completion.

In summary, recruitment and retention in academic librarianship is an important factor in evaluating residency or internship programs. There is also a sense in the work of Lanier and Henderson (1999) and of Perez (2007) that competencies and skills developed during the post MLS period could be key to future career development.

RESEARCH DESIGN

This study was designed to establish whether Canadian internship programs have been successful in promoting recruitment into academic librarianship and whether former interns have been recruited into and retained in academic libraries. It also probed whether former interns perceive that particular experiences or elements of an internship program have aided in their overall skill and competency development and career development and experience.

- To what extent are former participants in academic library internship programs in Canada recruited into permanent positions in university libraries?

- To what extent do former participants in academic library internship programs remain in university libraries once they are recruited into university library positions?

- To what extent do former participants in academic library internship programs perceive that their experience in an academic internship program was a factor in
    - recruitment into professional positions in university libraries.
    - recruitment into professional positions in other library sectors.
    - developing skills and competencies used throughout their careers.
    - their overall career development.

PROCEDURES

Methodology

To capture the largest pool possible, the study population comprised library/program administrators and former participants in the three Canadian academic library intern programs identified at the University of New Brunswick, University of Winnipeg, and University of Alberta. Table 3.1 indicates the years that the various programs have operated and the number of participants at each of the institutions.

Table 3.1 Canadian academic library internship programs by institution, years of program, and number of participants

Institution	Years of program	Number of participants
University of Alberta	2000–2008	34
University of New Brunswick	1999–2005	6
University of Winnipeg	2001–2006	4
Total (all programs)		44

Program administrators from the academic library intern programs at the three universities were contacted and asked to describe elements of the intern program and provide a list of former interns. Preliminary contacts with these programs confirmed that lists of former interns existed and were complete and accurate. These former interns were contacted via e-mail and given the option of participating and contributing data to the study. Demographic, program experience, recruitment, and career development data about the former interns were gathered and compared. The study was conducted over a six-week period in spring 2009.

This study consisted of two phases: the first phase involved telephone interviews with library/program administrators from the three institutions; the second phase was a Web-based survey whose link was e-mailed to former participants of the Canadian academic library internship programs. Telephone interviews (see Appendix 3.1) were structured to collect qualitative data that could be used to describe the structure of the respective programs, and to identify the program elements that were provided to program participants. Through the interviews, program activities (such as work and/or training in reference service) were identified along with specialized program components, such as the opportunity to participate in a mentorship program. These interviews provided insightful information that was useful in developing the survey instrument used to collect data from former interns.

Brewer (1997) and Lanier and Henderson (1999) were contacted, and their survey instruments were requested. One survey instrument was received and examined for potential usefulness and questions utilized as appropriate for this study. The resulting Web survey instrument was based on the previously used survey instrument and the qualitative data collected in the telephone interviews. New questions were constructed as necessary to address issues related to program experience and career development. Both methodologies for collecting data (the telephone interview and the Web survey) have the same legal and ethical requirements to guarantee informed consent and protect individual privacy and confidentiality. To ensure compliance with these requirements, the research proposal was examined by the Institutional Review Board at Simmons College.

The question of whether to offer incentives to complete the survey was addressed by advising study participants that they had the opportunity to participate in a drawing for a one-year membership to the Canadian Library Association if they so wished. Once the survey was completed, the Web instrument directed study participants to contact an individual not directly connected with the study to be put into the drawing for the membership.

Data Quality

Telephone interviews ensured that the program experience and career development variables outlined in the objectives and research questions were fully explored. The telephone interviews also confirmed the variables that needed to be incorporated into the survey so as to enhance content validity. To improve reliability and validity, the survey and telephone interview questions were pretested by volunteer librarians familiar with intern recruitment to see whether instructions were clear and to determine whether the questions were posed so as to elicit meaningful information. Pretesting highlighted potential problems and increased the reliability of the survey instrument. The survey instrument was revised and retested to improve the quality of the data gathered (Lee 2004).

LIMITATIONS

One limitation of the study was the difficulty of locating current contact information for former interns; some were no longer active in the profession of librarianship. Additionally, not all former interns agreed to participate. One follow-up e-mail was sent to encourage participation of former interns.

Of the group that agreed to participate, professional experience ranged from approximately one to eight years in the profession. Not all former interns were established long enough in the workforce to identify a clear career path. They may have been in their first job since leaving the internship program and therefore found it difficult to compare how the experience of the internship program translated to other jobs. Also unknown was the number of former interns who would have remained in academic librarianship if there were jobs available that offered them opportunity and career growth potential.

FINDINGS

A total of 35 responses were received as a result of the 44 survey requests sent. The group of 35 participants produced a response rate of 79.5% for the Web survey.

Survey Participant Profiles

As shown in Table 3.2, the vast majority of the study group were former residents of the U of A Academic Librarian Internship Program, female, and born between 1970 and 1979. Only four interns identified themselves as a member of a designated group.[5] Three were members of visible minorities, one identified as a person with disabilities, and none identified as a member of an aboriginal group. The majority of participants spent one year in an internship program. Only the University of New Brunswick and the University of Winnipeg programs had hired interns for more than one year at the time that the survey was done.

Table 3.2 Canadian academic library interns by program, gender, year of birth, designated group, and length of time in internship program

	Frequency	%	Cumulative %
University of Alberta	29	82.9	82.9
University of New Brunswick	2	5.7	88.6
University of Winnipeg	4	11.4	100.0
Total (all programs)	35		
Female	27	84.4	84.4
Male	5	15.6	100.0
Transgender	0	0	100.0
Total (all genders)	32		
1950–1959	1	3.3	3.3
1960–1969	1	3.3	6.6
1970–1979	25	83.4	90.0
1980–1989	3	10.0	100.0
Total (all birth years)	30		
Visible minorities	3	75.0	75.0
Persons with disabilities	1	25.0	100.0
Aboriginal peoples	0	0	100.0
Total (all designated groups)	4		
One year	30	85.7	85.7
Two years	3	8.6	94.3
Three years	0	0	94.3
Other	2	5.7	100.0
Total (all years)	35		

Participation in Program Work and Training Activities and Perceived Importance to Career Development

Survey questions about participation in various work and training activities established a fairly common program profile among the three programs under review. Almost all new professionals participated in reference service training (82.9%, $n = 29$) and reference service work (100.0%, $n = 35$), bibliographic instruction or information literacy training (60.0%, $n = 21$), and bibliographic instruction or information literacy work (100.0%, $n = 35$), along with collection development/evaluation training (54.3%, $n = 19$) and collection development/evaluation work (80.0%, $n = 28$).

A majority of interns participated in liaison with faculty or other members of the university community work (74.3%, $n = 26$) and technology/Web development/digital initiatives work (74.3%, $n = 26$) but were provided with lower levels of training for the work performed, 31.4% ($n = 11$) and 40.0% ($n = 14$), respectively. Few interns were trained in cataloging (2.9%, $n = 1$) or provided with work in cataloging of materials (5.7%, $n = 2$). Table 3.3 indicates the perceived importance of these experiences or activities to the career path and development of the intern participants.

The greater majority of interns agreed that they perceived that reference service training (81.3%, $n = 26$) and work (96.6%, $n = 31$), along with bibliographic instruction or information literacy training (64.6%, $n = 20$) and work (93.4%, $n = 28$), were important. In addition, the perception of a majority of interns indicated that collection development/evaluation (67.8%, $n = 21$), liaison work with faculty or other members of the university community (77.5%, $n = 24$), and technology/Web development/digital initiatives (68.7%, $n = 22$) were important.

Training in these activities, however, was not perceived to be as important as the tasks themselves, 42% ($n = 13$), 42% ($n = 13$), and 46.7% ($n = 14$), respectively. Unlike the aforementioned tasks, cataloging training (6.6%, $n = 2$) and work (10%, $n = 3$) were not perceived to be as important to career path and development as other activities, but it must also be noted that few interns participated in cataloging compared with other activities.

Participation in Specialized Program Components: Perceived Importance to Career Path and Development

Program participation in identified specialized program components indicates that all three Canadian programs are structured to employ fairly common program activities. The vast majority of interns (85.7%, $n = 30$) participated in a mentor relationship/program, and 68.7% ($n = 22$) agreed that it was important to their career path and development. All interns (100.0%, $n = 35$) agreed that they had the opportunity to participate in professional development (e.g., workshops, conferences), and 96.9% ($n = 31$) agreed or strongly agreed that these opportunities were important as well.

The great majority of interns (97.1%, $n = 34$) had the opportunity to participate in project work, and 90.6% ($n = 29$) agreed or strongly agreed that it was important. Only 42.9% ($n = 15$) of interns had the opportunity to take a leadership role, and all ($n = 15$) perceived that it was important or very important to their career path and development. The "other" program components (8.6%, $n = 3$) that were identified as ones in which interns had participated were marketing and communications, liaison with students with special needs, and managing a service and staff. There was a clear perception that these opportunities were beneficial to their career path and development as well. See Table 3.4.

Table 3.3 Participation in library work and training components and perceived importance to career development

Program component:	1 Strongly disagree	2	3	4	5 Strongly agree	N/A	Mean value
Reference service							
Training (n = 32)	3.1% (1)	3.1% (1)	0.0% (0)	43.8% (14)	37.5% (12)	12.5% (4)	4.25
Work (n = 32)	3.1% (1)	0.0% (0)	0.0% (0)	31.3% (10)	65.6% (21)	0.0% (0)	4.56
Bibliographic instruction or information literacy							
Training (n = 31)	3.2% (1)	6.5% (2)	0.0% (0)	19.4% (6)	45.2% (14)	25.8% (8)	4.30
Work (n = 30)	3.3% (1)	3.3% (1)	0.0% (0)	16.7% (5)	76.7% (23)	0.0% (0)	4.60
Collection development/evaluation							
Training (n = 31)	3.2% (1)	9.7% (3)	0.0% (0)	19.4% (6)	22.6% (7)	38.7% (12)	3.79
Work (n = 31)	3.2% (1)	9.7% (3)	6.5% (2)	35.5% (11)	32.3% (10)	12.9% (4)	3.96
Liaison with faculty							
Training (n = 31)	3.2% (1)	0.0% (0)	0.0% (0)	9.7% (3)	32.3% (10)	54.8% (17)	4.50
Work (n = 31)	3.2% (1)	0.0% (0)	0.0% (0)	19.4% (6)	58.1% (18)	19.4% (6)	4.60
Technology/Web/digital initiatives							
Training (n = 30)	3.3% (1)	3.3% (1)	0.0% (0)	20.0% (6)	26.7% (8)	46.7% (14)	4.19
Work (n = 32)	3.1% (1)	3.1% (1)	0.0% (0)	28.1% (9)	40.6% (13)	25.0% (8)	4.33
Cataloging							
Training (n = 30)	0.0% (0)	0.0% (0)	3.3% (1)	3.3% (1)	3.3% (1)	90.0% (27)	4.00
Work (n = 30)	0.0% (0)	3.3% (1)	3.3% (1)	6.7% (2)	3.3% (1)	83.3% (25)	3.60

Table 3.4 Participation in other program components and opportunities and perceived importance to career development

Program component	1 Strongly disagree	2	3	4	5 Strongly agree	N/A	Mean value
Mentorship relationship/program (n = 32)	6.3% (2)	12.5% (4)	3.1% (1)	28.1% (9)	40.6% (13)	9.4% (3)	3.93
Professional development (n = 32)	3.1% (1)	0.0% (0)	0.0% (0)	34.4% (11)	62.5% (20)	0.0% (0)	4.53
Project work (n = 32)	3.1% (1)	0.0% (0)	3.1% (1)	28.1% (9)	62.5% (20)	3.1% (1)	4.52
Leadership role (n = 30)	0.0% (0)	0.0% (0)	3.3% (1)	6.7% (2)	43.3% (13)	46.7% (14)	4.75
Other (n = 17)	0.0% (0)	0.0% (0)	0.0% (0)	5.9% (1)	11.8% (2)	82.4% (14)	4.67

Career Path and Development Path of Former Interns

Career path and development of former interns was a major focus of the study because it aids in understanding how much the internship experience contributed to developing a career in academic librarianship. Most former interns would have preferred to stay in the university library where they had done their internship (81.8%, n = 27) or would have preferred to continue to work in a university library (97.0%, n = 32). When asked why they wanted to continue to work or not work in the university library organizations in which they had done their internships, more than thirty responses (n = 32)[6] were received.

The responses clustered into eight categories or reasons for wishing to stay. The majority of the responses stated that former interns enjoyed the workplace (flexibility, great colleagues, supportive environment, challenging initiatives, etc.; n = 20), appreciated the work they were assigned (work was varied, project work was interesting, etc.) (n = 6), and felt they could contribute more and apply what had been learned during the internship (n = 5).

Three reasons were given by those former interns who would not have wanted to continue to work in their host institutions (18.2%, $n = 6$). The primary reason was that they needed to relocate to another city for personal reasons ($n = 4$). Not feeling that they fit in ($n = 1$) and lack of position availability ($n = 1$) were also mentioned.

Table 3.5 suggests that almost all former interns would have preferred to continue to work in a university library (97.0%, $n = 32$). When asked for reasons for this choice, responses ($n = 32$) indicated the most common reason was preference for an academic environment (challenging and stimulating work, variety of responsibilities, continuous learning, range of clients, etc.; $n = 18$), followed by the feeling that university libraries were a "good fit" for the individual ($n = 7$). Other responses indicated their career goal to work in a university library developed as a result of or reinforced by the internship opportunity ($n = 7$), and they felt they had the ability to contribute through research and appreciated academic status ($n = 5$). The sole dissenting voice raised for not wanting to work in a university library expressed the perception that career advancement would happen more quickly in a smaller organization where there were greater opportunities for leadership ($n = 1$).

As can be seen in Table 3.5, the great majority of former interns applied for jobs first in university libraries (72.7%, $n = 24$), followed by special libraries (36.4%, $n = 12$) and college libraries/technical institute/university college libraries (30.3%, $n = 10$). Over half (54.5%, $n = 18$) of former interns found their first job in a university library, followed by special libraries (18.2%, $n = 6$) and in a nontraditional workplace (12.1%, $n = 4$). Second and subsequent jobs were most often found in a university library (50.0%, $n = 12$) or a college/technical institute/university college library (25.0%, $n = 6$).

Table 3.5 Applying for and finding jobs after completion of academic library internship program

Type of Library	Applying for a first job by type of library ($n = 33$)*	First job found by type of library ($n = 33$)	Second and subsequent jobs found by type of library ($n = 24$)*
University library	72.7% (24)	54.5% (18)	50.0% (12)
College library/technical institute/university college	30.3% (10)	12.1% (4)	25.0% (6)
Regional library or consortium	9.1% (3)	6.1% (2)	4.2% (1)
Public library	18.2% (6)	0.0% (0)	4.2% (1)
Special library	36.4% (12)	18.2% (6)	12.5% (3)
School library	0.0%	0.0% (0)	0.0% (0)
Nontraditional library workplace	15.2% (5)	12.1% (4)	0.0% (0)
Other	3.0% (1)	0.0% (0)	12.5% (3)

*More than one possible response.

Recruitment into Permanent Positions in University Libraries

Although almost all former interns would have preferred to work in a university library, only slightly more than half of the program participants found a job in the university sector. As shown in Table 3.6, 60.6% ($n = 20$) of former participants in internship programs are currently working in university libraries. Of those, 70.0% ($n = 14$) are in tenure-track or continuing appointment positions. A majority of former interns (57.1%, $n = 8$) who are not currently working in a university library plan to apply in the future, and 42.9% ($n = 6$) are not sure whether they will apply to a university library in the future.

Those respondents who said they would apply for a university library job in the future had two primary reasons: they enjoyed the academic environment (teaching, research, technology) and work with faculty, students, and other clients. Respondents who were not sure about applying for a university job in the future gave three reasons. Having a stable position in another library sector and wanting to have a specific position or opportunity in applying to university libraries were mentioned most often.

Retention in University Libraries

By and large, former interns who have been recruited into university libraries intend to stay. Table 3.6 also indicates that 90.0% ($n = 18$) of those former participants in academic library internship programs currently working in university libraries intend to continue to work in them. Of that percentage, 68.4% ($n = 13$) expect to work in university libraries for their entire career, others for lesser periods of time.

Over half of those currently working in university libraries and intending to stay (66.6%, $n = 12$) responded to a question asking why they chose to remain in university libraries. Most of the responses centered on the nature of the work in university libraries. Respondents described how they enjoyed subject specialization and the opportunity to do research ($n = 8$); the challenging, interesting and rewarding nature of the work ($n = 7$); and the opportunity to work with students and faculty ($n = 6$). One respondent indicated the decision to stay depended on the opportunities for research, interesting projects, and professional development.

Table 3.6 Recruitment and retention of intern participants in university libraries

Currently working in a university library ($n=33$)	Yes	No	Not sure
	60.6% (20)	39.4% (13)	
Type of appointment ($n=20$)			
o Tenure track	45.0% (9)		
o Continuing appt	25.0% (5)		
o Temporary/sessional	30.0% (6)		
o Other	0.0%		
Intend to continue working in university libraries? ($n=20$)	90.0% (18)	0.0% (0)	10.0% (2)
How long will you continue to work in university libraries? ($n=19$)			
o 1-5 years	10.5% (2)		
o 6-10 years	5.3% (1)		
o 11-15 years	10.5% (2)		
o 16-20 years	5.3% (1)		
o entire career	68.4% (13)		
Not currently working in a university library ($n=13$)			
Intend to apply for work in a university library in the future ($n=14$)	57.1% (8)	0.00 (0)	42.9% (6)

Perception of Intern Program Experience as a Factor in Career Path and Development

Former interns were asked directly about their perceptions of program experience and subsequent career path and development. As seen in Table 3.7, the bulk of former participants in academic library internship programs perceive that their experience in an academic internship program was a factor in developing skills and competencies used throughout their careers (96.9%, $n = 31$) and overall career development (87.5%, $n = 28$). A substantial number of former interns (65.6%, $n = 21$) felt their experience contributed to recruitment into a professional position in a university library, and almost a third (31.3%, $n = 10$) felt it contributed to recruitment into a professional position in another library sector. It is noteworthy that none of the former participants of internship programs felt their participation did not have an impact on their subsequent career path and development.

Table 3.7 Perception of intern program experience as a factor in career path and development (n = 32)

Perception that internship program contributed to:	Response rate (more than one response possible)
Recruitment into a professional position in a university library	65.6% (21)
Recruitment into a professional position in other library sectors	31.3% (10)
Developing skills and competencies used throughout your career	96.9% (31)
Your overall career development	87.5% (28)
Participation had no impact at all	0.0% (0)
Other	3.1% (1)

Respondents were asked to comment about how they felt participation in an internship program contributed to their career path and development. This question elicited nine reasons. The reason most commonly given was the program confirmed skills, developed a knowledge base, and provided experience that would have been difficult to gain otherwise ($n = 22$). Former interns also commonly expressed the program provided status within the library community, particularly when searching for jobs ($n = 10$), the opportunity to make connections, network and learn from many colleagues ($n = 9$), a chance to gain a broad view and the "big picture" of academic librarianship ($n = 7$), and valuable mentorship ($n = 6$).

Former interns were asked how their career path and development would have been different if they had not participated in an academic library internship program. Their responses indicated that their participation had developed skills that made them competitive in looking for jobs ($n = 10$), and they would have ended up in jobs in other sectors or areas other than academic librarianship ($n = 7$). Responses directed to reasons career path and development would not have been different were related to already knowing their career direction and knowing what they wanted in developing their career ($n = 2$) or to the fact that the program gave them a head start on a career direction they had already decided upon ($n = 2$).

Asked about what changes they would suggest to academic library internship programs, former interns suggested a number of improvements programs could consider. Chief among these was the provision of a longer internship period, more structured opportunities for training, feedback/supervision and direction, self-selection of mentors, and the development of more internship programs in Canada.

DISCUSSION

Have academic library interns attained permanent positions and remained in Canadian academic libraries? Responses from former participants of academic library internship programs provide evidence that most interns would have preferred to stay in the university library in which they completed their internship or one of a similar nature. However, only about half of the intern respondents found their first job in a university library, and only slightly more than half are now working in university libraries. Three-quarters of former interns are in permanent professional positions.

A number of reasons were advanced concerning the desire to work in university libraries, most of which related to the nature of the work assignments, the workplace setting, and the academic environment. On the basis of the findings expressed by survey respondents, it is clear that former interns not currently working in university libraries will apply to work in them in the future.

Questions about job market and opportunities to apply for university library positions were not asked of former interns. However, when assessing the results of the survey, it seems possible from responses given that there were limited opportunities and fewer jobs to apply for than interest of the respondents warranted. Those currently working in university libraries intend to continue working in that sector of librarianship, many reporting they intend to stay for their entire careers.

Do former interns perceive career development experiences or elements of an internship program provided opportunity and informed their decision to stay in academic libraries? Most participants of academic library internship programs had a fairly common experience. They mentioned the opportunity to engage in a variety of activities, including reference service, bibliographic instruction or information literacy, building liaison relationships with faculty, technology initiatives, and how each was perceived as important to their career paths and development. The high levels of agreement overall suggest that the current work and training components of Canadian academic library internship programs are appropriate for the career development of intern participants.

An examination of other program components, such as mentorship, professional development, and project work, indicates high levels of participation with the exception of leadership roles. Although many interns had the chance to participate in a mentor relationship or program, the opportunity to engage in such a relationship and program was not perceived as being as important as the other program components. Few interns had the opportunity to take a leadership role, but it was perceived as most important to career path and development by the small number of those who were allowed to engage in the role. These are points for further exploration, and academic library internship programs should pay special attention to the mentorship and leadership components of programming.

Given the data about the perceived importance of the library work, training and other components of academic library internship programs, it is noteworthy that almost all former interns felt they acquired skills and competencies as a direct result of their participation in academic library internship programs. Further, not one of the respondents perceived that participation had no impact on their career path and development. It is unfortunate, but not unexpected, that not all former interns were recruited into university libraries or that a majority perceived the intern program experience was a factor in their recruitment into a professional position in a university library.

The data provides ample evidence that academic library internship programs succeed overall in providing valuable experience and the opportunity to develop professional skills and knowledge. Both are very important to career development and to help make interns attractive to future employers.

Future studies might examine the reasons former interns are not finding job opportunities in academic libraries. Academic library recruiters could probably provide some insights into position availability and recruitment opportunities. The personnel administrators of university libraries could be surveyed to establish their view of recruitment opportunities for former participants in academic library internship programs. They may also provide some insight as to whether new recruits bring the needed experience and the necessary skills and competencies that the interns perceive they have to offer university library organizations; this will be important to their future career path and development.

CONCLUSION

The three Canadian academic library internship programs examined in this study have developed largely on the premise that there is a long-term advantage to offering internships to new professionals. As baby boomers continue to exit the ranks of academic libraries, there is the expectation that developing a cadre of competent, experienced librarians allows for movement into increasingly more responsible university library positions. Thus, evaluation of these programs is important in determining whether former interns recruited through internship programs are retained in academic librarianship.

Data obtained through this study provides half of the larger story about Canadian academic library internship programs. The perceptions of former program participants are valuable, but also needed is the view of academic library recruiters and their assessment of whether academic library internship programs provide well-qualified candidates to enrich recruitment pools and whether their program experience is of benefit to the institution.

The results of this study have the potential to revitalize interest and promote further investment into academic library internship programs in Canada, particularly in institutions where programs have been suspended. Many postsecondary institutions with library schools collaborate to provide work and developmental experiences for their respective students. This study provides a solid basis on which to begin or advance a conversation regarding the importance of academic library internship programs and the need for further development of internship programming in Canada.

NOTES

1. For the purpose of this study, "academic library internships" are defined as taking place in university libraries, not in community college, technical institute, or university college libraries.

2. John Teskey, e-mail message to the author, November 4, 2007.

3. Karen Hunt, e-mail message to the author, November 5, 2007.

4. The various studies use different terminology to refer to the same subject: post-MLS training programs. Therefore, both terms "intern" and "resident" are used.

5. In Canada's federal Employment Equity Act, four designated groups are defined for employment equity purposes: women, aboriginal peoples, persons with disabilities, and members of visible minorities.

6. A percentage is not given when respondents could give more than one response.

REFERENCES

Association of Research Libraries. 1992. Internship, residency and fellowship programs in ARL libraries. SPEC Kit 188. http://www.eric.ed.gov/ERICDocs/data/ericdocs2sql/content_storage_01/0000019b/80/14/01/9b.pdf

Brewer, J. 1997. Post-master's residency programs: Enhancing the development of new professionals and minority recruitment in academic and research libraries. *College and Research Libraries* 56:528–537.

Brewer, J. 1998. Implementing post-master's residency programs. *Leading Ideas* 4. http://www.arl.org/bm~doc/li4.pdf

Brewer, J. 2007. An overview of research library residency programs. *Synergy: News from ARL Diversity Initiatives* 2. http://app.e2ma.net/campaign/c954cfadf699bb98dc59e2c4d617f7a1

Brewer, J., and M.D. Winston. 2001. Program evaluation for internship/residency programs in academic and research libraries. *College and Research Libraries* 62:307–315.

Hepburn, P. 2001. Residency programs as a means of nurturing new librarians. *Feliciter* 47(3):142–144.

Lanier, D., and C. L. Henderson. 1999. Library residencies and internships as indicators of success: Evidence from three programs. *Bulletin of the Medical Library Association* 87:192–199.

Lee, D. 2004. Survey research: Reliability and validity. *Library Administration and Management* 18:211–212.

Perez, M. 2007. From new graduate to competent practitioner: Rethinking the architecture of post-MLS residency programs in ARL libraries. Master's thesis, University of North Carolina at Chapel Hill.

APPENDIX 3.1

Interview Guide

Opening Statement

Thank you for agreeing to participate in this interview. Your participation is voluntary, and you will be free to withdraw from the interview at any time. The intent of the interview is to ascertain information about your library's internship program. I don't anticipate that any information you are providing will be considered confidential; however, do inform me if you feel that it is and that it should not be published or disseminated further. Direct quotations from this interview may be used in any publications resulting from this research study. The interview is not expected to take more than a half hour of your time.

Interview Schedule

1) In what year did your institution's internship program begin?

2) Is the program still running?

    2.1) If no, in what year did it end?

    2.2) Do you anticipate that it might revive?

3) How many interns have you had over the years of the program to 2008?

    3.1) Approximately how many interns each year?

4) Explain how the internship program was/is structured?

    {possible prompts for program components}

    4.1) Library work and training components – reference, instruction, cataloging, collections?

    4.2) Mentorship program or opportunities?

    4.3) Professional development opportunities?

    4.4) Project work?

    4.5) Leadership role?

5) Have you recruited interns from your program into permanent, tenure–track positions?

    5.1) If no, why not?

    5.2) If yes, how long were they retained within your library?

Closing

Do you agree to be contacted again for follow-up questions and/or clarification of information you have provided? You will be provided with a summary of your responses to the interview questions and will be free to add or subtract from the information you have provided.

Thank you for participating.

Chapter 4

The Development of the University of Louisville Libraries' Diversity Residency Program

Latisha Reynolds, Caroline Daniels, John Chenault, and Toccara Porter

In March 2007, the University of Louisville's Dean of Libraries charged a committee with restructuring the existing diversity residency, with an eye to enhancing both the participants' experiences and the services offered by the libraries. Through a process of research into other institutions' models, interviews with current and past residents and interns, and discussion with the libraries' leadership, we developed a new structure for our residency program. This chapter describes and discusses that process, as well as the outcomes. Adjustments that occurred after the program was initiated and that were necessitated by developments in the residents' interest and the economy, are also addressed.

The University of Louisville is a large publicly funded metropolitan research institution. Although the institution puts an emphasis on enhancing its research capabilities, it also values its position as an urban institution. The university was originally a municipal university, funded in part by the city of Louisville. It joined the state university system in 1970, but its location in the largest city in the state of Kentucky remains an important part of its identity. With a current enrollment of nearly 22,000, it is the second-largest university in the state, behind the flagship University of Kentucky.

The University of Louisville Libraries, which joined the Association of Research Libraries (ARL) in 2002, consists of five individual libraries. The main library, named in honor of former faculty member and administrator, William F. Ekstrom, is located on the Belknap Campus and serves undergraduates, graduate and professional students, and faculty in arts and sciences, engineering, business, education, and social work. The Kornhauser Health Sciences Library, which is the second-largest of the university libraries, is located on the Health Sciences Campus, closer to the urban business district. It serves students and faculty in medicine, dentistry, nursing, and public health. In addition, smaller libraries serve the school of music and the fine arts department, and the University of Louisville Archives and Records Center serves as a repository for the history of both the university and the community. The libraries serve large and diverse communities, and the original internship program was designed to enhance diversity among University of Louisville librarians.

ORIGINAL INTERNSHIP PROGRAM

For more than a decade, the University of Louisville Libraries has worked diligently to increase the number of librarians from underrepresented groups, especially the number of African Americans, which make up the largest minority population in the city and at the university. The University of Louisville Libraries' Dean, Hannelore Rader, felt there was a need for more diversity within the libraries because the University of Louisville has one of the most diverse student populations in the state. Also, diversity is an important component of the University of Louisville's overall goals. The libraries initiated an internship program in 1999 as a way to diversify the faculty of the libraries while helping to create a more welcoming environment for students.

This program, which was a precursor to the current residency program, was aimed at students in the University of Kentucky's School of Library and Information Science's MLS program. Interns received up to three years' paid tuition toward their degree program, which was the only MLS program in the state at that time. Interns were hired as lecturers in the Ekstrom Library Reference Department. The position was structured as a regular librarian position. Interns shared reference librarian duties including working at the reference desk, teaching general orientation to the library classes, serving as a liaison to faculty in academic units, creating subject guides, ordering books for the collection, serving on committees, and other special projects. The interns had faculty status and were also encouraged to participate in professional activities such as publishing and presenting at professional conferences.

The internship program was funded with vacant positions, with the expectation they would be hired into permanent positions upon finishing their master's degrees. However, this was dependent on the dean's final approval. A few years after the first position was created at the Ekstrom Library, a second intern position was funded at the Kornhauser Health Sciences Library. In all, there were six interns between 1999 and 2006.

Overall, the internship met with mixed results. Three interns left before completing the MLS program, including the first two. After the departure of these two, the libraries revised the guidelines for acceptance into the internship program to require that applicants be admitted to the MLS program prior to admission to the internship. Although interns left for various reasons, this change in criteria may have led to the selection of individuals who were more likely to finish the internship program by reducing the likelihood that an intern would fail to be accepted into the MLS program, or decide after enrolling that library science was not something they wanted to pursue.

The program found greater success after the guidelines were revised. Three of the last four interns completed the internship, received degrees from the University of Kentucky, and obtained tenure-track librarian positions with the University of Louisville Libraries. Two of those librarians remain with the university, and one moved on to a management position at another institution.

The committee that was charged with developing the residency program based their analysis, in part, on feedback from several previous interns and residents of the earlier programs. However, the specific experience of John Chenault, as the final participant in the internship program and the only intern to serve in Kornhauser Health Sciences Library, was particularly informative.

LIBRARY RESIDENCY EXPERIENCE (JOHN CHENAULT)

I became aware of the University of Louisville Libraries' internship program in 2002 while attending the university to earn a graduate degree in Pan African Studies (PAS). I immediately recognized the extraordinary opportunities it afforded any student interested in pursuing a career in library and information science. In addition to receiving full tuition to attend the University of Kentucky (UK) School of Library and Information Science (LIS), the qualified candidate also was given a faculty appointment (with the rank of "lecturer") for the three-year period needed to complete the degree.

The faculty appointment came with a full benefits package and the other perquisites of faculty status: faculty rank and the opportunity to pursue tenure, for example. I was in the last year of my PAS master's program and decided to apply for the library internship to further my education and earn a second master's degree. To my disappointment, I was not accepted the first time around. However, when the opportunity presented itself the following year, I reapplied. In the interim, the application requirements were revised to strengthen the pool of candidates. Beginning in 2003, applicants were required to confirm acceptance in the University of Kentucky's LIS program before applying for a library internship. I successfully negotiated the application process and soon was interviewed and selected to fill a newly created internship in the University of Louisville's Kornhauser Health Sciences Library (KHSL).

The KHSL director, with the support of the dean of the university libraries, restructured a recently vacated faculty position to create the internship to which I was appointed. Prior to my official start date, KHSL administrators also drafted a comprehensive plan for my orientation and training. The orientation introduced me to the library, the health sciences campus, and their respective cultures. The training program identified the skill sets needed to perform my duties and responsibilities and provided a blueprint and timeline for their acquisition and implementation. I truly appreciated the thoroughness of the training regimen, because it introduced me to every department in the library and its functions.

Thus, for the first year of my internship, I spent time learning and working in technical services, circulation, interlibrary loan, and archives. Some of my assignments included the routine activities involved in providing services to library clients and patrons. Other duties included special projects related to electronic resources, instructional classes, and archival work. I rotated daily or weekly through these departments in addition to working regular shifts on the reference desk. I received training on the reference desk from my direct supervisor and from the other reference librarians in the department. Throughout the training process, my new colleagues were generous in their support of the internship and of me personally. Their expert guidance during my transition to the new job also gave me a distinct advantage in meeting the challenges of completing my LIS degree program.

I began the job and the degree program with high expectations but not quite knowing what to anticipate. My expectations were based on the way the internship program was designed, organized, and structured. The unknown factor for me had to do with the challenges presented by earning my degree online from the University of Kentucky while working full-time at the KHSL. I had never taken a course on Blackboard, and I was a little intimidated by the prospect of doing most of my coursework in cyberspace. At the same time, I was grateful for not having to commute 75 miles (the distance between Louisville and Lexington) on a weekly basis to attend class.

As it turned out, I quickly took to distance education and have since taught undergraduate courses on Blackboard for the University of Louisville's Pan African Studies Department. Although I did take three courses in a physical classroom setting to complete my University of Kentucky degree program, all of the classes were held on the University of Louisville's campus in the Ekstrom Library. However, as a result of being a distance education student, I do not feel any real connection to University of Kentucky as my alma mater. I visited the campus only a few times for orientations, midterm and final exams, and the comprehensive examination required to graduate from the program. Nevertheless, I am grateful for the instruction I received in University of Kentucky's LIS School, the curriculum, and coursework that prepared me to meet the challenges and demands of academic librarianship.

The three years I spent as an intern seemed to go by very quickly. One day I was starting classes, and soon thereafter I was sitting for the comprehensive examination. This is indicative of how smoothly I progressed through the process from beginning to end. I attribute two central features of the University of Louisville Libraries' internship program with making my matriculation an unqualified success: opportunity and organization. The program gave me the opportunity and financial support needed to enter the dynamic field of library and information science and, at the same time, provided the professional development and training needed to meet the demands and challenges of clinical librarianship in a health sciences library. Upon my completion of the internship, the university libraries hired me as a reference librarian in the KHSL, a tenure-track position. I have since been promoted to the rank of assistant professor. I am the only African American male librarian on the faculty of the university libraries. None of this would have been possible without the University of Louisville Libraries' commitment to and support of the University of Louisville's diversity program and initiatives. I am grateful for the opportunity I received, and hope that others will enjoy similar benefits in the future.

FROM INTERNSHIP TO RESIDENCY

Although John Chenault's experience in the internship program was positive, several factors prompted the change from an internship program that supported students through an MLS program to a post-MLS residency. In 2006, the libraries hired its first resident, and an (informal) residency program was established. The resident was a recent graduate from the University of Kentucky, and the dean agreed to hire him for one year after he finished the MLS program. This first resident would work in the reference department and have duties similar to those of the interns. He started just as the last intern was completing the program and subsequently hired into a permanent position. After the last two interns were hired, funds were not available to continue the internship program because the two vacant positions were filled. Even if there had been a vacant position available, there was a growing awareness that there was a limited supply of entry-level positions.

In addition, there were concerns about the extra risk involving internships as opposed to post-MLS residencies. If successful, internships are an excellent way to improve library diversity.

However, because the intern is earning the degree while working, he or she may not have the same commitment to the field that a graduate would.

Also, the libraries received feedback from several surveys conducted in 2006 and 2007 that addressed diversity and staffing concerns. Respondents expressed that our internships and residencies needed more structure in the program and recruitment process. The staffing concerns survey also provided information about departments and specific types of activities that library faculty and staff felt needed more resources—personnel in particular. Members of management also felt the searches should be national given the library system's Association of Research Libraries (ARL) status. All of these issues were factors taken into consideration as the program changed.

CREATING A FORMAL RESIDENCY PROGRAM

On the basis of the experiences with the internship program and feedback from the surveys, the libraries determined that the program needed additional structure and forethought to produce results that were useful to both the resident and the institution. The residents needed to gain valuable experience and exposure to working in an academic library, perhaps even experiencing a variety of settings within that environment. The program needed to serve the needs of the libraries but also needed to provide sufficient personnel to undertake specific goals and activities, as identified in the staffing survey.

A three-person committee was charged with identifying best practices and developing the structure of the program, including possible areas of assignment, along with creating a recruitment and assessment plan. The committee was aware that there were many residency programs already in existence. They therefore sought to create something unique—something that would be successful in attracting candidates to Louisville.

The three-person ad hoc committee—consisting of Reference Librarian and former intern Latisha Reynolds; Associate Director of the University Archives, Carrie Daniels; and Associate Dean for Assessment, Personnel and Research, Melissa Laning—began meeting in early 2007 and started developing a plan for identifying best practices. The key feature of this plan was to speak with individuals from other academic libraries that were involved in the development or oversight of similar programs. Working from ARL's Research Library Residency and Internship Programs database, the committee identified and contacted programs that seemed similar to the type of residency they hoped to develop.

Specifically, the ad hoc committee was interested in developing a residency program, which would require that the participant already hold an MLS and include rotations or some other means of sampling a variety of areas of specialization within an academic library setting. The committee's discussions with representatives from academic libraries covered a broad spectrum of issues from basic administrative considerations such as the duration of the program, salary, and methods of recruitment to more structural issues such as whether the program involved rotations (and, if so, how they were determined) and how the residents were supervised and evaluated.

In addition, discussions with librarians who were responsible for other residency programs covered more evaluative and perceptual areas and included questions about the residents' opinions on the value of the program, as well as the opinions of other librarians and staff about the program. The committee also asked these individuals what they would do differently and what the key factors in their success were. These interviews yielded useful observations, many of which were echoed by several institutions.

Additionally, committee members spoke with former interns and residents to get their assessment of earlier programs and suggestions for improvements for which they provided similar advice. Mentoring was identified as an important component, as was the idea of providing an orientation to the libraries as a whole—not just to the home department or first assignment. Further, the identification of the resident as a professional was viewed as important to the past participants. They appreciated when people treated them as fellow professionals who already possessed the training and skills to do the job, and they advised against "dumping" the work no one else wanted to do on the resident. There was interest in sampling the work of more than one environment, either from a positive experience in doing so or because they would have liked to have had this opportunity. Clearly, both the social environment and the work itself were important.

INITIAL DESIGN

On the basis of our research into other residencies and our knowledge of the libraries' goals for this program, we developed an initial structure for the redesigned residency program. The document that laid out our proposal included a statement of the purposes of the residency: to promote and contribute to diversity in the University of Louisville Libraries as well as in academic librarianship more broadly, to provide valuable staffing to departments, and to provide a useful experience to residents. Our initial proposal established a two-year program. Residents would begin in a home department where they would remain for six months to get grounded in that area and become acclimated to the libraries, the university, and the community.

After that initial period, they would rotate into other areas of the libraries. The first rotations would be selected following a general orientation and introduction to participating departments and would be based on the resident's skills and interests. The resident would spend six months in the rotation while continuing to work 20 percent of the time, or the equivalent of one day a week, in his or her home department. In this model, the resident would have the opportunity to work and gain experience in a different area of librarianship, yet still maintain a home base and thus have some continuity of community.

At the end of the second six-month period, the resident would move to his or her next rotation. During the final six months of the program, the resident would return full time to the home department. The idea here was to balance the need for support with the value of exposing the resident to different areas within the libraries. Because the residents were considered valuable resources, we also wanted to be sure they were shared across departments. The rotations would be proposed by the various libraries and departments, with an eye toward working on projects that would be valuable to the unit while giving the resident useful, marketable experience. It was stressed that these were to be professional-level projects. Projects that promoted diversity were encouraged.

Providing mentoring and a sense of community were high priorities in the redesign. In addition to providing the resident with a home department, the program also provided for a mentor. Former intern Latisha Reynolds agreed to serve in this capacity. This was a formal mentoring arrangement intended to supplement the mentoring the resident might receive through his or her home department, in rotations, and through other, less formal means. The resident was also assigned to serve on the diversity committee. In order not to overburden residents until they were acclimated to the position, this would be their only committee assignment for their first six months, after which they could opt to serve on other committees or teams.

The supervisory structure was clearly defined to identify who would be responsible for evaluations, work assignments, and similar tasks. The head of the home department was designated as the primary supervisor. However, program directors in the departments through which the resident rotated would have responsibility for supervision and evaluation of work done during the resident's rotation in their area. Residents, like other faculty librarians, would be subject to the same evaluation process as other library faculty. Specifically, the supervisor of the home department would prepare an annual review using feedback gathered from program directors that hosted rotations.

This initial design elicited seven rotation/home department proposals from diverse areas such as the university archives and records center, special collections and technical services departments, and the libraries' scholarly communications specialist.

Although there was enthusiasm for the residency program, the initial design met with some critical feedback. The two structural features that were raised as issues and discussed further with the libraries' leadership committee were the duration of the residency and the organization of the rotations. There was a suggestion that two years might not be sufficient, given that it may take a semester or more to develop enough competency to "fly solo." In a similar vein, it was noted that some of the rotations might need to be longer than others—in fact be twice as long—for the same reason. The committee charged with redesigning the residency and the leadership committee responded positively to these suggestions and added an option for the resident to be appointed for a third year.

Another area that elicited comments was the proposed salary. Initially, the minimum salary was established above the normal rate for entry-level librarians, in recognition that we would be competing in a nationwide employment environment and would need to offer extra incentive for someone to relocate to Louisville. There were concerns that this was unfair to others who had been hired at lower rates and to nonprofessional employees (many of whom, as elsewhere, held MLS degrees). The minimum salary was ultimately brought into alignment with the standard entry-level minimum starting salary for University of Louisville librarians.

A final part of the design of the program was the development of an orientation plan for new residents. Many of the aspects of the libraries and the university with which the resident needed to be familiarized were common to all new faculty and staff members. This ranged from parking and benefits to how the home department "works." Mentoring specifically in areas such as professional development, annual review documentation, and generally "getting along in the libraries" were included in a schedule of meetings stretching from the resident's first day to the end of the calendar year six months later. In addition, an article in the libraries' newsletter, the *Owl,* featured the resident, and monthly "lunch dates" were scheduled with the residents' assigned and informal mentors, along with the head of their home department.

SEEKING AND PREPARING FOR THE RESIDENT

In summer 2007, as the committee and the leadership group worked out these final details, the search committee began their work. Two of the three members of the residency restructuring committee were formal members of the search committee, and one served as an ex officio member. Five other faculty members and a staff member rounded out the search committee, which was chaired by Katherine Burger Johnson, archivist for manuscript collections.

Working from the program outline developed by the residency restructuring committee and the rotations proposed by libraries and departments, the committee developed the job ad, including requirements and preferred qualifications. Because the proposals were the heart of the position—and, we hoped, the uniquely attractive feature of the job—the proposed rotations were posted, along with the job description, to the libraries' diversity webpage and the libraries' jobs webpage. The associate dean for assessment, personnel, and research developed a list of local and national recruitment sources that included venues for underrepresented groups. This list was used to promote the position. Some organizations on the list included the American Library Association (ALA) and Association of Research Libraries (ARL) websites, the ARL residency database, the Kentucky Library Job Hotline, African American Librarians in Kentucky e-mail list, Asian/Pacific American Librarians Association job list, Chinese American Librarians Association job list, Reformanet, Black Caucus list, NewLib-L, LISjobs, and several library school lists.

The committee developed the position description, questions for the applicants, and questions for references. The position, along with the residency proposals from each department, were then posted to the library's website. Approximately thirty applications were received. Based on the qualifications, cover letter, and responses to the rotation proposals, the committee narrowed the number of prospects to five. After checking references, three people were chosen for interviews.

There was a brief delay during the search due to a hiring freeze, but, in spring 2008, the search committee received word that they could continue. Preparations began to bring in the candidates. The two-day interview process included dinner with faculty and staff members the first night, followed by a full day of activities. The schedule included a meeting with the dean, a library tour, interview with the search committee, a presentation open to library staff, a meeting with the proposal developers, and lunch with selected faculty members.

The search committee collected evaluations from each person involved in the process including the presentation attendees, proposal developers, search committee members, and even the lunch and dinner attendees. The evaluation asked participants to rate the prospective residents on their qualifications as observed. Once this process was completed, the committee identified and recommended a top candidate. The committee also submitted second and third choices in case the first choice did not accept the position. The dean accepted the committee's choice, and the committee contacted the top candidate, Toccara Porter, with the offer. The offer was accepted, and she was scheduled to start in June 2008.

After Ms. Porter accepted the position, the residency restructuring committee resumed meetings to plan for her arrival. On the basis of Ms. Porter's preferred areas of interest, which included the proposals made by the main library's reference and information literacy departments, the scholarly communications specialist, and the oral history center, the rotation areas were selected. The group met with proposal developers to determine the logical choice for a home department, as well as a likely sequence of rotations in the other areas. Reference was chosen as the home base where she would spend at least the first nine months of the program. The information literacy rotation, focusing on teaching library instruction classes, would also be incorporated into the first rotation, because most of the reference librarians teach and the departments work closely together.

The resident's mentor, in collaboration with the head of the reference department, developed the learning outcomes/work plan and an orientation schedule. Development of a work plan is a regular yearly requirement for faculty, so this served as a document that could be further developed by the resident as work duties expanded. The mentor worked with the restructuring committee, other departments, and staff to ensure that Ms. Porter received both proper training in reference and a general orientation to the main areas of the library. Ms. Reynolds and Ms. Porter also met regularly during the first six months to make sure the process was running smoothly and that Ms. Porter was comfortable with her learning goals, in addition to the overall workings of the program. To date, Ms. Porter is still working in the reference department and has also gained valuable experience in teaching, outreach (another area of interest), exhibits, scholarly communications, collection development, and liaison work.

There have been some changes to the original rotation plan due, in part, to retirements in the reference department, a downturn in the economy, and the resident's interest in reference and teaching. It was originally expected that Ms. Porter would do a summer rotation in the oral history center, but this was postponed until 2010. In the fall of 2009, she completed a scholarly communications rotation that involved work in special collections. Although there were unexpected changes, flexibly in this respect was also an original part of the planning for the program, and this has proved to be advantageous. The residency restructuring committee continues to meet as needed to evaluate the program in process and to oversee changes in the rotation structure and progression. As with the previous internship and residency programs, the resident's own words, in addition to our analysis, are instructive.

LIBRARY RESIDENCY EXPERIENCE (TOCCARA PORTER)

As a resident at the University of Louisville Libraries, my primary concentration has been in reference. This is significant for me given that, throughout my short career in librarianship, I can vividly recall my encounters with reference librarians in both academic and public libraries. Their confident demeanor in answering questions at the reference desk and their considerable knowledge base in locating items left me in awe. I wondered whether I would ever attain that level of ability and whether I would be given the chance to be a professional reference librarian in an academic library.

The University of Louisville was and has been that place for me. The residency has allowed me to improve my reference skills. In working to enhance these skills, I had to become familiar not only with the services of the university libraries but of the academic departments and organizations at the University of Louisville. This is necessary for me to become an effective communicator when promoting the library and collaborating with students, faculty, and staff. Essentially, I am maturing into a professional academic librarian, and for that I am very grateful.

As of this writing, I am in the second year of my residency. I saw the ad for the Diversity Residency position at the University of Louisville in October 2007. The timing was fitting, as I would graduate from Kent State in December of that year and had planned on moving back to Louisville, Kentucky, my hometown, to find employment. Information about library residency programs was not covered during my time in library school. However, I remember that several months prior to seeing the University of Louisville ad, Ohio State University had advertised an opening for a library resident.

At first glance, residency positions seemed to be no different from any other job, with the exception that most place an emphasis on hiring minority candidates who had recently graduated from library school. However, after reading the job description, applying for the position seemed appealing for several additional reasons.

First, it is no secret that securing jobs in academic librarianship is challenging. Applicant pools are highly competitive, and many university employers are seeking candidates with extensive library experience. As a recent library school graduate with less than five years experience working in libraries, I did not meet that criterion. Second, the position was advertised as entry level. The term "entry level" can be understood in various ways, some of them unsuitable for holders of advanced degrees. I focused more on the aspect that this library was seeking a candidate who wanted to work in academia but who did not have a significant amount of experience. This was an indicator that the candidate chosen would have room to grow by actively learning on the job.

Third, specific courses in library school prepared me for what is to be expected when interviewing for an academic librarianship position. For example, even though the residency was a non–tenure track position, I felt my exposure in library school to the concept of the tenure process for academic librarians would better my prospects as a viable candidate who was familiar with some of the systems involved in an academic library. The library school course, "The Academic Library," covered several aspects, including the tenure process, resume building, the importance of being concise in your writing, and how library faculty and administrative status employees influence the operations and decision-making process of an academic library.

Another example is the aspect of research and publication. As part of my school's requirements for graduation, I had to complete a culminating experience. Therefore, when I entered my last semester of library school, I chose to write a research report, "The Black Experience in Library School." The research, which surveyed the encounters of racism among black students in ALA-accredited library schools, was being edited for publication at the time of the interview. Considering that research and publication are high priorities in academic librarianship, I believed my research paper demonstrated my potential for becoming a tenure-track academic librarian.

For those reasons, I decided to apply; but I still needed to find out exactly what a diversity residency program entailed. In looking through the literature, I came across *Diversity in Libraries: Academic Residency Programs* (Cogell and Gruwell 2001). This work profiled residency programs from three perspectives: first, from the standpoint of administrators in charge of the program; second, from those who were current residents; and third, from the retrospective viewpoint of former residents looking back on their experiences in library residency programs. The residents' examples reinforced for me that applying for the job was a good decision. I received notification three months later, around early April 2008, that I had been selected as one of the final candidates to interview for the residency position. My first day of work was June 3, 2008.

Thirteen months have passed since my first day as the Diversity Resident at the University of Louisville. During the first week, my schedule consisted of touring the university libraries and being introduced to library faculty and staff. I spent the first few months getting oriented to the library through activities such as working at the reference desk and observing library instruction sessions. The overall plan was to get me acclimated to the library culture during the course of the residency through departmental rotations in reference, information literacy, scholarly communications, and archives.

Those first three months were a bit confusing and frustrating. Inside, I felt lost. I was a new librarian trying to figure out my place in the landscape of this library community and, honestly, I did not know how to reconcile that. Everyone in the work environment was very supportive, from my mentor to the reference librarians to others I met in the media resources department. Yet my daily thoughts centered on proving to colleagues that my employment was not a fluke; that the level of potential I demonstrated during the interview would materialize for the library. Knowing that I would contribute was helpful, but the question of "how" remained. I did not realize that the answer would later appear in the form of teaching.

In the interim, I focused my energies on the area that was most enjoyable: reference, my home department. The work primarily consisted of six to eight hours of desk coverage each week during the semester and supervising students with their shelving duties. At the reference desk, I was always paired with veteran reference librarians who offered additional support and taught me more about their subject areas of expertise. I started working during the summer session, which was also helpful because this is normally a slow period in terms of student traffic in the library. I used this time to practice my reference skills, knowing that, as a new employee without extensive knowledge of the layout of the library, I was sure to get some questions wrong; and initially, that was okay. During this time, the reference department experienced staff shortages. One librarian resigned, and another retired. That left the remaining librarians in the department compelled to take on more responsibility to balance the workload. This balance was specifically needed in the area of library instruction within the information literacy department.

Library instruction was a scary thought for me given my anxiety with public speaking. Hence, when I interviewed for the residency position, I listed library instruction last in terms of preferred areas of focus. However, given the staff shortages in reference, I saw teaching as the solution to that sense of feeling lost. After teaching a few classes, I realized that library instruction, as an extension of reference work, was a facet of librarianship that I enjoyed. The majority of the library instruction classes I taught were one-shot classes at the 100-level in the areas of communication and English, but later would include EndNote.

Library instruction instilled in me an awareness of the need for open communication between the librarian and student, and the librarian and professor, to engage in relevant collaboration to promote critical thinking in the classroom. Further, I am continuously reevaluating best practices to implement active learning techniques to promote student engagement. I have learned much from observing other library instruction sessions. As a result, library instruction has helped me to better understand the overall "process" of teaching research to students.

As of this writing, I am completing a scholarly communication rotation and am in the final stages of completing a joint scholarly communication/special collections project that focuses on copyright and agreements with donors of collections. The project entailed my looking through more than one thousand files to determine whether copyright was transferred to special collections. In 2010, I began my rotation in the University of Louisville's Archives and Records Center.

Looking back on the experience thus far, the residency has placed me in situations that have challenged me to develop leadership and teaching skills. The experience also demonstrated that the steps I took prior to the residency were appropriate. Graduating from library school and my previous work in libraries as a reference student assistant, volunteer, and circulation worker were the proper foundations that enabled me to contribute actively as a professional librarian shortly after arriving at the University of Louisville. My achievements to date include presenting my research report, "The Black Experience in Library School," as part of the 2008 poster sessions at the Spectrum of the Future Conference in Louisville, Kentucky (Porter 2008); developing my teaching and information literacy skills in various library instruction classes; creating brochures to promote the library; and performing liaison work with various academic units.

The achievement that I am most proud of is establishing two funds to offer support for students employed in the university libraries and lesbian, gay, bisexual, and transgender students at the University of Louisville. The first fund is a scholarship I named the Toccara Porter Library Scholarship, which was established to show appreciation for students employed in the university libraries. The scholarship was awarded for a second time in 2010.

Applicants have to meet specific eligibility requirements, including enrollment as a part-time or full-time student at the University of Louisville, at least one semester of work experience in one of the university libraries, and a grade point average of 2.7 or above. There is also a requirement for applicants to submit an essay detailing how working in the library has impacted their life. The recipient receives $1,000 to use toward academic expenses such as tuition, housing, and books. Each year, a scholarship committee made up of three members of faculty and staff from the university libraries will select recipients.

The second fund I started, The Intersection Book Fund, provides $500 to be used toward purchasing books for the lesbian, gay, bisexual, and transgender collection in the Office of Lesbian, Gay, Bisexual, and Transgender (LGBT) Services at the University of Louisville. The fund was named by a group of lesbian, gay, bisexual, and transgender students at the University of Louisville and is derived from the section of the campus building where the Office of LGBT Services is housed. I was inspired to develop the fund in 2009 when I attended diversity training for library staff conducted by the Office of LGBT Services where three students told their coming-out stories.

One student detailed how the library played an important role in his discovery. His story made me think about how difficult it may be for lesbian, gay, bisexual, and transgender students to ask for help finding items on the LGBT experience in the library. For this reason, I focused my efforts in a manner that reflected my awareness for improving access to materials for lesbian, gay, bisexual, and transgender students without the help of a librarian.

In closing, I would like to thank the University of Louisville for the opportunity to learn and develop a working knowledge in the practice of academic librarianship. I would also like to offer some advice to current residents or to those who are considering the benefits of a library residency program in the future.

First, seek out a library residency program where the administrators or coordinators are conscious that their library has a responsibility to foster the resident's growth not only in the aim of diversity but also for professional development. You can do this by asking certain questions. What expectation does the library have regarding the impact of the resident on the library and on other academic units and organizations at the university? What are the library's views on the importance of diversity within the larger context of the organization and operations? Will the resident have any input in the structure of the residency work plan?

Second, the issue of diversity is important. Here at the University of Louisville, diversity is part of the strategic plan for the libraries and the university at large. Such models convey that diversity should not solely be the responsibility of one or two people who have that job title, but participation should involve a collective group of people. Look for opportunities to collaborate with other units in the library and on campus whose mission also supports diversity. Doing these things can help you meet others who can provide you with a sense of community.

Last, understand that you as the resident need to bring something to the table. Show initiative in your areas of interest and ability because this can make the residency experience more rewarding for you and the library. The list could go on, but these are a few of the aspects that will help you gauge whether a residency program is suitable for you.

CONCLUSION

Like Ms. Porter, the University of Louisville Libraries has had a rewarding experience with the newly redesigned, post-MLS residency program. Our experience with internship programs, which predated the current residency program, was largely satisfactory and provided a good base of experience on which to build a new program. Between 1999 and 2006, internships supported six library school students from underrepresented minority groups and resulted in three new academic librarians. This "grow-your-own" method worked well for the University of Louisville Libraries, and for many of its interns.

The move to a post-MLS residency program was motivated largely by the hope that we could do more to diversify the pool of academic librarians by working with individuals who had already shown a commitment to the profession by earning an MLS. Although we did not have a permanent position available to offer to one individual, we could help many new librarians to become stronger candidates for professional positions by providing them with academic library experience.

In addition, a resident can be expected to perform at a professional level. Although recent graduates cannot be expected to be as comfortable with a library instruction class as a more experienced librarian, our expectations were higher for Ms. Porter than they would have been for an intern. The transition from an internship program to a residency program made sense for the University of Louisville Libraries, given our needs and resources.

Another aim in redesigning the residency was to provide professional support for valuable projects. The University of Louisville's experience in this respect has been positive, perhaps because we were somewhat flexible about the structure. The residency was designed to offer a broad range of experiences within academic librarianship, but we found that the individual's interests and the economy played a role in the way those plans were implemented.

Once the residency began, the restructuring committee sought to ensure that the evolving needs of the departments and the interests of the resident were met. The committee also worked, however, to ensure that one of the unique features of the original design—the rotations through different departments within the University of Louisville Libraries—was retained. Given the reference department's needs and Ms. Porter's talents and interests, it was tempting to let her continue working full time with the reference and information literacy departments. However, if the position became a de facto reference residency, then part of the original plan, and part of its distinctiveness from earlier programs, would be lost.

Fortunately, the scholarly communications rotation could be arranged in a way that she could continue to spend a significant amount of her time in reference. The project she undertook in the main library's special collections department was not actually among the original proposals; however, it was a valuable project and will help support the department's ongoing work. By remaining flexible but always mindful of the ultimate goals of the program, we have been able to provide Ms. Porter with valuable and somewhat unusual professional experience, while also furthering the libraries' goals. As Ms. Porter notes, she has found a place and made valuable contributions to the work of the libraries.

Our plan for orientation and ongoing support was carried out with only slight modifications along the way. Our intent had been to provide enough support and information that she would feel at home. The extent to which we succeeded is revealed in her narrative. How quickly can someone feel at home in a new workplace? Did we provide enough of the right kinds of interaction? Did we provide enough support to enable Ms. Porter to move through the unavoidably tentative first few months in a new position? These will be questions we explore further as we continue to evaluate, adjust, and modify the program.

REFERENCES

Cogell, R. V., and C.A. Gruwell, eds. 2001. *Diversity in Libraries: Academic Residency Programs.* Westport, CT: Greenwood.

Porter, T. 2008. The black experience in library school. Poster presented at the Spectrum of the Future Conference, October 1–4, in Louisville, Kentucky.

Chapter 5

Program Management: Challenges and Lessons Learned: Purdue University

Scott Mandernack and Rebecca A. Richardson

Academic librarianship is undergoing a fundamental transformation. First, universities are increasingly called upon to create learning experiences that equip undergraduate students with core competencies in critical thinking, communication skills, information literacy, methods of inquiry, and information technology. Second, the delivery of information resources, course materials, and virtual learning opportunities are now available on desktops, and, at the same time, the growth in multimedia as a means of sharing knowledge is changing the way students regard and use library facilities. Third, continuous advancements in information technology continue to cross national and cultural boundaries creating new, intellectually labor-intensive roles for the librarians of our academies.

More specifically, these transformations in academic culture require research libraries to 1) integrate information literacy into the higher education curriculum and community outreach initiatives, 2) champion pedagogically sound and innovative learning environments, and 3) actively engage librarians as integral partners in collaborative and interdisciplinary research. The new challenges and demands on college and university libraries require a new generation of academic librarians. The Purdue University Libraries Diversity Fellowship Program was established in 2006 to address these challenges while contributing to the development of a more diverse, national pool of academic librarians.

ASSESSMENT OF NEED

Within the academy today, the interdisciplinary nature of research continues to intensify. There is now an increased impetus among scholars to share with broader constituencies not only the analysis of their research results but also the information that has been generated. Collections of massive data sets pose new problems of storage, organization, access, interpretation, and sustainability. Joining scientists and other scholars as investigators on significant research projects, academic librarians bring the principles of library science to these challenges and provide vital facilitation of interdisciplinary information.

Concurrent with this shift in the core mission of academic libraries is the critical challenge to effectively serve increasingly diverse constituencies with a professional workforce that is much less diverse than its user population. As reported by the Association of Research Libraries (Association of Research Libraries 2005), the proportion of libraries' professional staff from underrepresented populations (12.8% in 2004–5) lags behind that of U.S. faculty in universities and colleges (16.3%; U.S. Department of Education 2006b). An even more striking contrast exists with the largest group of potential users: college and university students (approximately 31%; U.S. Department of Education 2006a).

Unfortunately, the lack of diversity in the population of academic librarians undermines one of the academic library's core missions for public good, said Dr. Nancy Cantor, chancellor of the University of Illinois, at the 2002 Third National Conference on Diversity in Academic Libraries. She asserts that diversity and academic excellence are inextricably intertwined, and that the nation must attend to who we train as well as who we hire (Simmons-Welburn and McNeil 2004).

A key element of Purdue University's strategic plan is to enhance human and intellectual diversity to "build a student body, faculty, and staff that reflect our society, while fostering a climate that values inclusivity and equity, assures respect for human dignity, and positions Purdue as a place of choice, of support, and of pride" (Purdue University 2001). Campus initiatives, such as the diversity resource office, multicultural forums, and training for campus administrators, complement an already successful infrastructure, including the various cultural centers and the Purdue Black Caucus of Faculty and Staff. The Purdue University Libraries' (PUL) commitment to recruiting a more diverse national workforce of academic library professionals is a broader expression of the recognized need for practical diversity interventions in PUL's own faculty and professional staff. However, the libraries determined that more could be done within the scope of its own services and resources to represent more fully the diversity of user groups at Purdue and to foster a climate of inclusiveness within the library and campus environments.

PROGRAM DESIGN

The Purdue Libraries established the Purdue University Libraries Diversity Fellowship Program in 2006 with the goal of equipping a new generation of academic librarians with the skills, knowledge, and experience that would help them lead the transformation of academic libraries. Further, the program sought to rigorously foster human and academic diversity and address the needs of an increasingly diverse academic user population. We pursued this goal through the following measurable program objectives:

- Enhance fellows' understanding of the unique needs and requirements of an academic library

- Enable fellows to gain expertise in a focused area of interest within academic librarianship

- Improve fellows' ability to identify and develop services that meet the needs of diverse populations
- Increase fellows' understanding of the changing role of academic librarians in collaborative research
- Develop pedagogical skills of fellows for effective library instruction
- Provide opportunity for fellows to participate in needs assessment projects
- Increase placement of fellows in academic library positions
- Facilitate fellows' ability to incorporate elements of fellowship program experiences into professional positions and responsibilities.

The Purdue program was designed to fulfill a unique niche among fellowship/residency programs by reflecting the existing strengths of the Purdue Libraries. The program incorporated a focus on integrating information literacy into the higher education curriculum and community engagement initiatives, building on the successes of a multifaceted information literacy instruction program already in place. The program also provided opportunities to promote and engage the fellows in collaborative, interdisciplinary research, a strategic direction for librarians at Purdue.

To provide a broadly balanced and valuable experience in academic librarianship, the two-year diversity fellowship program provided each fellow with an overview of foundational principles and practices of librarianship as well as a concentrated experience in an area of specialization. The program was open to recent graduates of master's degree programs in library and information studies who wished to expand their skills to serve diverse user populations in the context of the academic library arena.

After a period of general orientation to the libraries, the campus, and the community, the fellows would engage in a series of rotations through various libraries or units to expose them to different aspects of librarianship. This general introduction led to the selection of a more in-depth experience in a particular library or unit in which the fellows would develop a capstone project in that area of specialization based on their interests.

Throughout the fellowship program, each fellow developed a portfolio that included all work relevant to the program and culminated in a product that highlighted their capstone experiences. The portfolio was to include assessment instruments and analysis, publications, presentations, and reports about programs or services implemented during the two years. Fellows were asked to also include goal statements, reflections on experiences, and any other relevant information that summarized their experience as a fellow (see Appendix 5.1).

Underlying the entire fellowship experience was a strong mentoring program that served to provide fellows with both psychosocial and career advancement support throughout their fellowship appointment. Mentors helped acclimate the fellows to the libraries' environment, the campus community, and the local community. They also served as liaisons to the program directors and provided general guidance and support.

Year One

Discussions regarding the nature of the fellowship program, the campus and PUL organizational climates, key personnel, and available resources characterized the first few weeks of the program. At the same time, fellows began their portfolios with a statement of intended goals and outcomes for the fellowship experience. Within the first month of the program, each fellow chose a primary mentor with whom he or she met regularly throughout the fellowship. Discussions between the fellows, their mentors, and supervisors from units throughout PUL informed the development of an individually tailored program that met the fellows' career and professional development goals, as well as the needs of PUL.

In the first year, fellows rotated through three or four departments or libraries in PUL that best matched their individual interests. For example, one fellow chose to rotate through archives and special collections, the undergraduate library, and the management and economics library during her first year. Another fellow worked in the undergraduate library, the Purdue University Copyright Office, and in the chemistry library in association with the Purdue University Libraries' Advancement Office. Each fellow, in consultation with the appropriate supervisor, wrote a statement of intent with expected learning outcomes for each rotation. For the duration of each rotation, the fellow participated in the general operation of the unit and also worked on special projects, as appropriate. Some of the projects included using EAD (Encoded Archival Description) software to create finding aids for digital collections, evaluating Purdue's collections using the World Cat Collection Analysis Tool, and assisting in teaching a general studies course.

Upon completion of the first year of the program, fellows added to their portfolios a summative statement reflecting on the first year experience. The portfolio was reviewed and discussed by the fellow, his or her mentor, and the unit supervisors. This discussion assessed the success of the fellow's overall experience to date, from the perspective of both the fellow and PUL, and informed the development of the second year experience.

Year Two

In year two, each fellow departed from the rotation schedule and engaged in an in-depth, concentrated experience in one or two areas of specialization within academic librarianship. This in-depth experience led to the development and implementation of a capstone project, designed to foster cultural diversity in the library environment. It also included a form of assessment, both of which are components critical to the success of the new generation of academic librarians. Fellows were also encouraged to participate in collaborative research projects with PUL faculty and staff and researchers from academic departments across campus.

At the beginning of the second year, all fellows, mentors, and supervisors of capstone projects met with program directors to coordinate year-two capstone projects. While the fellows chose their own projects, these discussions ensured that potential projects were well formulated, advanced the PUL strategic plan, and could be accommodated by existing PUL resources; each project had to be approved. Training needs of the fellows were also addressed to better equip them for successful completion of their capstone projects. This additional training could include instructional design, diversity awareness, application software, and assessment methods. Before embarking on the capstone project, each fellow added a statement of intended second-year goals and outcomes to his or her portfolio.

Upon completion of the capstone projects, fellows prepared presentations for PUL faculty and staff outlining the nature of their projects and the impact on users. These presentations were then added to their portfolios.

PROGRAM MANAGEMENT

The PUL Diversity Fellowship Program was codirected by the staff development coordinator and the head of the undergraduate library, with oversight provided by the associate dean for planning and administration. The codirectors were responsible for the overall implementation of the program, including all of the operational aspects: coordinating rotations, monitoring rotation goals and outcomes, conducting performance reviews, and overseeing the mentoring program. The associate dean for planning and administration provided oversight and guidance for the program and served as liaison with the libraries and campus administration.

An advisory board played a vital role in assessing the progress and success of the fellowship program. National leaders with expertise in academic librarianship and diversity issues provided valuable guidance and direction in the pursuit of program objectives. Advisory board meetings were held several times over the course of the program and included interactions with fellows as well as planning and oversight discussions with the program directors and other key individuals from PUL.

Participant Roles and Expectations

With so many individuals involved in both the fellowship program and the mentoring program, clear and articulated roles and expectations for all participants would be critical. As previously stated, communication was a constant challenge, and the success of the fellowship program would be dependent on timely dissemination of information to a diverse and dispersed group of individuals. In addition to the sheer number of individuals involved, the variety of roles comprising the program design also demanded a clear delineation of expectations for each role. As a result, a set of expectations was identified that offered structure and guidelines for each role (see Appendix 5.2).

Clearly stated expectations allowed those individuals who volunteered to have a clear understanding of the activities in which they were asked to participate. Expectations addressed the frequency and nature of communications required and gave volunteers a sense of the amount of time they might anticipate devoting to the program. A number of individuals served in multiple capacities over the course of the program (e.g., primary mentor, resource mentor, rotation supervisor, and capstone supervisor), so these expectations also helped articulate the unique responsibilities of each of the roles they assumed. Further, these sets of responsibilities established a firm baseline on which much of the program assessment would be based.

Program Assessment

A detailed evaluation rubric was developed to guide the assessment initiatives throughout the duration of the program. A mixed methodological approach that incorporated both quantitative and qualitative techniques was used to evaluate the program on two levels: the progress of the individual diversity fellow and the success of the fellowship program in general.

In the initial weeks of the fellowship program, each diversity fellow crafted a statement of intended goals and outcomes of their fellowship experience. At the end of year one, this statement was reviewed by the program directors and mentors as part of a formative feedback process to confirm that appropriate progress was made or to make modifications to the fellow's plan as needed.

At the beginning of each rotation in year one, and each project in year two, the fellow collaborated with his or her mentor and rotation supervisor to prepare a plan outlining performance expectations, with measurable outcomes, for the rotation or project. Formative evaluation was provided during the rotation via informal feedback from the rotation supervisor, with fellows encouraged to also seek feedback from other colleagues. At the conclusion of each rotation, summative feedback was prepared by the rotation supervisor, with input from the fellow, in the form of a written performance summary that relates to the performance plan expectations.

Throughout the two-year program, the fellow's mentor provided informal feedback on the developing portfolio. At the conclusion of each individual's fellowship, the program directors reviewed the portfolios and rotation summaries of each fellow, discussed with the fellow his or her self-evaluation of performance, and prepared a final summative report. Each fellow was also asked to comment on his or her appraisal of the program. Analysis of the verbal feedback regarding the program and the fellows' responses to an anonymous questionnaire provided an initial assessment of the program. A final analysis was planned using input from follow-up surveys of diversity fellows and their employers within one year post-fellowship.

A particularly strong component of the program assessment was the inclusion of an advisory board, which was established to assess the progress and success of the program, asking questions to see that the stated objectives were being fulfilled, and offering feedback, guidance and direction. The composition of the advisory board included a dean/director of an academic library, a dean/director of an accredited school of library/information science, a representative from the Association of Research Libraries' (ARL) Diversity Initiative, and a practicing academic librarian from a historically underrepresented group.

Regular e-mail communication bulletins from the program director kept board members apprised of program activity and progress, while providing a consistent avenue for input. The board also convened on-site several times a year throughout the fellowship program to meet with the fellows, the program directors, primary mentors, rotation supervisors, and other key individuals from the Purdue Libraries. Each visit included presentations by the fellows on their progress to date, highlighting projects on which they were working, as well as individual and group meetings. Following each on-site visit, the board submitted a progress report of their findings and observations, which was shared and reviewed by the program directors, the associate dean for planning and administration, and the dean of libraries.

PROGRAM STRENGTHS

The Purdue Libraries Diversity Fellowship Program included a number of components that were particularly valuable and that made substantial contributions to its overall success. Included among these were the flexibility of the program to be tailored to each fellow's interests, the very generous levels of support provided to the fellows for professional development, and the unique structure of the mentoring program. Of course, all elements of a program had to be well-coordinated and well-managed to work together, but these components of the Purdue program were noted for their particular value to the program's success.

Program Flexibility: Rotation Schedules

A core principle of the program's design was its flexibility. While some residency/fellowship programs allow their participants to choose rotations, many programs are designed around a set rotation schedule that each participant follows. In many library organizations, a predetermined rotation schedule is a logical design. However, in PUL, which has a decentralized library system with no main library, the fellows had the opportunity to combine areas of professional interest with subject orientations or other focuses. To optimize the experience of each fellow in the program and to address the unique combination of interests, issues, and expectations of each, it was specifically designed to allow each fellow to choose the areas, and to some extent the duration, of their rotations.

Early in the fellows' appointments, they were asked to submit an outline of the rotation areas in which they were most interested and their expectations for each rotation. These statements were shared with the program directors, who then discussed with the supervisors of each represented library/unit, the possibilities and options for a successful rotation in that unit, as well as an appropriate timeframe. On the basis of the mutual needs of the fellows and the respective libraries/units, the rotations were coordinated and sequenced to accommodate potential projects and equitable distribution of time. The resulting arrangements allowed for rotation schedules ranging from four 3-month rotations, three 4-month rotations, and two overlapping 6-month rotations followed by two 3-month rotations. The diversity of scheduling was challenging but manageable and, in the end, very productive and uniquely beneficial to the individuals involved.

Professional Development

Throughout the fellowship, fellows were encouraged to attend and participate in workshops, seminars, and other professional development offerings to further inform their awareness and understanding of the broader issues within academic librarianship. Several times each year, for example, national leaders are invited to campus to speak with the libraries' faculty and staff on emerging issues or creative innovations in academic libraries. Furthermore, open discussion forums are regularly presented by PUL colleagues on such topics as distributed institutional repositories, the future of U.S. government documents, and guidelines for the selection of electronic publications, to name a few.

The first year of the program included campus-wide opportunities to increase pedagogical skills and reinforce "best practices" in developing active, collaborative, problem-based learning. Purdue's Center for Instructional Excellence (CIE) provides workshops and seminars on such topics as effective utilization of instructional technologies, building rapport with students, constructing well-designed tests, and more. Offered as one-time sessions or ongoing series, fellows were able to engage in numerous campus offerings to gain new experiences and insights into creative approaches to teaching and learning.

Deepening their perspectives and insights into the broad array of diversity-related issues, the fellows also participated in professional development opportunities that focused on such concerns within the profession and in society at large. They received support to attend the Joint Conference of Librarians of Color, the ARL Leadership Symposium, and the ARL National Diversity in Librarianship Conference. Additionally, they were encouraged to participate in the various ethnic caucuses of professional associations, such as the Black Caucus of the American Library Association (BCALA), the Chinese American Librarians Association, and REFORMA.

Fellows focused mainly on attending larger, more general conferences, such as ALA Annual, ALA Midwinter, and those of the Association of College and Research Libraries (ACRL). Between these conferences and the various conferences focused on diversity, the fellows attended, on average, four conferences a year excluding workshops and institutes. Purdue provided generous monetary support for their registration and participation. In fact, they were fully supported for almost every professional development opportunity they requested to attend despite the absence of a budgetary allowance in the program for these activities. This was an incredible act of support from the PUL administration, because many other institutions set a limit on the amount of support faculty and professional librarians receive annually for development opportunities.

Mentoring Program

Mentoring has long been recognized as an invaluable element of any new faculty appointment to help a new colleague make the transitions necessary for success. According to Haring, "Mentoring is significant career assistance that is given by more experienced person(s) to less experienced one(s) during a time of transition" (Haring 1999). Numerous models have been employed, ranging from informal mentoring among colleagues to very formal and highly structured programs.

The Purdue fellowship program reflected its deep commitment to integrating the fellows into the campus community through a strong mentoring program. With the programmatic goals of preparing librarians for successful career advancement as well as fostering a more diverse climate throughout the libraries' organization, a strong mentoring program that encouraged and promoted learning among all participants was considered essential.

The model on which the Purdue program was based identifies eight roles that a mentor plays with a protégé: educating, role modeling, consulting and coaching, encouraging, sponsoring, protecting, counseling, and moving from transitional figure to friend. These roles follow through a series of phases over the course of a mentoring relationship (Haring 1993).

Mentoring Program Goals

The goals of the fellowship's mentoring program (distinct from the goals of the overarching fellowship program) were as follows:

- Aid in the fellows' transition from being students of library and information science to professional academic librarians.
- Prepare fellows for successful careers in academic librarianship.
- Aid in the fellows' transition to the Purdue community and the greater West Lafayette/Lafayette community.
- Enable the fellows' success as diversity fellows at Purdue University.
- Transform the Purdue University Libraries.

Many mentoring programs tend to focus on the professional development and career advancement of the protégés, typically viewed as the primary purpose of the program. Although this was indeed a critical component of the Purdue program, acclimating the fellows to the campus and community environments was considered just as critical to their overall success. During a meeting on July 20, 2006, Dr. Marilyn Haring suggested that the success of mentoring programs is often dependent, in large part, on the psychosocial aspects of the mentor-protégé relationships. Realization of this critical factor determined the structure of the Purdue mentoring program and informed the nature of the discussions and associated activities of the mentoring network. As a result, deliberate attention was given to providing mechanisms that would help the fellows identify and take advantage of campus and community resources, support networks, and the like to support their transitions to the new community. The focus of this mentoring program, then, was to provide all types of assistance, with an emphasis on psychosocial assistance.

Hybrid Model

Given the breadth of these goals, it was recognized that the work of the mentors would be significant and, if left to a single mentor for each fellow, extremely difficult to meet all the expectations. To meet the needs of the fellows and of the program, we developed a mentoring program that blended two mentoring models: grooming and networking. The grooming aspect of the program allows a dyadic relationship between a chosen primary mentor and a fellow, and the networking aspect of the program would provide a broader cohort, or network, of resources. The mentoring cohort would consist of the fellows, primary mentors, resource mentors (those interested in mentoring but who were not chosen as a primary mentor), and program directors. This network of interested participants would enable the various needs of the fellow to be met by multiple people, creating a climate of inclusion and openness that might not have been found with the traditional grooming model.

The matching process of fellows and primary mentors was accomplished through a series of steps taken early in the program. Prior to the arrival of the fellows, all libraries faculty and administrative/professional (A/P) staff members who were interested in serving as mentors were asked to write a brief narrative statement describing their interest in serving as a mentor, their professional interests, as well as any personal interests or other information that they felt would offer a sense of "who they are." Within the first week following the initial appointment of the fellows, each fellow was also asked to write a narrative statement articulating their individual goals and expectations for the program and their professional and personal interests. These statements were made available to all potential mentors and the fellows. Additionally, a number of gatherings were scheduled over the first few weeks to allow for interaction between these parties and for a chance to become acquainted with each other. By the end of the first month, fellows were to select a primary mentor, who would serve as their principal coach and point of contact for the duration of the program.

Once chosen, the fellows then met with their primary mentor to develop a relationship. It was during this initial meeting that the fellows were asked to identify specific needs and to share them with their primary mentor. Stating needs clearly allowed both the primary mentor and the fellow to be able to assess whether those needs were being met as the program progressed. It was understood by all participants in the mentoring program that mentor-protégé matching is more an art than a science and that pairings are not always successful. Therefore, if at any time, either the fellow or the primary mentor felt that the mentoring relationship was not working successfully, the pairing would be reconsidered, and another mentor would be assigned to the fellow.

Because this mentoring program was a blend of the grooming and networking models, utilization of all interested libraries' faculty and A/P staff members as resource mentors was possible. This allowed for a fellow to gain guidance and assistance from multiple mentors—or resources—with multiple perspectives, areas of expertise, and interests. Perhaps just as important, however, this model was also based on a belief that all members of the cohort could learn from each other. Because one of the mentoring program goals was to transform the Purdue University Libraries, mutual and collaborative learning was expected from all participants and was accomplished through this blended, hybrid model.

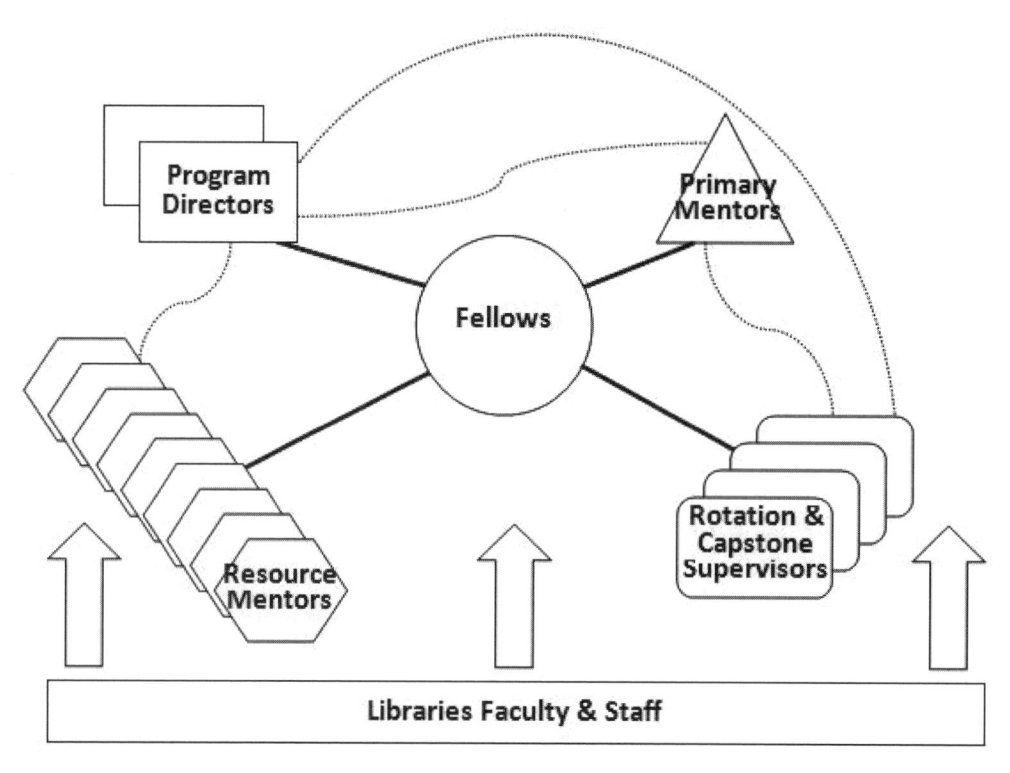

Figure 5.1. Purdue University Libraries Diversity Fellowship Program network mentoring model.

Resource mentors met monthly with all fellows, primary mentors, and the program directors. They were also available to offer insights, knowledge, experience, or other assistance, as needed. In many instances, the types of assistance that the resource mentors provided was not necessarily something the primary mentor was not able to provide. This was not viewed as a failure of the primary mentor. Rather, the purpose of this mentoring program, which emphasized networking, was to utilize resources within the organization, such as these additional mentors, in order to meet the needs of the fellow.

Communication

Communication is one of the more difficult and constant challenges within a complex, decentralized organization. Expectations for each role of the mentoring program cohort, therefore, were established to offer structure and guidelines (see Appendix 5.2). Primary mentors were expected to meet regularly with the fellows, as well as with other key figures. Regular meetings with key figures, such as the program directors and the rotation supervisors, ensured that communication occurred across the organization and across the fellowship program.

Each month, fellows, primary mentors, resource mentors, and program directors met, either within the libraries and focusing discussion on an issue of interest to the group or, at other times, outside of work for a purely social gathering. Everyone was encouraged to share ideas and opinions and to feel safe without feeling vulnerable. These meetings also served as an opportunity to gather informal formative feedback on various program elements. This open exchange of ideas and opinions is what would help transform the libraries, and ultimately the profession. Considerable attention, therefore, was given to the development of group rules and expectations.

LESSONS LEARNED

New programs, no matter how well planned and considered, inevitably face challenges. Purdue's Diversity Fellowship Program was no different. Some of the lessons learned included a need for better preparation of potential rotation supervisors, the establishment of clear parameters for professional development and travel funding, and a reconsideration of the requirement that fellows focus on diversity-related issues.

Several months before the start of the program, a meeting of libraries' faculty and staff was held for all those who were interested in participating in the program in some fashion. At this meeting, the general program design was outlined, the various roles were articulated, and a discussion on mentoring was presented by a campus expert. Although it was suggested to potential rotation supervisors at this meeting that they consider specific tasks or projects to which the fellows might contribute during a rotation in their unit, the intent was not to require that every fellow complete a project in each rotation. However, as the program evolved, the fellows expressed concern that their rotation expectations were too focused on project completion, adding undue stress and anxiety. Even though the program directors met with the rotation supervisors and fellows at the beginning and end of each rotation, clearer expectations for the supervisors and more sustained communication with them throughout each rotation would likely result in more positive experiences.

One might presume a commitment to nearly unlimited professional development and travel support would only result in tremendous benefit to the individuals and the organization, but, in fact, such dedicated support became an organizational complication by the end of the fellowship program. A major component of the program was to offer generous support for fellows' professional development and travel, providing opportunities to learn and grow while also establishing professional networks. With no stated budget, the fellows took advantage of numerous conferences and other professional development offerings, from very general conferences to workshops and symposia on focused issues within librarianship and archival management.

Unfortunately, there was a perception among other faculty and staff that the fellows received special treatment, and this became a concern for the libraries. Untenured faculty members, in particular, did not receive the same levels of monetary support to attend professional development activities. This discrepancy resulted in negative feelings toward the program (although, fortunately, not toward the fellows themselves). Future programs would continue to support professional development and travel but at a level consistent with that of junior tenure-track librarians, eliminating any notion of special treatment.

Debate continues over the focus and roles of participants in diversity residency and fellowship programs. Many, if not most, tend to incorporate elements of diversity services, often explicitly including residents or fellows on library or university diversity committees or channeling them into roles that focus on developing and offering services to underrepresented groups. Such was the case with the first cohort in the Purdue program. However, the question remains whether this deliberate focus "typecasts" young professionals from underrepresented groups into similar roles in subsequent career positions.

Although the broader goal of most residency programs is to develop leaders in the profession with alternate cultural values and perspectives so that we, as a profession, continue to offer the most relevant and useful services and resources to diverse communities of users, we must also be careful not to establish a professional focus that limits the development of these young professionals in all the other aspects of library and information sciences.

CONCLUSION

The first-ever Purdue University Libraries Diversity Fellowship Program was a tremendous success in many ways, incorporating a number of unique elements which may be successfully applied in other contexts. The complexity of the distributed libraries' organization at Purdue required close attention to program structure and communication channels. Clear expectations and regular communication with all the participants was a critical factor in its success. Although the program design was carefully constructed, it also offered significant flexibility to be tailored to the unique needs and interests of the individual fellows. Such flexibility, often cited as a strength of the program, necessitated significant oversight and management by the program directors. Strategies for greater standardization and efficiency throughout the various elements of the program, while still retaining the flexibility, will be key considerations in future offerings of the program.

REFERENCES

Association of Research Libraries. 2005. *ARL Annual Salary Survey 2004–05*. Compiled and edited by M. Kyrillidou and M. Young. Washington, DC: Association of Research Libraries.

Haring, M. J. 1993. Mentoring for research: Examining alternative models. In *Research Mentorship and Training in Communication Sciences and Disorders: Proceedings of a National Conference*, edited by Minghetti, N. J., J. A. Cooper, H. Goldstein, L. B. Olswang, and S. F. Warren, pp. 117–126. American Speech-Language-Hearing Foundation, National Institute on Deafness and Other Communication Disorders, and National Institutes of Health.

Haring, M. J. 1999. The case for a conceptual base for minority mentoring programs. *Peabody Journal of Education* 74 (2):5–14.

Purdue University. 2001. *Strategies and Metrics. The Next Level: Preeminence: Strategic Plan 2001–2006*. http://www.purdue.edu/strategic_plan/2001-2006/pages/westlafayette/wl_strategies.html.

Simmons-Welburn, J. 2004. Creating and sustaining a diverse workplace. In *Human Resource Management in Today's Academic Library: Meeting Challenges and Creating Opportunities*, edited by J. Simmons-Welburn and B. McNeil, pp. 9-17. Santa Barbara, CA: Libraries Unlimited.

U.S. Department of Education, Institute of Education Sciences, National Center for Education Statistics. 2006a. *Digest of Education Statistics, Table 210*. http://nces.ed.gov/programs/digest/d06/tables/dt06_210.asp

U.S. Department of Education, Institute of Education Sciences, National Center for Education Statistics. 2006b. *Digest of Education Statistics, Table 232*. http://nces.ed.gov/programs/digest/d06/tables/dt06_232.asp

APPENDIX 5.1

Portfolio Guidelines

Each diversity fellow will develop a cumulative portfolio that will include all work relevant to the program objectives and will culminate in a portfolio that highlights capstone experiences.

Items to include:

- **Resume**—upon entrance to program; need not include personal information (i.e. address, phone numbers, references, etc.)
- **Statement of Interest**—broad professional/career directions and what fellow hopes to gain from program to advance their career
- **Preliminary Rotation Expectation**—preliminary statements about rotation possibilities and expectations from each
- **Rotation Expectations with Outcomes**—to be drafted at the start of each rotation. Fellow, rotation supervisor and primary mentor discuss fellow's preliminary expectations and coordinate with unit needs to establish set expectations for rotation. Form the basis of performance review for each rotation.
- **Rotation Summative Essays**—to be drafted at the end of each rotation. This summative essay should include reflection on impact of rotation on career goals, etc.
- **Professional Development Activity Reports** (workshops, conferences, etc). Record of each professional development opportunity fellow has attended and participated in; to include expectations, what was learned, and how what was learned can be integrated into fellow's professional work (at PUL or in the future).

End-of-Year-Two Summary—reflection on how year one impacted activities in year two, as well as the impact of year two (beyond your capstone work) on career goals, etc.

Resume—upon departure from program

Optional items to include:

Reflection(s) on Key Learnings/Realizations/Observations (intermittent)—general statements, as they may occur throughout the rotation experience.

APPENDIX 5.2

Participant Expectations

Fellow Expectations

- Establish individual goals and outcomes for fellowship experience; write statement of professional interests
- Participate in Purdue Libraries orientation activities
- Identify individual needs/preferences regarding mentoring relationship
- Establish relationship/build rapport with chosen primary mentor
- Connect with primary mentor on regular basis (3–4 times/month), at least 2 times/month face-to-face
- Identify 3-4 units/libraries for first year rotation; write statement of intent for each rotation, with learning outcomes
- Meet with primary mentor and rotation supervisors at beginning of each rotation (clarify roles and responsibilities)
- Participate in performance review with rotation supervisor at conclusion of rotation
- Write summative essay of each rotation experience, with statement of outcomes
- At end of year one, write summative essay, reflecting on first year experience; discuss with primary mentor and program directors
- Identify area of specialization for year two and write statement of intent, with goals and outcomes for capstone project; discuss with capstone advisor, primary mentor and program directors
- Develop and complete capstone project throughout year two
- Present results of capstone project to Libraries faculty and staff
- Attend monthly meetings with program directors, all mentors, and all fellows
- Attend diversity fellowship functions/events
- Communicate with and provide feedback to program directors
- Be open to modifications of mentor/fellow relationships if needed

Program Director Expectations

- Willing to commit to a 2-year program
- Meet with each other weekly
- Conduct mentor orientation/training
- Meet with fellows monthly over lunch

- Meet with primary mentors & resource mentors monthly
- Facilitate fellow/mentor cohort monthly meetings
- Distribute monthly meeting minutes to cohort via mentoring program listserv
- At end of year one, meet with fellow and primary mentor and program directors to discuss summative evaluation essay
- Meet with fellow, capstone advisor, and primary mentor at the end of year one to discuss capstone project goals and objectives
- Organize and attend diversity fellowship functions/events
- Organize monthly fellow/mentor cohort meetings: location, refreshments, activities
- Communicate with fellow/mentor cohort via mentoring program listserv, as needed
- Develop and implement evaluations: formative and summative
- Report progress of program to Libraries administration at the end of each year
- Assist primary mentors and resource mentors, as needed (provide resources, psychosocial assistance, etc)
- Modify mentoring program, based on evaluation feedback, as needed
- Modify mentor/fellow relationships, if needed

Primary Mentor Expectations

- Willing to commit to a 2-year program
- Participate in mentor orientation / training
- Attend monthly meetings with program directors and all mentors
- Attend monthly meetings with program directors, all mentors, and all fellows
- Attend diversity fellowship functions/events
- Establish relationship/build rapport with assigned fellow
- Connect with fellow on regular basis (3-4 times/month), at least 2 times/month face-to-face
- Help acclimate fellow to campus community and greater Lafayette community
- Be available for questions/consultation, as needed by fellow
- Provide general guidance and support
- Help resolve problems/difficulties in accomplishing expectations
- Give professional career-related advice
- Meet with fellow and rotation supervisors at beginning of each rotation (clarify roles and responsibilities)
- Serve as liaison between fellow and rotation supervisor, as appropriate

- Serve as liaison with capstone advisor; meet with capstone advisor and fellow at least quarterly throughout duration of project
- Review fellow's portfolio throughout the fellowship program
- Communicate with and provide feedback to program directors
- Be open to modifications of mentor/fellow relationships if needed

Resource Mentor Expectations

- Willing to commit to a 2-year program
- Participate in mentor orientation / training
- Attend monthly meetings with program directors, all mentors, and all fellows
- Attend diversity fellowship functions/events
- Support network-mentoring model, as needed:

    - Establish relationship/build rapport with fellows
    - Help acclimate fellow to campus community and greater Lafayette community
    - Be available for questions/consultation
    - Provide general guidance and support
    - Help resolve problems/difficulties in accomplishing expectations
    - Give professional career-related advice
    - Review fellow's portfolio throughout the fellowship program
- Communicate with and provide feedback to program directors
- Be open to modifications of mentor/fellow relationships if needed

Rotation Supervisor Expectations

- Willing to commit to up to 4 rotations within one year
- Identify potential projects for fellow participation/involvement
- Provide desk/office space for fellows
- Meet with fellow and primary mentor at beginning of rotation to establish fellow's roles, responsibilities, and expectations
- Inform staff of unit/library of fellow's roles and responsibilities
- Orient fellow to operations of unit/library
- Provide general guidance and support
- Be available for questions/consultation, as needed by fellow
- Help resolve problems/difficulties in accomplishing expectations
- Conduct performance review with fellow at conclusion of rotation

- Attend diversity fellowship functions/events, as able
- Provide feedback to program directors

Capstone Advisor Expectations

- Willing to commit up to a year
- Meet with fellow, primary mentor, and program directors at beginning of project to establish project scope and definition
- Meet with fellow, primary mentor, and program directors at least quarterly throughout duration of project
- Provide general direction and guidance in support of project
- Be available for questions/consultation, as needed by fellow
- Help resolve problems/difficulties in accomplishing project expectations
- Assess capstone project
- Attend diversity fellowship functions/events, as able
- Provide feedback to program directors

APPENDIX 5.3

Program Objectives/Activities

Program Objectives	Program Activities
Increase general familiarity with unique needs and requirements of a Research 1 academic library	General orientation to academic library environment Work in 3–4 functional units Participate in PUL teams / committees Participate in professional development opportunities Participate in mentorship program
Gain expertise in focused area of interest within academic librarianship	Participate in project(s) within area(s) of specialization Portfolio Project: • Report / presentation re: project
Identify and develop services that meet the needs of diverse populations	Develop program/service for identified user group(s) Portfolio Project: • Assessment instruments • Assessment analysis • Report / presentation re: program/service
Expose fellows to opportunities for collaborative research	Participate in disciplinary faculty research projects Attend seminars / workshops / symposia on Libraries research initiatives
Increase pedagogical skills for effective library instruction	Co-instruct GS 175 Conduct instructional sessions Portfolio project: • Instructional resources (e.g. online tutorials, website redesign, handouts) • Report / presentation re: instructional activities / projects Attend seminars / workshops / symposia on Libraries instruction initiatives Coursework in education or educational psychology
Participate in needs assessment projects	Portfolio Project: • Assessment instruments • Assessment analysis • Report / presentation re: program/service

APPENDIX 5.4

Evaluation Plan, Diversity Fellows

Program Objectives	Program Activities	Evaluation
Diversity fellows will identify and develop services to meet the needs of diverse populations	Fellow develops program or service for identified user group(s) Fellow builds portfolio project, including assessment instruments and analysis, and publication, presentation, or report about program or services	Formative: Informal feedback on portfolio and performance Summative: Written performance summaries Exit interviews
Diversity fellows will increase their understanding of the unique needs and requirements of an academic library	Fellow participates in general orientation to academic library environment Fellow works in 3–4 functional units Fellow serves on library teams and committees Fellow participates in professional development opportunities and mentorship program Fellow begins to build portfolio project, including assessment instruments and analysis, and publication, presentation, or report about program or services	Formative: Informal feedback on portfolio and performance Summative: Written performance summaries Exit interviews
Diversity fellows will gain expertise in focused area(s) of interest within academic librarianship	Fellow participates in project(s) within area(s) of specialization Fellow builds portfolio project, including assessment instruments and analysis, and publication, presentation, or report about program or services	Formative: Informal feedback on portfolio and performance Summative: Written performance summaries Exit interviews
Diversity fellows will increase their understanding of the changing role of academic librarians in collaborative research	Fellow participates in interdisciplinary research between PUL and academic departments across campus and/or assists associate dean for research with partnership development Fellow attends seminars, workshops, or symposia on PUL research initiatives Fellow builds portfolio project, including assessment instruments and analysis, and publication, presentation, or report about program or services	Formative: Informal feedback on portfolio and performance Summative: Written performance summaries Exit interviews

Program Objectives	Program Activities	Evaluation
Diversity fellows will increase their pedagogical skills for effective library instruction	Fellow co-instructs General Studies 175: Information Strategies course Fellow conducts instructional sessions Fellow attends seminars, workshops, or symposia on PUL instruction initiatives Fellow builds portfolio project, including assessment instruments and analysis, and publication, presentation, or report about program or services	Formative: Informal feedback on portfolio and performance Summative: Written performance summaries Exit interviews
Diversity fellows will participate in needs assessment projects	Fellow builds portfolio project, including assessment instruments and analysis, and publication, presentation, or report about program or services	Formative: Informal feedback on portfolio and performance Summative: Written performance summaries Exit interviews
Diversity fellows will increase their potential for placement in academic library positions	Fellow participates in local, regional, and/or national conferences (networking) Fellow develops resume Fellow uses career resources, such as the ARL Resume Database	Survey of former fellows within first post-fellowship year
Diversity fellows will incorporate elements of their fellowship program experiences into their professional positions and responsibilities	Fellow utilizes portfolio contents as the groundwork for incorporating diversity in future professional positions	Survey of employers within first post-fellowship year Survey of former fellows within first post-fellowship year

Chapter 6

Come Be a Part of the University of Tennessee Libraries' Diversity Librarian Residency Program

Jill Keally

INTRODUCTION

The University of Tennessee (UT), located in Knoxville, is a Carnegie Research Level One institution and enrolls approximately 26,000 students from the United States and more than one hundred foreign countries. The UT Libraries, with an annual budget exceeding $16 million, holds 3 million volumes and employs more than two hundred staff members, including forty librarians. Diversity, as an organizational value, has been in place at the University of Tennessee Libraries since 1994 when it was incorporated into the libraries' strategic plan.

The libraries' first formal diversity initiative occurred in 2001 when the dean formed a diversity committee to develop a comprehensive proposal to address diversity at the library. Initial priorities included the creation of a welcoming environment and the assessment of the current state of the libraries' diversity awareness. A year later, in response to the campus strategic plan that included a goal to "build a diverse inclusive campus community" (University of Tennessee 2004), the diversity committee recommended a new library initiative: to establish a minority resident librarian program at the University of Tennessee Libraries.

PROGRAM DEVELOPMENT

Purpose

Launched in January 2003, the purpose of the Minority Librarian Residency Program is to attract recent library school graduates from underrepresented groups to a challenging and rewarding career in academic librarianship. According to the first announcement:

> Residents will be expected to do the following: work closely with librarians to develop skills and career paths, develop collegial relationships with faculty outside the library, participate in library committees, and become involved in professional associations. In addition, the candidates will receive guidance from a mentor with the goal of completing a specialized project during the second year of their residency. Each resident will select several areas of the library in which he/she will work and take part in a variety of initiatives and projects. (University of Tennessee Libraries 2002)

Candidates are expected to have the "ability to work effectively in a team environment; excellent oral and written communication skills; demonstrated interest in scholarship and professional growth; strong service orientation; knowledge of issues and trends in academic libraries" (University of Tennessee Libraries 2002). Residents were appointed for two years at the rank of Research Assistant Professor with a salary commensurate with an entry-level librarian at UT. The package also includes financial support for attending conferences, workshops, and relocation assistance.

Recruitment, Selection, Orientation

The search committee used the standard faculty application process, requesting a cover letter addressing the required qualifications, a current resume, and three references. Recruitment materials including brochures and posters were sent to library schools and research libraries. The position was advertised in various journals and posted on websites and online discussion lists. Consistent with the university's employment practices, the committee accepted, reviewed, and considered equally all applications, regardless of the individual's "race, color, national origin, religion, sex, pregnancy, marital status, sexual orientation, gender identity, age, physical or mental disability, or covered veteran status" (University of Tennessee 2007). Finalists were invited to campus for daylong interviews. Candidates met with various groups and individuals, including the diversity committee, library administrators and department heads, and other faculty and staff. They were required to make a short presentation addressing the question: "How might this residency program benefit the UT Libraries?"

The committee received forty-three applicants for the two positions. In addition to talking with the preferred candidates' references, the search committee conducted phone interviews and then invited six of the applicants to interview; five accepted the invitation. At the conclusion of the process, library faculty and staff submitted evaluations of the finalists. After lengthy deliberations, the search committee recommended to the dean that the libraries secure funding to hire an additional resident, bringing the total to three.

The university agreed to pay the salary and benefits for one; the library used endowment funds to cover the cost of the other two residents. Even though one of the candidates selected for the program lived in Knoxville and was available to begin working immediately, the diversity committee, which was responsible for administering the program, thought it was important for all of the residents to begin working on the same date. Letters of offer were extended in July 2003, and the first cohort group of three residents was hired to begin working on September 1.

Throughout the summer, diversity committee members assisted with locating and arranging housing for two of the residents and began planning for their arrival. Library administrators selected and organized workspaces to enable the residents to be located in the same department and in close proximity to one another. The libraries purchased laptops to make it possible for residents to move easily from one rotation to another. Prior to their arrival on campus, activation of e-mail accounts enabled residents to begin communicating with library staff and with each other. Diversity committee members scheduled and organized a welcome event so that all library staff and university administrators would have an opportunity to meet the residents. They also participated in the design of a monthlong orientation to familiarize the residents with the campus and the library.

Orientation consisted of tours of the library and campus, social occasions, including lunch with staff and faculty, one-on-one meetings with department heads, and opportunities to attend committee meetings. Residents met frequently with the head of human resources and the training coordinator, who served as the primary program directors and mentors for the first cohort group, to discuss expectations and anticipated outcomes. As a group, the residents spent several days in most of the library departments and units to become knowledgeable enough about the functions and services to make informed choices about their preferred rotational assignments.

At the conclusion of the monthlong orientation, the residents completed a questionnaire about the experience. They were asked to comment about what they found most helpful. Responses included suggestions to keep a daily journal, to write goals, and to learn about the libraries' policies, procedures, and practices. They replied positively to the question about the welcoming events and expressed appreciation for the offers of assistance they received from so many of the libraries' staff and faculty. They all had one suggestion for improvement: advise future residents to wear appropriate footwear for the extensive walking that would be required during orientation.

PROGRAM COMPONENTS

Job Assignments

Residents work with the program administrators and mentors to select their rotational job assignments. Normally, selections are made several weeks prior to the anticipated start dates for each rotation so that there is adequate time to locate temporary workspace in the department. In collaboration with the residents, rotational supervisors discuss and establish goals, develop training plans, and choose a short-term project that will benefit the department and allow the resident to showcase his or her skills. At the conclusion of the rotation, the supervisor completes an evaluation describing the individual's accomplishments and contributions. As faculty, residents devote about a fifth of the workweek to service activities and scholarship so that the evaluation form includes a section for the supervisor to summarize these achievements as well. The selection process for the yearlong job assignment follows the same pattern as the rotation. However, the departmental experience is intended to give the residents the skills they need to qualify for specialized positions in academic libraries.

Professional Development

One of the most valuable components of the program is the opportunity for residents to attend conferences and participate in local, state, and national meetings and training events. Service to the library, profession, and even the community is an expectation of faculty, and residents are appointed to committees and encouraged to volunteer their services to campus and community groups. All residents serve on the libraries' diversity committee.

Residents also attend and participate in at least one American Library Association (ALA) annual conference. Many of the residents choose to join ALA's New Members Round Table, which provides networking opportunities and enables new librarians to join committees and take part in social activities. Residents in the first cohort group expressed an interest in leadership training. All three submitted applications for the 2004 Minnesota Institute for Early Career Librarians from Traditionally Underrepresented Groups (Minnesota Institute). The library provided full financial support and released time for this purpose.

Some of the other Minnesota Institute participants were also residents in academic libraries, so the group had the opportunity to share experiences. Residents report that long after the completion of the program, they rely on the colleagues they met at the institute for ongoing advice, encouragement, and support. With the current emphasis on the importance of succession planning in academic libraries, all residents are now expected to apply for and, if selected, participate in the Minnesota Institute program.

Mentoring

Graduates of UT's residency program report that mentoring is one of the most important aspects of the program. Mentors serve multiple purposes: trainers, collaborators, coauthors, local guides, advisors, confidantes, problem solvers, liaisons to librarians in other academic institutions, and referees for future positions. Residents select individual mentors. As with the library's tenure-track faculty who are expected to choose a mentor to provide support and assistance, today's residents benefit as well from the opportunity to work closely with another library colleague to develop career plans, conduct research, and select appropriate service activities.

During their two-year assignments, the residents work with and report to various library department heads and colleagues who may also serve in the role of mentor and coach. Program directors, one of them a library administrator, serve primarily as mentors for the entire group, meeting frequently to discuss progress, ideas for continued development and growth, and plans for the future.

Creative Accomplishments

As faculty, librarians at the University of Tennessee must engage in scholarly activities. Publications, presentations, and submission of grant proposals for external funding are a few of the ways faculty contribute to the discipline and demonstrate professional excellence. As prospective employees of academic libraries with similar expectations, resident assignments include specific objectives for creative activity. All cohort groups have met these criteria, conducting meaningful research and producing scholarly results that benefit the library community as a whole.

For example, members of the 2003–2005 residency program received a grant to develop a minority librarian electronic discussion list and website (Keally 2004). Funded by a Cultural Development Grant from a division of the ALA, the website, the Diversity Librarians' Network (DLN), was designed to provide up-to-date information on diversity training programs and a forum for diverse librarians to share their experiences and expertise. For example, in 2006, members of the second cohort group replicated a study conducted at the University of Washington by Dr. Scott Walter to determine how students from international/intercultural centers on campus used the library. They conducted a survey, evaluated the data, and publicized the results of the research in an article in *Reference Services Review* (Puente 2009).

Residents Damon Campbell and Shantrie Collins (2007–2009) along with training coordinator Thura Mack presented "Assessing Academic Library Diversity Residency Programs from a Resident Standpoint" at the 2008 National Diversity in Libraries Conference. The paper was subsequently published in the conference proceedings (Mack 2008). Examples of other creative works the residents completed during their two-year assignments have been published in journals (Mundava, Chaudhuri, and Bright 2004) and in contributed manuscripts (Mundava, Bright, and Chaudhuri 2006; Bright et al. 2006).

PROGRAM CHANGES

To date, three cohort groups comprising eight librarians have completed the Diversity Resident Librarian Program at the UT Libraries. At this writing, a fourth group, hired in February 2010, has begun the first rotational assignment. There have been no changes in the anticipated outcomes for the program since its implementation in 2003. For the residents, the program continues to offer an opportunity for career growth. They learn new skills and develop collegial relationships with other librarians in the field. As research faculty, they become involved with professional associations and produce a scholarly record that includes presentations and publications. Their resumes also include a variety of work experiences, committee activities, and projects that enable them to compete successfully for permanent positions in other academic libraries.

They report that the training and mentoring they received during the program have enabled them to compete well in the national marketplace. However, it is not only the residents who benefit from participation in the program. The library benefits from the diversity the residents bring to the work environment, as well as from their contributions to and assistance with important tasks and priorities. The university, its faculty, and its students, are the beneficiaries of the experience and perspective offered by these librarians.

Normally, there is some overlap between the end of one program and the beginning of the next. This intersection has allowed departing residents to serve on the search committee to select the next class of residents, assisting with recruitment efforts, evaluating the candidates' qualifications, responding to applicants' questions and concerns, and in some cases, facilitating the selected residents' moves to the Knoxville area. Over the course of the program, mentors, supervisors, and administrators talked frequently with the residents about whether the program is meeting their needs. Occasionally, rotational assignments needed to be changed or the timeframe for some expanded or shortened. They were expected to begin and end their rotations at the same time.

At the conclusion of each 2-year program, residents made suggestions for improvements. On the basis of those results, the length of time for orienting the residents to the library and the campus environment was reduced to two weeks. This change meant there was less time for the residents to become familiar with the various departments before being asked to select their first rotational assignment. On the other hand, many of the residents had prior library work experience and had already identified the preferred department for the first assignment.

In 2007, the library began using the term "diversity" instead of "minority" in its descriptions and announcements to emphasize the breadth of the intended applicant pool. Some additional changes occurred during the 2009 search. First, the length of the rotational assignments was shortened from four months to three to expand the primary assignment to fifteen months. Second, in these difficult economic times when the library is unable to fund full-time faculty positions, the committee identified priority areas from which the residents would select their work assignments. This change ensured that some of the libraries' highest-priority needs would be met during the two-year appointments. The priority areas included instructional services, special collections and archives, and digital initiatives. Finally, the commitment to advancing the libraries' and university's diversity goals was added to the required qualifications for the position.

Program leaders also asked librarians, including department heads, to evaluate the program and its impact on the libraries, especially on those units where the residents had worked. Although there were some suggestions for improvement and change, most said the program had exceeded their expectations and the participants' enthusiasm, energy, and commitment to service had contributed to a positive work environment.

HOW IS THE PROGRAM UNIQUE?

Residency programs had been in place at other academic libraries when UT's program was implemented in 2003. In fact, some of this program's components were modeled after those in place at other institutions including the University of Iowa and the University of Michigan. What is unique about UT's program, however, is reflected in the accomplishments of the residents and contributions they have made as a group and as individuals. As members of an academic environment, librarians must work well with their colleagues and be open to collaborating with their peers. Therefore, during the selection process, the committee looks for residents who can work individually but also as members of a cohort group.

Commenting on UT's cohort experience in an article published in a 2006 issue of *Versed,* Shantel Agnew, LaVerne Gray, and Mark Puente point out that the experience working as a group has several advantages. "One is the built-in accountability and support network that is created in this model. The UT residents remind each other of deadlines, meetings, or tasks, to take notes if one misses a meeting, and are each other's best advocates in the workplace." They acknowledge as well that "each resident brings something unique to the table and these varying perspectives enhance the collaborative environment" (Agnew, Gray, and Puente 2006).

Another unique feature of the program is the requirement for resident librarians to become actively involved in the profession. They join committees, participate in programs, and serve as discussion leaders, panel members, and presenters. Their visibility and their leadership, especially in the national library community, have been invaluable to UT's diversity efforts, raising awareness about the program, the library's diversity committee, campus and library-sponsored events, resources, and other programs.

LESSONS LEARNED

The development and implementation of a residency program requires an investment in money, time, and most important, the concept that diversity, broadly defined, is a high priority for both the university and the library. The hiring of resident librarians enabled the library to incorporate diverse perspectives into programs, activities, and recruitment strategies and to expand partnerships with other campus and diverse communities. In addition, all cohort groups have played an important role in the provision of library services to diverse users.

One of the major challenges in developing and sustaining a residency program is ensuring there is ongoing funding support, not only to cover salaries and benefits but also recruitment and moving expenses along with professional development and travel. Prior to the inception of the program, the libraries proposed a matching funding model that would use university funding to pay for the salary and benefits for one librarian and income from library endowments to cover the second resident's salary and benefits and all other additional expenses.

During the first cohort experience, residents participated in and contributed to campus-wide events and programs. Among other activities, they taught classes, presented workshops, and conducted tours. In many ways, they served as the library's ambassadors to diverse student populations. Their visibility in the campus community played a role in helping to secure additional funding from the university to support the hiring of two additional residents for the second cohort group. That practice of shared funding between the university and the library continues today.

Residents' involvement in the campus community had a positive outcome on future funding requests. However, their involvement and contributions to the library's goals and projects helped cement the importance of the resident positions to the library organization. The investments the library made in training and preparing the residents for positions in academic libraries enabled them to make significant contributions to the UT Library as well.

Diversity residents cataloged backlogs, served on the reference desk, and made significant contributions to committees. They were eager to learn but equally eager to help. Even during the first few months on the job, they became proficient enough to take on assignments and assume responsibilities for tasks that were critical to the library's ability to achieve important objectives. The progress that units and departments were able to make as a result of the residents' involvement in the workplace was an unexpected outcome of the first residency program. What mentors and program administrators learned from this experience, however, was that the residents expected to be given meaningful assignments and projects to accomplish. It was important for them to feel like equal partners in the community they were hired to serve.

THOUGHTS FOR THE FUTURE

Expectations for the Residents

In the future, the library will continue to look for residents who will complement not only the skills of others in the cohort group but also the skills of the current faculty. Applicants will be required to demonstrate an interest in leadership training and contribute to the library's succession planning. Residents may be expected to assist in recruiting students, especially master's level graduate students for the School of Information Sciences. Serving on search committees, they will also function as advocates for increasing diversity among the libraries' faculty and staff. Nearly a decade after its formation, the libraries' diversity committee continues to "provide programs and resources that enhance knowledge and encourage understanding of diversity" (University of Tennessee Libraries 2010), and residents are active participants in the program planning and dissemination of information. At the national level, residents will be encouraged to connect with other residents, to volunteer for committees, and to represent the library at diversity events and functions.

Expectations for the Library

Program sustainability will require the library to secure ongoing, permanent funding. One current strategy to achieve this goal includes a successful capital campaign that, among other funding priorities, seeks to secure a $1 million endowment that would provide sufficient annual income to hire one resident per year. Other potential, but as yet untapped, funding sources include partnerships with other colleges and centers and with sponsored projects and research grants through the office of research. In addition to funding, assessment and evaluation, including feedback from the residents as well as the librarians and staff, is essential to the ongoing quality of the program. Finally, while the program has continued to flourish and grow without a lot of documentation, important next steps include the delineation of program principles as well as policies and procedures.

CONCLUSION

In 2009, the invitation to apply for the diversity librarian residency program at the University of Tennessee Libraries resulted in more than 130 applications, three times the number received in 2003. This surge in interest may result from the attention the program has received in the library literature and at various conferences, much of it coming from the residents themselves who attribute their current successes in the field to the experiences they had in the program. Other than the changes described earlier, not much else has changed in the local environment.

As was the case in 2002 when the program was launched, the library diversity committee and the University of Tennessee Council for Diversity and Interculturalism, appointed by the office of the chancellor, continue serving as advocates for increasing diversity among students, faculty, and staff (University of Tennessee 2010). Both the campus and the library remain committed to funding the program. Librarians still value and appreciate the fresh perspective and initiative the residents bring to the organization and, consequently, are willing trainers, research partners, and mentors.

Finally, and perhaps most important, residents remain our most effective ambassadors for the university and the library. Their pictures and comments, featured on the current brochure, tell the story best. Kawanna Bright, Diversity Resident in 2003–2005 and currently Instructional Services Librarian, Research and Information Services, North Carolina State University Libraries, says the program provided "the chance to experience being a librarian while truly finding my place in the field." Mark Puente, Diversity Resident in 2005–2007 and currently Director of Diversity Programs for the Association of Research Libraries, gained "valuable skills and experience that will benefit my career long into the future." Maud Mundava, Diversity Resident in 2003–2005 and Curriculum Materials Librarian at the RW Woodruff Library, Atlanta University Center, appreciated the "well-structured mentoring program, opportunities to publish, and the ability to interact and network with fellow librarians." Asked to reflect on the two-year residency experience, one of the recent graduates of the program, Damon Campbell, Diversity Resident in 2007–2009 and currently serving as Acquisitions Librarian at the Florida Coastal School of Law, summarized his experience as follows: "accepting this position is one of the best decisions I've ever made" (University of Tennessee Libraries, 2009).

REFERENCES

Agnew, S., L. Gray, and M. Puente. 2006. Diversity toolchest: Academic residency programs, the cohort experience. *Versed: Bulletin of the Office of Diversity, American Library Association* (June): 4.

Bright, K., S. Agnew, T. Arnold, L. Gray, M. Hristov, J. Keally, M. Puente, and W. Robinson. 2006. Recruiting the under-represented: The science links experience. In *Recruiting, Training, and Retention of Science and Technology Librarians*, edited by P. Kreitz and J. Devries. New York: Haworth Press.

Keally, J., and University of Tennessee Libraries' Minority Librarian Residency Program. 2004. *Minority Librarian Mentoring and Networking Initiatives and Opportunities: Electronic Discussion List and Website.* American Library Association, Library Administration and Management Association Cultural Diversity Grant.

Mack, T., D. Campbell, and S. Collins. 2008. Assessing academic library diversity residency programs from a resident standpoint. Conference Proceedings, National Diversity in Libraries Conference, Louisville, KY.

Mundava, M., K. Bright, and J. Chaudhuri. 2006. The Diversity Librarians' Network. In *Achieving Diversity: A How-to-Do-It Manual for Librarians,* edited by B. Dewey and L. Parham. New York: Neal Schuman Publishers.

Mundava, M., J. Chaudhuri, and K. Bright. 2004. Preparing diverse graduates for careers in professional librarianship: A focus on the University of Tennessee Libraries Minority Residency Program. *The Tennessee Librarian* 54:2.

Puente, M., L. Gray, and S. Agnew. 2009. The expanding library wall: Outreach to the University of Tennessee's multicultural/international student population. *Reference Services Review* 37.1:30–43.

University of Tennessee. 2004. "A Plan for the New Century."

University of Tennessee. 2007. Office of Equity and Diversity. http://oed.utk.edu/statement/

University of Tennessee. 2010. Office of the Chancellor. Advisory Groups. Council for Diversity & Interculturalism. http://chancellor.utk.edu/advisory/diversity.shtml

University of Tennessee Libraries. 2002. *Minority Librarian Residency Program* [brochure].

University of Tennessee Libraries. 2009. *Diversity Librarian Residency Program* [brochure].

University of Tennessee Libraries. 2010. Diversity Committee. http://www.lib.utk.edu/diversity

Chapter 7

Nurse Preceptors and the Academic Library: A Model for New Graduate Development

Megan Zoe Perez

INTRODUCTION

The nursing profession has employed various approaches to address new graduate nurses' lack of preparation and to attract and retain the new nurse. Nursing residency programs (NRPs) have been documented in the literature as demonstrating success in achieving these goals (Altier and Krsek 2006). One of the most critical components of an NRP, however, is the nurse "preceptor," a component that is absent from library residency programs.

The nursing preceptor is an indispensable element in the transfer of skills and knowledge from an experienced practitioner to a new learner. The description of a "learner" by Speers, Strzyzewski, and Ziolkowski (2004) includes seasoned employees, staff members who are new to any given area, and, most important for the purpose of this discussion, the new graduate. Preceptors are the mentors and guides for the new graduate. They are experienced staff members who possess, for example, outstanding communication skills and teaching skills and who facilitate the new graduate's learning through instruction, evaluation, socialization, and workplace orientation.

Numerous studies suggest that the use of preceptors can enhance the recruitment and retention of both new graduate nurses and nurses transitioning into a new setting. They provide the new nurse with the opportunity to become socialized into the profession and acquire the requisite skills and knowledge for effective practice (Oermann and Moffitt-Wolf 1997). This chapter, however, is not about nursing preceptors. It is about the systematic development and advancement of new graduates' levels of skills proficiency—a development that is based on concepts of adult learning that can be applied in our own profession. It is about viewing the nursing profession's use of preceptors as a model for the development of both library residents and library residency program coordinators.

The work opens with a brief description of the value of studying the nursing industry and continues to examine the history of nurse preceptors, different models of support for preceptors, and a comparison of nursing residency programs with library residency programs. Results of a survey conducted by the author are presented and discussed, and the chapter concludes with recommendations for future action. Although this chapter pays close attention to the concept and use of preceptors in the nursing industry, I encourage you to read it with an eye toward how we can apply the principles, concepts, and practices to the structure and design of post-MLS library residency programs.

WHY STUDY NURSING?

Murray (2002) describes a nursing workforce that is facing challenges similar to the library workforce. First, there is a nursing shortage expected to extend into 2020 with an estimated 400,000 registered nurse vacancies. An aging nursing pool, a decline in nursing school enrollment, increased career opportunities for women in traditionally female-dominated professions, nurse "burnout," and a public misconception of a nurse's responsibilities are cited by Murray as some of the factors contributing to this shortage. She also notes that one out of every three nurses under age thirty plans to leave the profession within a year due to dissatisfaction with scheduling, mandatory overtime, and high levels of stress (Murray 2002).

Their challenges are not unlike those currently faced in librarianship, and these similarities have not escaped the notice of members of our own profession. Davis and Hall (2007), for example, determined the anticipated exodus of librarians out of the workforce due to retirement would not only be delayed but that even more librarians would reach retirement age than previously thought (Table 7.1).

Table 7.1 Number of librarians reaching age 65, 2000–2019

Time period	Number
2000–4	5,479
2005–9	12,898
2010–14	23,208
2015–19	25,014

Source: Adapted with permission from Davis and Hall 2007, fig. 9.

Holt and Strock (2005) report the number of library and information science (LIS) graduates is relatively stable at approximately 5,000 graduates a year. The most current Association for Library and Information Science Education (ALISE) data available shows the total number of MLS degrees from American Library Association (ALA)-accredited schools during the 2003–2004 year is 5,951 (ALISE 2005). The authors of an Association of College and Research Libraries (ACRL) white paper incorporated a discussion of nursing shortage and supply issues in its discussion of recruitment and retention issues for librarianship (ACRL Ad Hoc Task Force 2002). Important themes regarding the recruitment of new librarians that were identified by ACRL's white paper included additional professional opportunities for new graduates, a negative image of the profession, and a stagnant number of new graduates. Table 7.2 compares factors contributing to workforce shortages in both nursing and librarianship.

Table 7.2 Factors contributing to workforce shortages

Factor	Nursing	Librarianship
Aging workforce	Yes	Yes
School enrollment	Declining	Stagnant
Lingering negative image	Yes	Yes
Increased opportunities for women outside librarianship	Yes	Yes

In terms of workforce demographics, the data reported in the ALISE *Statistical Report* is significant (2005). According to the most current report, the percentage of students of White origin in ALA-accredited library science programs is 72.5% (ALISE 2005). The percentage of students in ALA-accredited library science programs who are female is 79.1 percent, and the largest group of students is in the twenty-five to twenty-nine year old category. Davis and Hall (2007) found that the nearly 110,000 credentialed librarians are predominantly white women aged forty-five to fifty-four. They also reported a 3 percent decline in the "under thirty-five" age range and a 41 percent decline in the thirty-five to forty-four age range.

According to the American Association of Colleges and Nursing (AACN 2009), the percentage of students enrolled in a generic, baccalaureate nursing program in 2008 and who declared themselves to be of white origin was 74 percent. The gender of nursing students enrolled in the same kind of program was 89.5 percent female in the fall of 2007 (AACN 2008). Altier and Krsek (2006) found nurse residents have an average age of twenty-six. This profile is not unlike that of the library and information science student (Table 7.3).

Table 7.3 Demographic profiles of nursing and library information science students

	Nursing	Librarianship
Gender	89.5% female	79% female
Ethnicity	74% white	72.5% white
Age	26 (average)	25–29

These similarities in worker demographics, workforce challenges for the new graduate, and concern for recruitment and retention to the profession make nursing an appropriate professional model for study and emulation.

PRECEPTORS: THEN AND NOW

The works of Goode and Williams (2004) and Oermann and Moffitt-Wolf (1997) both discuss the increasing difficulties, stresses, and challenges experienced by new graduates in transitioning to the professional role. Various approaches have been employed by the nursing profession to address these concerns and to attract and retain the new graduate nurse. One of the most widely used techniques in undergraduate and postgraduate nursing education is the use of a nurse preceptor (Usher et al. 1999).

Countless models for preceptor support and development can be found in the literature (Beecroft, Hernandez, and Reid 2008; Jackson 2001; Kertis 2007; Neumann et al. 2004; Nicol and Young 2007). Some programs are designed to offer incentives and rewards for preceptors. Other programs are designed to address the learning needs of preceptors. Still others are designed to include a tiered, team-based approach to precepting; an experiential learning approach; or a broader, institutionally integrated approach.

The term "preceptor," when compared with other theories, models, and concepts of adult education, is relatively new. It is approximately three decades old and first made its appearance in the nursing literature in 1975 (Beecroft, Hernandez, and Reid 2008). Traditionally, the roles of the preceptor are to serve as a socializer, an educator, and a role model for a new graduate nurse. They are responsible for the socialization of the new graduate into the workplace, and they assist the preceptee in settling into his or her new role and environment. In their role as educator, preceptors assess learning needs, plan learning activities, and develop the capabilities of the new nurse. Last, as a role model, preceptors lead the preceptee by example and serve as an exemplar of professionalism by adhering to standards of practice.

In more contemporary models, however, the preceptor's role has undergone a series of transformations. Traditionally, the preceptor serves as an experienced practitioner who teaches, instructs, and supervises new nurses (Usher et al. 1999). The customary preceptor serves as a clinical skills facilitator (Speers, Strzyzewski, and Ziolkowski 2004). Previously, the preceptor also functioned as a link between theory and practice, a guide, supporter, evaluator, and teacher of the new nurse (Kertis 2007), and as a delivery agent of the workplace culture (Boyer 2008).

In fact, contemporary preceptors now fill the roles of protector, evaluator, and team builder in addition to their traditional roles of socializer, educator, and role model (Boyer 2008). As protectors, preceptors help create a safe learning environment for the new graduate to practice and learn. As evaluators, they assess and document the new practitioner's level of skills competency; as team builders they are responsible for communicating the purpose and value of the preceptorship to, and ensuring its support from, the administration, managers, and staff.

Research shows that, given the multifaceted role of the contemporary preceptor, there are a variety of obstacles to the development of successful relationships between preceptor and new learner. Some of these obstacles include burnout (Usher et al. 1999) and lack of guidance and education (Kertis 2007). An absence of qualified staff to precept (Jackson 2001), time constraints (Yonge et al. 2002), and lack of administrative support and recognition (Neumann et al. 2004) are also cited in the research as barriers to successful relationship development.

Preceptors are typically selected on the basis of the level of expertise, tenure with the organization, interest in precepting new hires, and staff availability. "Many preceptors," writes Kertis (2007, 238), "have limited or no educational experience for this expanded nursing role. Excellent clinicians do not necessarily make excellent preceptors." A study by Speers and others (2004, 128) expresses a similar sentiment with regard to preceptors' abilities to fulfill their roles:

The philosophy of the hospital is one that focuses on the patient and the concept that all are responsible for teaching. In theory, this is a wonderful concept, but in reality, some staff are better suited for this responsibility than others.

These obstacles will continue to remain in place and will be further exacerbated by the aging of the nursing workforce. As the baby boomer generation moves toward a mass exodus out of the profession due to natural attrition, the need for new nurses will increase. This demand for new nurses will consequently require a new generation of mentors and teachers who can develop the new graduate nurse into a fully functional, independent practitioner in a shorter amount of time—that is, the demand for qualified preceptors will be even greater than before as both skills and expertise depart from the profession.

PRECEPTOR MODELS

Preceptors need support just as new graduates do. A variety of programs and models have been developed and documented in the nursing literature, which describes different strategies for preceptor support and development. There are incentive programs (Jackson 2001), five-step preceptor teaching tools (Kertis 2007), and formal, centralized preceptor development programs (Neumann et al. 2004). There are also models that recommend the inclusion of nursing educators in the preceptorship (Yonge et al. 2002). Some programs include educators, practitioners, and a standardized preceptor curriculum (Boyer 2008), and still others rely on experiential learning activities (Nicol and Young 2007) or use a team-based approach to precepting (Beecroft, Hernandez, and Reed 2008). Despite this variety, specific themes can be identified throughout the literature. There is, for example, consistent recognition of a dwindling pool of preceptors and acknowledgment that preceptors need support, additional instruction, training, education, and practice developing empathy and giving feedback.

Roughly speaking, however, these different approaches that support preceptors can be divided into two categories: 1) short-term or quick administrative fixes and 2) long-term institutional approaches.

Short-Term or Administrative Approaches

The Preceptor Incentive Program

At the University of California at San Diego Medical Center, preceptors are selected by managers and given one or two days of training. As older, more experienced preceptors leave the workforce, the pool of preceptors shrinks. In addition, medical center administrators learned that increasing numbers of nurses were unwilling to serve as preceptors because of the responsibility and additional workload it required (Jackson 2001). In response, the medical center's nursing education department created the Preceptor Incentive Program (PIP).

PIP provides a variety of rewards for nurses who are willing to precept new graduates. Under the program, preceptors can, for example, earn education credit for each hour spent as a preceptor. The credit can be spent for approved educational purposes (academic courses, continuing education courses, and conference fees), enabling preceptors to participate in additional professional development opportunities. They can attend a conference on paid educational leave and use their PIP credit to pay for conference fees and expenses.

During the first 6 months of the program, more than 100 RNs spent nearly 12,000 hours acting as preceptors to 180 new nurse graduates. Cumulative PIP credit totaled nearly $15,000, and more than 70 additional nurses have been added to the program (Jackson 2001). Nurse managers, clinicians, and specialists report that PIP has been effective in increasing the willingness of experienced nurses to serve as preceptors of new nurses and has improved staff morale. It also provides new nurses with an incentive to develop their teaching and learning skills so they can serve as preceptors in the future and earn PIP credit that will fund their continuing education later in their career.

The One-Minute Preceptor

The One-Minute Preceptor, or OMP, is a teaching tool that has been used in NRPs since the early 1990s. It was developed to address the learning needs of preceptors with two specific premises in mind: 1) the ideal preceptor is responsible for guiding, supporting, teaching, evaluating, and orienting the new graduate and 2) many preceptors do not have the educational preparation for this expanded nursing role. The creators of the OMP argue that the preceptor needs to be exposed to adult learning principles, strategies that promote critical thinking, and evaluation methods and techniques (Kertis 2007).

There are five steps to the OMP. They include:

1. Getting the learner to state the problem. (What is going on in this situation? What is your plan for resolving it?)

2. Probing the learner's thought process to look for rationale leading to the problem's resolution. (Why did you choose that action? Did you consider alternatives?)

3. Teaching general rules. If the learner misstates the problem in Step 1, direct the learner to resources which can help resolve the problem. ("The procedure for X is detailed in Y.")

4. Reinforcing what was done correctly through positive feedback and encouragement.

5. Correcting mistakes through both positive and negative feedback.

These five steps have their theoretical foundation in principles of adult education such as Malcolm Knowles's andragogy (1984) and Donald Schön's (1983) theory of reflective practice. Educational theorists regard Knowles's andragogy as a series of guidelines for how to teach adult learners rather than as a cogent theory of general education (Kaufman 2003). His work resulted in the development of seven principles that could be used to provide the novice with a structure for self-directed learning. In the case of the OMP, the steps listed above are drawn from the principles of Knowles's andragogy. "Correcting mistakes" and "reinforcing what was already done," for example, are two activities that actively involve the learner in the evaluation process (Kertis 2007). This directly corresponds to one of Knowles's principles: involve learners in evaluating their own learning (Kaufman 2003).

Schön's theory of reflective practice involves the process of a practitioner's analysis and reflection on a past experience to learn and develop problem-solving strategies and new response techniques to similar problems that may arise in the future. Activities that help support this process of reflective learning include peer gatherings, moderated group discussions, and personal reflection in the form of journaling (Kaufman 2003; Martin 2007). One of the most important features of the

OMP is that it promotes the reflection process in learning, making it possible for both the teacher and learner to gain something from the experience (Kertis 2007).

In May 2004, nurses were invited to a one-hour education program on the OMP. The program included a lecture, handouts introducing the objectives and the five steps of the OMP, and case studies. Pre- and post-program surveys were used to determine differences in preceptors' perceptions of their teaching abilities before and one month after attending the OMP program.

Before attending the OMP, more than 30 percent either agreed or strongly agreed that it was difficult to evaluate new employees, provide feedback, and promote self-directed learning. Kertis (2007) also notes that preceptors were receptive to education on methods that promoted critical thinking, stimulated dialogue, and encouraged feedback. One month after the OMP program, 92 percent said they had already used the skills they learned in the program and indicated they would continue to do so. Participants reported less difficulty in advancing the clinical setting's educational goals (establishing a positive environment, controlling the teaching session, communicating goals, promoting understanding, evaluating, providing feedback, and promoting self-directed learning).

Although most preceptors indicated commitment to the preceptor program, burnout remained an issue. Fifteen percent in both the pre- and post-survey felt tired and drained from being a preceptor. On the basis of the data collected and analyzed, however, the OMP tool provides useful information for nurses in the preceptor role—information that is easy to learn and easy to apply. It is a teaching tool that can be taught to nurse preceptors in a one-hour program and that can contribute to a successful training program.

Experiential Learning

Research demonstrates that new graduates with limited work experience undergo a highly emotional and stressful transition into the cultural and social environment of the nursing work setting (Keller, Meekins, and Summers 2006). Predominant stresses are lack of experience, lack of organizational skills, dependence on others, and a lack of supervisory support. Further, job stress was identified as a factor in decreased work satisfaction and graduate nurse turnover (Nicol and Young 2007).

Preceptors are often chosen for their expertise and familiarity with the workplace. This is both a strength and a weakness. It can be a weakness in that preceptors may have forgotten what it is like to be a new learner in an unfamiliar setting. A teaching-learning program that exposes preceptors to new methods and skills in a different setting provides preceptors with an opportunity to experience anxiety once again, a re-creation of the stresses that new graduates feel. Experiential learning can be an effective way for preceptors to develop empathy, improve teaching skills, and practice giving feedback. The crucial elements in experiential learning are challenging activities that include an aspect of new skill acquisition and facilitated debriefing time to reflect, process, and transfer the learning to the workplace. Nicol and Young (2007) contend that this process of experiential learning will help preceptors develop additional competence, rendering them more effective.

To recreate the new nurse experience, a hospital in Perth, Australia, selected a one-day sail training program using small sail crafts as a method of experiential learning. Sail instructors provided the training and supervised the sailing. Participants were given sufficient instruction ahead of time to alleviate safety concerns but were not given enough detail to remove the element of the unknown (Nicol and Young 2007). Before the training, participants were asked to complete a self-evaluation instrument regarding their role as preceptor. At the end of the sailing experience, a nurse educator facilitated a debriefing period, during which the participants discussed the feelings of learning a new skill, explored the impact of emotions on learning, and identified teaching methods used by the sailing instructors, barriers to learning, and the role of feedback.

Six weeks after the program, participants were again asked to complete the self-evaluation tool. Overall, preceptors evaluated their performance in the role of preceptor more highly following the program. Nicol and Young (2007) divided the open-ended responses to the evaluation instrument into two categories: empathy (how the sailing day made them feel) and skill acquisition (how the program improved their role as preceptor).

Regarding empathy, the researchers found that remembering the emotions of being new was a theme. One participant noted, "learning a new skill can be a very stressful experience and it opened my eyes to how a new grad feels." Dependence on another is a second theme in the empathy category: "remembering what it was like to be a new learner again—floundering and looking for someone to be a mentor/supporter." The third theme regards the challenges of learning a new skill and recognized "the importance of a good introduction to new skills and environment" (Nicol and Young 2007, 301).

Regarding skill acquisition, Nicol and Young (2007) identified three themes: personal qualities, providing support, and enhancing learning. After completing the sail training program, the preceptors began to develop an "understanding [of] what they [new graduates] are going through and confronting each day" and began "being more aware of their [new graduates'] apprehension." The preceptors also began to recognize the need for "making myself more available" or to make "more time for them." The researchers also note that many comments were given addressing the importance of giving regular and constructive feedback and in assessing the learning needs of the new graduate (Nicol and Young 2007, 301).

For Nicol and Young (2007), the preliminary results of their study suggest experiential learning activities can be an effective way to develop the skills of nurse preceptors. Providing feedback, the development of personal qualities (such as being more aware of what the new graduates are going through), and the responsibilities of the preceptor are among the lasting effects of the experience that Nicol and Young (2007) identified. A benefit of the program they did not anticipate is an improvement in morale. Participants reported, for example, an improved positive feeling toward their employer for allowing them to develop their skills in a nontraditional setting and to have some fun.

Long-Term or Institutional Approaches

The Centralization Model

Researchers from the Mayo Clinic in Rochester, Minnesota, based their creation of a centralized preceptor program on the beliefs that a formal support program would enhance the effectiveness of preceptors and that without the resources of time, education, and finances, preceptors will burnout, experience sustained frustration, and provide potentially substandard patient care (Neumann et al. 2004). They began this project by creating a workgroup consisting of nursing education specialists, preceptors, directors, nurse managers, and nurse specialists.

The workgroup found that support of nursing leaders provides both the philosophical and financial support for the program. Getting the administration on board is pivotal. Identified selling points to the administration included the following:

1. Standardized selection process and criteria for preceptors

2. Ongoing staff development plans for preceptors

3. Mechanisms for preceptor reward and recognition
4. Ongoing evaluation with an annual report to nursing leadership
5. Creation of a preceptor oversight group to provide guidance for the improvement of the formal program

In terms of preceptor education, the researchers devised a three-tiered approach to meet the learning needs of novice preceptors, the needs of preceptors with one year of precepting experience, and the ongoing needs of more experienced preceptors. Courses were designed for each level of experience. The topics of the first-level courses included learning styles, providing feedback, and role-modeling. The second level focused on adult learning theory and teaching and learning strategies.

The last level is a forum. These are designed to keep preceptors informed and educated but also as a way to meet the learning outcomes of critical thinking and reflective practice. The result should be the development of a pool of preceptors who can observe, analyze, and evaluate current practice (Neumann et al. 2004, 20). Each forum focuses on a central theme, includes a question-and-answer period, and is repeated at specific intervals. Teaching and learning methods used here include pairing activities, total group interaction, discussion, and analysis. More experienced preceptors are expected to attend at least two forums each year.

The researchers found the nursing leadership and administration to be essential to the centralization of the program. Financial and educational resources must be available (Neumann et al. 2004, 23). Second, the preceptor's value must be understood throughout the organization. This suggests clear communication throughout the institution and strategic timing of program rollout.

Third, recognition is also an important element in preceptor program centralization. It is necessary to maintain and enhance staff morale, to reinforce the integrity of the program, and to recruit and retain employees who can be added to the preceptor pool. The researchers also found that methods for improving institution-wide preceptor development and education are necessary for the provision of outstanding and quality-driven orientation experiences for the new graduate.

The Support Model

Through a survey of 295 preceptors in Alberta, Canada, Yonge and others found that preceptors experience time constraints, increased workloads, increased stress, and lack of financial support, all of which lead to preceptor burnout and withdrawal from preceptor programs. They also reported that preceptors experienced complications with the preceptor-preceptee pairing process, with preceptee evaluation, and with a lack of recognition. Preceptor selection is not based on established criteria. Instead, student and preceptor pairings are often based on staff availability, and this form of selection can lead to unsuccessful matches (Yonge et al. 2002, 74).

Standardized assessment forms and/or evaluative instruments are often unavailable to preceptors. This creates difficulty for preceptors when evaluating new nurses in isolation from one another and can cause the preceptor to question their ability to appraise a learner's progress accurately. Although most preceptors wanted recognition for their role, only a few received it, and only slightly more than half of preceptors found their peers supportive. In most cases, support was provided by staff development departments, and not by the administration.

Of those who felt most supported, nursing educator availability was the category most often cited by preceptors. Other categories included prearranged meetings and/or interviews, support from the preceptors' coworkers and supervisors, and open communication between educator and preceptor (phone calls and visits to the preceptor by the educator). Preceptors need support with students' skill deficits—lack of confidence and poor communication skills, for example (Yonge et al. 2002, 75). Nursing educators assist preceptors in developing their skills to navigate these challenges, and for Yonge and others, the critical element of support for preceptors is the availability of nursing educators for feedback and open communication. It is significant that of those who felt least supported, insufficient communication with nurse educators was often cited as a reason why they received insufficient support.

For preceptors to receive as much support as possible, nursing instructors need to view themselves in an educational, collegial partnership with preceptors (Yonge et al. 2002, 76). Nursing educators, however, need support for this role as well. Nursing deans and directors will have to recognize the time, flexibility, energy, and thought necessary for a successful preceptorship.

To achieve these goals, Yonge and others recommend the creation of an onsite coordinator or liaison for the preceptor who can serve as a consultant for preceptors and who can maintain a formal relationship with the instructors. The development of a partnership between educators and preceptors is also an important strategy for increasing support for preceptors. This partnership should support each of the three parties involved: the preceptor, the educator, and the liaison; it should also jointly address the preceptor's responsibility for new nurse preparation and evaluation. Although Yonge and others (2002) recognize the best form of support comes from sustained educator involvement, they also acknowledge that preceptors will feel better supported if educators as well as deans and directors view themselves as partners in the preceptoring process.

The Vermont Nurse Internship Program

The purpose of the Vermont Nurse Internship Program (VNIP) is to create a formal nursing internship program that provides sufficient experience for novice nurses to function at a competent level when they enter the workforce, to increase the use of clinical staff as preceptors, and to develop a comprehensive support program for preceptors. The program is designed to be a marriage of schools of nursing and fields of practice that could strengthen both institutions. Central to the VNIP's success is research- and theory-based educational preparation for the preceptor role.

In 2001, nurse educators and staff development specialists drew from principles of novice-to-expert theory to modify an existing curriculum. The new curriculum provides a foundation for both teacher and learner to understand both *how* and *why* to do something in practice. This approach brings together both educators and practitioners and builds a "cadre of care providers and educators" who can utilize communication, teaching and learning, and interpersonal skills with both patients and colleagues in everyday interactions (Boyer 2008, E3). A curriculum that involves preceptors, learners, educators, and staff development officers, then, provides for a culture of learning within an institution.

When preceptors were first introduced into the nursing profession more than thirty years ago, the role of the preceptor was threefold. The preceptor was to acclimate the new nurse to the new working environment, to provide a model of professional behavior, and to develop critical thinking skills in the new nurse. The preceptor served as a socializer, a role model, and an educator. While developing this new curriculum for preceptors, the researchers maintained these traditional roles but also identified three additional roles of the preceptor: protector, team builder, and evaluator.

As a protector, the function of the preceptor is to provide a safe learning environment—an environment where the resident feels comfortable asking questions and making mistakes, where there is a teaching-and-learning approach that builds from the simple to the more complex; an environment where the resident is encouraged to engage in independent practice, and where there is consistent observation, ongoing feedback, and regular encouragement.

According to Boyer (2008), communication, teamwork, and interpersonal interactions are the preconditions for a safe learning environment. To create this environment, the preceptor must build a team consisting of members from the entire health care staff. The preceptor's role is to lead this team and help build a workplace culture of support and nurture, a culture that sees the success of the resident as a joint responsibility and not simply as "the preceptor's job." In addition to being a protector, the preceptor is also a team builder.

Defining expectations, ensuring adherence to standards of practice, discussing performance issues, and documenting a resident's abilities are all part of the preceptor's role as evaluator. In this role, preceptors can use the performance categories listed in the Dreyfus model to define and demonstrate levels of skills proficiency, but they first need education and preparation in Dreyfus model theory. The same can be said of their other roles and responsibilities. Before preceptors can successfully fulfill their role as educator and teach a skill such as critical thinking, for example, they first must have an understanding of what it is, how it is done, and, ultimately, how to develop it in others.

To help prepare their preceptors, the VNIP included a two-day workshop as a critical component of the program. The topics addressed during the workshop included preceptor roles, novice-to-expert theory, competency assessment, teaching/learning theory, communication, personality styles, critical thinking, and team building. Teaching methods included small-group work, case studies, and individual surveys. The VNIP also included standardized coaching plans for the preceptor to follow. The plan provided guidelines for educational processes to follow with the new nurse learner and offerd specific learning activities.

Managers, educators, and colleagues reported a marked improvement in the transition process after implementation of the VNIP. Quantitative data indicates a positive impact on recruitment and retention. In 1999, retention of those who completed their orientation was 75 percent; following completion of the internship program, retention was 93 percent. Boyer (2008) concludes that preceptors require development and support in fulfilling their performance expectations as socializer, team builder, role model, evaluator, educator, and protector roles but that they can meet those expectations effectively if they are supported by a standardized curriculum, the inclusion of the entire health care team (including staff development officers and educators), clearly defined expectations, and the development of clinical coaching plans.

Team Preceptorships

In 1998, Beecroft, Kunzman, and Krozek (2001) created a Registered Nurse Residency program to help bridge the gap between skills learned in nursing school and the concrete needs of the workplace. To help develop their program, they used a task force to coordinate a formal orientation period for new nurses. After surveying the clinical orientation of new nurses, the task force made a number of unexpected discoveries. For example, they learned that newer nurses did not feel competent to precept and, second, that older nurses did not feel younger nurses were qualified to precept.

Additionally, fewer expert nurses were available to precept because of the nursing shortage described by Murray (2002). As a result, the same individuals were always assigned as primary preceptors directly contributing to a high risk of preceptor burnout (Beecroft, Hernandez, and Reid 2008). Previously, an eight-hour preceptor preparation class was used to make preceptors ready for their duties and responsibilities. Beecroft and others (2008) found this eight-hour class was insufficient for the needs of the preceptors. It did not address the unique learning needs of nurse residents, and it did not address the distinctiveness of the residency program, which included a novice-to-expert framework.

A new program would, therefore, be modified to address the learning needs of the nurse residents, and it would include a new structure for training that would prevent preceptor burnout (Beecroft 2008, 144). It would also accommodate the increased timeframe necessary to reflect novice-to-expert framework and guided learning experiences for new preceptors.

Drawing on the work of Modic and Schloesser (2008), who suggest that newly competent nurses can easily remember what it was like to be new and can sympathize with the stresses and strains of learning in an unfamiliar environment, the team approach to precepting took shape. New grads were paired with both a novice nurse and an expert nurse. The novice nurse would socialize the new nurse into the workforce, teach basic nursing skills, and introduce policies and procedures. The more experienced nurse would then take over precepting responsibilities once the new nurse was ready to take on more challenging and complex activities. The expert nurse also oversees the instruction offered by the novice nurse.

Selection criteria were developed for the preceptors before making these new pairings. To participate in the program, preceptors must have at least one year of clinical experience; role model the values of the facility; consistently seek out learning opportunities; demonstrate communication, critical thinking, and leadership skills; and inspire independence in others.

The eight-hour workshop was also completely revamped to include a novice-to-expert framework. During the workshop, participants learned to distinguish novice work from that of more expert practices. Additional content covered during the workshop included principles of adult learning styles, critical thinking and problem solving, conflict resolution, reflective practice, and strategies for providing effective feedback. At the conclusion of the workshop, a notebook was given to participants providing information about the residency program and the role of the preceptor and new graduate.

The advantages of this structure include the development of a new preceptor (the novice nurse), thereby increasing the pool of available preceptors; a reduction in the skills gap between new graduate and preceptor (expert nurse), saving the expert nurse frustration; the provision of support and empathy for the new nurse from the novice nurse because the two are closer in skills level; an increase in the amount of information available regarding new graduate performance (for evaluation purposes); and an increase in educational opportunities as the new graduate is exposed to different preceptors.

Despite these listed advantages, the researchers found that implementation of the model proved difficult for at least three reasons. First, selection of the expert and novice preceptors was hard despite the developed selection criteria. Second, nurse educators found they needed buy-in from the expert preceptors to precept two people (the new nurse and the novice nurse). Third, expert nurses were also vocal about their distrust and skepticism of novice nurses serving as preceptors. To quell some of this distrust and generate buy-in, individual education classes were given to explain the program and to allow discussion of expert preceptor concerns.

Overall, the research suggests promising effects of the new program structure. During the first year, experience with the structure and increased availability of preceptors resulted in expert preceptors becoming advocates for the new team-based system. Further, during the same year, more than 94 percent of preceptors indicated satisfaction with being a preceptor. After seven years, the new preceptor training system is now fully integrated into the residency program, and obstacles were overcome as expert and novice preceptors began to see the benefits of the new structure.

SUMMARY AND REVIEW

These seven models of preceptor programs vary in duration, scope, design, and strategy. Some are intended to provide participants with rewards and recognition or quick, short-term training. Some provide exposure to the needs of the new graduate through experiential learning programs. Others look to develop preceptors' skills and abilities through the use of standardized curricula and coaching plans. Still others hope to create a culture of teaching and learning through the simultaneous involvement of educators, administrators, staff development officers, nurses, and new graduates.

Despite these variables, however, these models share several consistent themes. First, all of these programs demonstrate a concern for the development of the new graduate vis-à-vis the use of a preceptor. Second, there is an implicit, and sometimes explicit, acknowledgment that preceptors require additional skills to satisfy their expectations efficiently. Third, the research shows there is a growing concern over new graduates' inability to function independently, a concern that is rooted in insufficient preparation, inadequate training, and absent systems of support for preceptors.

Fourth, although formal preceptor training programs are being developed in different settings around the world, the content of these programs is similar: critical thinking, adult learning principles, teaching styles, delivering effective feedback, novice-to-expert theory, and evaluation and assessment. It is important to note that these skills are not unique to the nursing profession. They are applicable and have value in any organization within any industry and within any program, particularly those that concern the ongoing development and educational needs of adult learners.

Fifth, and also of particular importance to us as library professionals, the deeper purpose of preceptor programs is not to develop new graduates, and it is not to better train preceptors; it is to ensure the profession has a steady flow of competent practitioners ready and available to provide superior levels of quality service and to do so with high degrees of self-satisfaction. In other words, the purpose of preceptor programs is to recruit and retain talent in the profession.

Additional models of preceptor development are available in the literature, but these seven illustrate approaches that have been adopted recently and that have shown promising results. The models also provide us with examples of tools and strategies that can be used to enhance the structure of library residency programs in general and to support the development of program coordinators in particular.

Yet how do currently active library residency programs compare to these models? Do they teach and evaluate critical thinking skills? Do they use formal programs to train their residents' supervisors in adult learning theory, novice-to-expert theory, and delivering effective feedback? Research regarding library residency programs is extant but not current. In fact, the majority of research in this area predates the turn of this century, with the lone exception of Brewer and Winston (2001). Hence, a survey was developed to examine these questions.

METHODOLOGY AND RESEARCH QUESTIONS

After receiving Institutional Review Board approval from the University of Arkansas, an online survey was distributed via e-mail to human resources and personnel online discussion lists and to an ACRL Residency Interest Group discussion list in January 2009. The instrument used was identical to the instrument used in a 2007 study of library residency programs (Perez 2007). In 2007, the total number of respondents was nineteen. In 2009, the number of respondents increased to twenty-four.

The instrument included a total of 47 questions that were a combination of open-ended, closed-ended, and Likert-type scale questions. The target population of the survey included program coordinators of residency programs in the United States and Canada. A unique difference between this instrument and previous residency program surveys is that it contains questions regarding evaluation factors cited as being important or useful for future investigations by both library and nursing researchers (Brewer and Winston 2001). The present survey, however, was designed to measure residency program status, residency candidate identification, resident development, program visibility, and reputation. For the purposes of this specific chapter, only the results concerning resident development are discussed.

Questions in the resident development section addressed the design of resident program assignments, the use of personality and critical thinking inventories, and the structure of mentorship arrangements. Specifically, the survey had a fundamental interrogative: Do library residency program coordinators use the skills, tools, tactics, strategies, and techniques that are used in nursing residency programs?

Results

Assignment Design

In terms of assignment design, an overwhelming majority of respondents in 2007 (92.3 percent) indicated that they did not include the residents' input. Only one respondent indicated that the participants' assignments were created through consultation with supervisors and program directors, and only one respondent indicated that they were designed by the library director and a faculty member from the library school. A different respondent indicated that his or her program allowed residents to choose which assignments are preferred, but these assignments were proposed by the staff before the interview process.

The landscape has changed somewhat during the two years since the original survey. In 2009, 29 percent of respondents (5 out of 17) indicated resident involvement in the design of the resident's work assignments. The level of involvement, however, varied. For example, one respondent indicated that the resident worked with senior management and project managers to design the work assignment and then completed a learning contract. Another respondent indicated that the assignments were part of a portfolio of projects put together by the program coordinator, department heads, and the resident.

Personality and Critical Thinking

In regard to the use of personality inventories and critical thinking skills, results from both surveys suggest library residency programs simply do not use them. In 2007, only one respondent (8 percent) indicated that his or her program used learning style measurements on the resident. In 2009, this figure dropped to zero. Table 7.4 compares the responses to the question regarding the use of learning style assessments. Table 7.5 shows responses to the question regarding the use of critical thinking skills inventories.

Table 7.4 "Are learning style measurements performed on the resident?"

Year	Yes	No
2007 (N = 13)	8%	92%
2009 (N = 18)	0%	100%
% change	−8%	+8%

Table 7.5 "Are the resident's critical thinking skills inventoried?"

Year	Yes	No
2007 (N = 13)	0%	100%
2009 (N = 16)	6%	94%
% change	−6%	+6%

Confidence, Stress, and Job Satisfaction

In terms of confidence, stress, and job satisfaction, there was a reversal of practice from 2007 to 2009. In 2007, seven of twelve (58 percent) respondents indicated the levels of residents' confidence and ability were measured during the course of the program. Four of these seven respondents indicated the confidence and ability measures were informal: verbal assessment or conversation/discussion, for example. Between 2007 and 2009, confidence assessment dropped 11 percent. In 2009, only 47 percent of respondents (8 of 17) indicated that they measured residents' levels of confidence and ability (Table 7.6).

Table 7.6 "Are the levels of the resident's confidence and ability measured during the course of the program?"

Year	Yes	No
2007 (N=12)	58%	42%
2009 (N=17)	47%	53%
% change	−11%	+11%

One possible cause for this decrease in confidence assessment may be that there were more new programs in 2009 than in 2007. These newer programs may not have had all of their methods of assessment in place yet. Further, it is possible that several of the seven respondents from the 2007 survey were included in the eight respondents from the 2009 survey. The number of coordinators using these measures may have remained relatively constant, while the number of active programs increased, thereby reducing the percentage of programs using such measures.

Although the percentage of respondents measuring levels of confidence *decreased*, the frequency of evaluation among those who use any method of assessment *increased*. Three of these eight respondents indicated that the resident was evaluated after each rotation. This is a significant change from 2007, when none of the respondents indicated such regular assessment.

A similar decrease in usage is apparent with regard to the question of stress and job satisfaction. Between 2007 and 2009, levels of stress and job satisfaction measurement dropped 22 percent. In 2007, 69 percent of survey respondents indicated that levels of stress and job satisfaction were measured during the program. In 2009, only 47 percent of respondents indicated that levels of stress and job satisfaction were measured (Table 7.7).

Table 7.7 "Are levels of stress and job satisfaction measured at any point during the program?"

Year	Yes	No
2007 (*N* = 13)	69%	31%
2009 (*N* = 17)	47%	53%
% change	−22%	+22%

An important finding of the study is that among those who did implement such measures, respondents indicated level of stress was not measured *expressly*; formal measures were not used to determine levels of job satisfaction. Only one of these respondents noted that a formal assessment is used multiple times per year. The other respondents indicated that the assessment was either informal or part of regular performance reviews.

Another significant difference between the years 2007 and 2009 regards the availability of "downtime" for assimilation and reflection of material presented in rotations. Contrary to the measurement of confidence, stress, and levels of job satisfaction, the practice of journaling in library residency programs *increased* between 2007 and 2009. In 2007, downtime or journaling was available in only 36 percent of the programs. In 2009, 56 percent of respondents noted that such a feature was a part of the residency program.

Mentoring

Mentoring, in contrast, is a component that has remained relatively stable over this time period. In 2007, 85 percent of respondents indicated that it is a formal component of the program. In 2009, this figure dipped slightly to 81 percent. The basis on which mentors were identified during both survey periods, however, was widely variable.

The study revealed that the strategies used by respondents to identify mentors in both survey periods include the following: suggestion by the program coordinator, self-identification by the resident, solicitation for volunteers, administrative assignment, and common professional interest. A separate question was asked regarding the basis on which the mentor-mentee pairing is made. A majority of the responses in both 2007 and 2009 indicated this pairing is based on mutual interests, staff availability, staff interest in serving as a mentor, and resident identification of a mentor.

This is markedly different from the mentor selection process in NRPs. In nursing residencies, mentors are selected according to predetermined, formal criteria. They must have a minimum number of years of experience with the specific institution (not experience in the profession), model the values of the host institution, actively seek out additional learning opportunities (display qualities of a lifelong learner), and demonstrate the ability to communicate, think critically, and lead by example. Further, nurses selected to serve as resident mentors must be teachable and learn an additional set of skills, tools, and techniques for the development of new professionals.

Resident Evaluation

Finally, respondents were asked how the residents' performance is evaluated. In 2007, two-thirds of the respondents indicated residents are evaluated by the same formal process for librarian/faculty evaluation. The remaining respondents indicated an essay written by the supervisor or by both the participant and the supervisor was used for evaluation. Regarding evaluation frequency, one-third of all respondents conducted the evaluation process at the end of each rotation. A different third of respondents performed evaluations semiannually. The last third conducted them on an annual basis.

In 2009, the responses show a greater variety of evaluative strategies. Written evaluations, summative essays authored by both the resident and the rotation supervisor, and the same formal process for other library/faculty members were all cited as methods of evaluation. Informal conversations, peer reviews, informal feedback from staff, and a review of work or project assignments, however, were also cited as strategies for evaluation of resident work performance. The data suggests that these latter strategies were not used in 2007. Regarding evaluation frequency, the data also suggests the frequency of resident evaluation increased from 2007 to 2009. Six of sixteen respondents to the 2009 survey indicated the resident is evaluated more than twice per year, and five of these six indicated the resident is evaluated at the conclusion of each rotation.

FINDINGS/DISCUSSION

The purpose of this study was to examine the value of nursing preceptors and to develop an understanding of how we can apply preceptor principles, concepts, and practices to the structure and design of post-MLS library residency programs. The study first described the relevance of the nursing industry for librarianship, the history of nurse preceptors, and different models of preceptorship. Lastly, the study compared the findings of a survey of residency program coordinators administered at two time points.

The present work is limited by a number of factors. One disadvantage of this study is its sample size. Brewer and Winston (2001) reported a response from nineteen institutions with active programs. In 2007, fourteen respondents indicated they had a currently active program, and in 2009, eighteen respondents indicated they had an active program. Some of these questions—those regarding evaluation, for example—may not be applicable, particularly if a program is less than one year old and has not yet had an opportunity to evaluate the resident. Also, some potential respondents may have excluded themselves simply by not answering the survey. Specifically, those who responded in 2007 may not have felt the need to complete the survey again in 2009, or those who did not have an active program in 2009 may have felt they had little data to contribute.

Second, the findings are not generalizable. Some respondents may represent programs that do not have a typical, academic library structure. The University of Arkansas, for example, is a three-year program that includes one year of rotations, one year of specialization, and a final year designed as a capstone experience. Other responses may have come from specialized research libraries such as the National Library of Medicine or the Eskind Biomedical Library at Vanderbilt University. Still another response could have come from Georgetown University, which hosts a law library residency program.

Nevertheless, the survey findings provide some useful information regarding the current practice of mentor identification, mentor-mentee pairing, and resident development and evaluation in library residency programs. The data suggest that there have been numerous changes in the management and design of residency programs since 2007.

First, more programs are now including residents in the creation and design of their work assignments than in 2007. Second, fewer programs are now measuring their residents' levels of confidence, stress, and job satisfaction. The percentage of programs utilizing any kind of confidence assessment dropped from 58 percent in 2007 to 47 percent in 2009; and there was a 22 percent drop in the use of stress and job satisfaction measures.

Third, the percentage of programs allowing for downtime or journaling has increased from 36 percent to 56 percent. Fourth, the 2009 survey data report that there has been an increase in the variety of evaluative strategies used by programs and an increase in the frequency with which these strategies are used.

Despite these differences, it is significant that the process of mentor identification and mentor-mentee pairing has remained relatively stable. Although the respondents indicated a variety of processes used to identify mentors and pair them with the resident, *none of the respondents indicated the selection of mentors was based on established, standardized criteria*. These responses are mirrored by the responses to the question regarding mentor-mentee pairing, and, again, none of the respondents indicated the mentor-mentee pairing was based on established, standardized criteria.

It is as though librarianship is in the position nursing was in decades ago. At that time, the prevailing attitude regarding mentorship was that those who are more senior, experienced, available, and interested were assigned or suggested as mentors, or that individual mentors were not necessary as the institution aimed to develop a *culture* of learning and mentoring. In fact, one of the 2009 survey respondents stated the mentee-mentor pairing was not applicable. For this institution, "there is not a one-to-one mentor assigned. The focus is on developing a culture of mentoring."

These attitudes, however, as the review of the literature suggests, are outdated and anachronistic, and they are no longer sufficient to satisfy the needs of contemporary reality. Recall the statement by Speers, Strzyzewski, and Ziolkowski (2004, 128) regarding the mentoring and teaching philosophy of the William Beaumont Hospital: "In theory, this [the concept that all are responsible for teaching] is a wonderful concept, but in reality, some staff are better suited for this responsibility than others." This finding is made additionally significant given that Brewer found "residents identified mentoring skills and ability to provide constructive feedback as the two most important attributes for supervisors" (Brewer 1997, 533). In that same study, residents went on to describe the overall mentoring skills of their supervisors as relatively low.

RECOMMENDATIONS

Library residency programs have an opportunity to increase the efficiency of their residents' development and the overall quality of the resident experience by adding additional components to their programs. These components can be drawn from the nurse preceptor examples described in the literature review section. Taken together, the review of the literature and the survey data suggest that residency programs and their coordinators can be dramatically improved using the following tactics:

1. *Incentivize participation for library staff.* Jackson (2001) described one such program, but how can librarians be encouraged to actively and enthusiastically participate in new graduate development?

2. *Address learning needs.* The OMP preceptor program (Kertis 2007) provides a model for addressing the learning needs of the new graduate supervisors, mentors, and program coordinators.

3. *Incorporate experiential learning.* Nicol and Young (2007) described the purpose and value of experiential learning for preceptors. What kinds of experiential learning activities can librarians engage in to help remind them of what it is like to be a new learner in unfamiliar territory?

4. *Centralize program management.* Create a standing committee or working group to manage the coordination of the residency program. This model, similar to the one described by Neumann and others (2004), allows more staff to participate in the program and provides the resident with broader connections to the institution.

5. *Take a team-based approach to resident development, particularly in the area of mentorship.* A team-based approach alleviates a single individual of the pressures and responsibilities of managing a program in isolation and provides additional opportunities for varying qualities of mentorship: socialization, education, evaluation, and protection.

6. *Develop mentors according to preestablished, formal criteria.* Speers, Strzyzewski, and Ziolkowski (2004) developed a checklist that has been adapted for our purposes (see Appendix 7.1: "Resident Mentor Selection Criteria").

7. *Establish a mentor-mentee agreement plan with the resident* (see Appendix 7.2: "Resident Mentor-Menteel Agreement").

8. *Consult with ALISE.* Yonge and others (2002) described the need for garnering support from nurse educators. I cannot think of a single library residency program that consults regularly with LIS faculty regarding new graduate education, transition, evaluation, or other. Why is this?

9. *Standardize program coordinator education.* Boyer's (2008) VNIP offers us a model of preceptor education. Although the VNIP is an eight-hour workshop, there is no reason why library program coordinators cannot create a similar experience. An extended, centralized workshop, seminar, or symposium can be organized at an annual conference or provided over time through a series of online workshops, with support from a variety of sources. In recent years, the ARL Office of Diversity Programs coordinated an extended visit to an ARL library as a part of its Initiative to Recruit a Diverse Workforce (IRDW) program. Every two years, the University of Minnesota Libraries hosts the Minnesota Institute for Early Career Librarians from Traditionally Underrepresented Groups (Minnesota Institute). Both of these programs provide models for the development of a residency program institute for both program coordinators and residents. Topics for this educational program might include the following:

    a. Personality inventories
    b. Critical thinking skills inventories
    c. Learning style measurements
    d. Confidence assessment tools
    e. Stress and job satisfaction measurements
    f. Introductions to Knowles's andragogy and Schön's theory of reflective practice and novice-to-expert theory

10. *Include time for reflection and journaling as a formal part of each rotation.* The benefits of such formal training and coordinator development will have the effect of formalizing the structure within which residents are educated and will provide a wealth of evaluative data necessary to secure sustainable administrative, financial, and organizational support. A more formal training program will not only improve the skills

and abilities of resident mentors but will also improve a program's reputation and rate of success, thereby improving the quality of future applicant pools.

SUMMARY AND CONCLUSION

This study identified similarities in workforce demographics and workforce issues in the library and nursing professions. It introduced the concept of the nurse preceptor and reviewed, in detail, seven preceptor models that can be applied to librarianship. This study also compared the results of a library residency program coordinators survey which was administered once in 2007, and then repeated in 2009. From analysis of these surveys, recommendations for improving residency programs through coordinator development were created and then listed.

Although the nursing and library professions have similar demographic characteristics and similar workforce concerns, the structure and execution of their residency programs differs. Informal anecdotal and formal documented evidence indicates that library residency programs are successful in achieving their programmatic goals. These programs, however, may enjoy additional success and see sustained financial, institutional, and employee support if they continue to develop, expand, and evolve. They can do this by incorporating some of the practices and principles used by other models of residency program management—practices and principles that have been laid out in this chapter.

There is sufficient literature and research available to improve the practices of our programs. The issue is whether we are willing, as institutions, administrators, and coordinators, to invest the human and financial resources requisite for this improvement.

REFERENCES

ACRL Ad Hoc Task Force on Recruitment & Retention Issues. 2002. *Recruitment, Retention, & Restructuring: Human Resources in Academic Libraries*. Chicago: Association of College and Research Libraries.

Altier, M., and C. A. Krsek. 2006. Effects of a 1-year residency program on job satisfaction and retention in new graduates. *Journal for Nurses in Staff Development* 22:70–77.

American Association of Colleges of Nursing (AACN). 2008. *Enrollment and Graduations in Baccalaureate and Graduate Programs in Nursing*. Washington, DC: AACN.

American Association of Colleges of Nursing (AACN). 2009. *Enrollment and Graduations in Baccalaureate and Graduate Programs in Nursing*. Washington, DC: AACN.

Association for Library and Information Science Education (ALISE). 2005. *Library and Information Science Education Statistical Report*. Chicago: ALISE.

Beecroft, P., A. M. Hernandez, and D. Reid. 2008. Team preceptorships: Precepting new nurses. *Journal for Nurses in Staff Development* 24:143–148.

Beecroft, P., L. Kunzman, and C. Krozek. 2001. RN internship: Outcomes of a one-year pilot program. *Journal of Nursing Administration* 31:575–582.

Boyer, S. A. 2008. Competence and innovation in preceptor development: Updating our programs. *Journal for Nurses in Staff Development* 24:E1–E6.

Brewer, J. 1997. Post-master's residency programs: Enhancing the development of new professionals and minority recruitment in academic and research libraries. *College & Research Libraries* 58:528–537.

Brewer, J., and M. Winston. 2001. Program evaluation in internship/residency programs in academic and research libraries. *College & Research Libraries* 62:307–315.

Davis, D. M., and T. D. Hall. 2007. Diversity counts! American Library Association. http://www.ala.org/ala/aboutala/offices/diversity/diversitycounts/diversitycounts_rev0.pdf

Goode C. J., and C. A. Williams. 2004. Post-baccalaureate nurse residency programs. *Journal of Nursing Administration* 34:71–77.

Holt, R., and A. L. Strock. 2005. The entry level gap. *Library Journal*. http://www.libraryjournal.com/article/CA527965.html.

Jackson, M. 2001. A preceptor incentive program: Rewarding staff nurses for mentorship. *American Journal of Nursing* 101:24A–24E.

Kaufman, D. 2003. ABC of learning and teaching in medicine: Applying educational theory in practice. *BMJ* 326:213–216.

Keller, J. L., K. Meekins, and B. L. Summers. 2006. Pearls and pitfalls of a new graduate academic residency program. *Journal of Nursing Administration* 36:589–598.

Kertis, M. 2007. The one-minute preceptor: A five-step tool to improve clinical teaching skills. *Journal for Nurses in Staff Development* 23:238–242.

Knowles, M. 1984. *Andragogy in action*. San Francisco: Jossey-Bass.

Martin, T. 2007. Both technical and emotional skills needed to achieve Dreyfus Model. *ACGME Resident Review* Summer 2007:6–7.

Modic, M. B., and M. Schloesser. 2008. Preceptorship. *Journal for Nurses in Staff Development* 22:34–40.

Murray, M. K. 2002. The nursing shortage: Past, present, and future. *Journal of Nursing Administration* 32:79–84.

Neumann, J. A., K. A. Brady-Schluttner, A. K. McKay, J. J. Roslien, D. M. Twedell, and K. M. G. James. 2004. Centralizing a registered nurse preceptor program at the institutional level. *Journal for Nurses in Staff Development* 20:17–24.

Nicol, P., and M. Young. 2007. Sail training: An innovative approach to graduate nurse preceptor development. *Journal for Nurses in Staff Development* 23:298–302.

Oermann, M. H., and A. Moffitt-Wolf. 1997. New graduates' perceptions of clinical practice. *The Journal of Continuing Education in Nursing* 28:20–25.

Perez, M. 2007. *From new graduate to competent practitioner: Rethinking the architecture of post-MLS residency programs in ARL libraries.* Master's thesis, University of North Carolina at Chapel Hill.

Schön, D. A. 1983. *The reflective practitioner*. New York: Basic Books.

Speers, A. T., N. Strzyzewski, and L. D. Ziolkowski. 2004. Preceptor preparation: An investment in the future. *Journal for Nurses in Staff Development* 20:127–133.

Usher, K., C. Nolan, P. Reser, J. Owens, and J. Tollefson. 1999. An exploration of the preceptor role: Preceptors' perceptions of benefits, rewards, supports and commitment to the preceptor role. *Journal of Advanced Nursing* 29:506–514.

Yonge, O., H. Krahn, L. Trojan, R. Reid, and M. Haase. 2002. Supporting preceptors. *Journal for Nurses in Staff Development* 18:73–79.

APPENDIX 7.1

Resident Mentor Selection Criteria

University of Arkansas
Librarian-In-Residence Program

Name: _____

Department: _____

Date of application: _____

Criteria	Met	Not Met
Employed with library for at least 2 years.		
Demonstrates proficiency in assigned work area.		
Demonstrates ability to make thoughtful, timely decisions.		
Demonstrates excellent team behavior.		
Promotes positive, interpersonal relationships.		
Exhibits a positive, professional attitude at all times.		
Able to evaluate through both positive and negative feedback in a constructive manner.		
Demonstrates leadership skills in terms of setting priorities, making difficult decisions, and solving problems creatively.		
Serves as a positive role model.		
Creates an atmosphere of safety and security that promotes learning and trust.		
Displays characteristics of gregariousness and sociability; and possesses extended networks of professional peers.		
Shows ability to effectively educate, teach, and train new employees.		
Exhibits an interest in professional development through participation in scholarly activities such as conference presentations, independent research, and continuing education.		
States an interest in serving as a mentor.		

Recommendation: Approved Y/N

Role: Team Leader / Socializer / Role Model / Evaluator / Educator / Protector

Program Coordinator Signature: _____
Date: _____

Mentor Signature: _____
Date: _____

Adapted by permission from Speers, Strzyzewski, and Ziolkowski 2004, fig. 1.

APPENDIX 7.2

Resident Mentor-Mentee Agreement

University of Arkansas
Librarian-In-Residence Program

Libraries with successful mentoring programs typically experience increased retention and reduced turnover. Employees who participate in successful mentoring programs are inducted more quickly into the norms and performance expectations of the library, thus increasing their efficiency. Professional mentors can help socialize you into the culture of the organization, assist in your education of the cultural, organizational, social, and technical knowledge of the institution, provide you with useful feedback, and help create a safe environment for you in which to grow and develop. They can connect you with campus offices and faculty members as well as local, state, and national organizations. They can also help keep you aware of professional development opportunities. Most importantly, however, you will learn by association with a relevant role model.

Now that you have a mentor, what do you do next? The following are recommendations for developing and sustaining your mentor-mentee relationship:

- Think of the relationship as being a two-way learning process that requires commitment and mutual respect.
- Create a design for your interactions that is agreeable to both parties. Will your interaction be strictly virtual or live and in-person? Will it be formal and restricted to the borders of campus or are you both willing to meet someplace neutral and less traditional?
- Develop a schedule for yourselves. Consider how often you will meet and how long your meetings will be. Will you have a regular meeting schedule or will you meet irregularly and spontaneously?
- Articulate some clear objectives. What do you want to learn from your mentor? What skills are you trying to develop? How can you contribute to the relationship?
- Keep a journal about your conversations.
- Later in the relationship, go back and review the objectives you set for yourselves in the beginning. Are you on schedule? Have your needs changed? Do your objectives need some revision?
- Think of ways to learn together: See a speaker or lecture or film together. Invite each other over to your respective workplace and consider some abbreviated shadowing. Critique each other's resumes or engage in some mock interviewing.

Resident Signature: _____
Date: _____

Mentor Signature: _____
Date: _____

Program Coordinator Signature: _____
Date: _____

Chapter 8

The Residents Report

Megan Zoe Perez, Damon Campbell, and Shantrie Collins

INTRODUCTION

This chapter details the results of a February 2009 study of library residents in the United States and Canada. There are other publications that report data on post-master's program participants and on library and information science education. The Association for Library and Information Science Education's (ALISE) *Statistical Report,* for example, is an annual publication that reports data on accredited schools of library and information science and of students in such programs at all levels (bachelor's, master's, and PhD). This report also offers data on post-master's program participants. These participants, however, are defined specifically as "students who are working toward a post-master's degree or certificate in library and information science" (ALISE 2005).

There are still other statistical publications regarding library and information science education issued by the Census Bureau, the National Center for Science Education, the Association of Research Libraries (ARL), and the American Library Association (ALA). These publications, however, do not separate out data specifically regarding post-MLS residents from data regarding other kinds of degree-holding librarians. Also, on a local level, some institutional hosts of residency programs may keep demographic data on their own residents, but it is not openly, consistently, and regularly available for other program coordinators, and it has not been published in any of the available literature. Further, some library and information science programs—for example, the University of Michigan's School of Information—publish demographic data of their graduates as a group, but these publications do not provide information regarding resident demographics specifically nor in isolation from other aggregate data.

After reviewing the literature, the authors of this study recognized a gap in the study of library residency programs. Studies that focused specifically on the residents themselves, as opposed to the programs, and that assembled both quantitative and qualitative information into one coherent report could not be identified. Further, the definition of "resident" or "residency program" was not applied consistently across programs. The authors therefore decided to create such a study, one with the purpose of collecting, analyzing, and synthesizing statistical (and other descriptive) data that is specific to library residents and that used a standardized definition of "resident" and "residency program."

The participants in this study, therefore, were selected on a different basis. Contrary to the definition given in the *Statistical Report*, and for the purposes of this study, the researchers defined post-MLS residency according to the "ALISE Guidelines and Standards" included in ARL's SPEC Kit #188 (Brewer, 1992): postgraduate, entry-level work experience for recently graduated library and information science students. The participants in this study conform to this definition and are not students working toward a post-master's degree or certificate. They are degree-holding recent graduates with less than 3 years of full-time professional experience who have completed or are completing a post-MLS library residency program.

The researchers therefore devised a survey to fill in the gap left by these publications (see Appendix 8.1). The purpose of the survey is threefold:

1. to better inform residency program managers of the design and practice of other, comparable library residency programs;

2. to assist institutions and administrators who are considering implementing a residency program in the future; and

3. to provide library and information science students who are interested in learning more about residency programs with a centralized source of information.

This report was created as a model for other researchers to develop a regular, annual publication like it in the future. It is intended as a service to the community of professionals and researchers who are interested in reviewing current trends in library resident demographics, resident perception, and resident program satisfaction. We hope the report in hand will be similar to both the annual *Employment Report* (Kroll 2007) issued by the University of Michigan's School of Information and to the most current, annual ALISE *Statistical Report* (ALISE 2005), but focused specifically on resident demographics.

METHODOLOGY

In March 2008, the researchers first discussed the idea of assembling a report of this type. Initially, a simple spreadsheet was created and used to gather as much public information as was available from websites, personal contacts, and publications. The sheet generated data from the respondents regarding their activities and experiences as residents. More specifically, the first instrument asked respondents to answer questions concerning their residency location, degree granting institution, rotation departments, project assignments, and professional association memberships.

Campbell and Collins analyzed and presented the results of this project at the 2008 National Diversity in Libraries' Post-Conference on Residency Programs in Louisville, Kentucky. After reviewing the program's evaluations and incorporating feedback from its audience, the researchers decided to continue their work on this subject. Although their initial efforts were met with some skepticism, the researchers' further investigation indicated that only limited information of this kind could be found. Hence, the decision was made to fill this gap and continue the project. True, collecting data from more than forty individuals spread across more than fifteen institutions presented a challenge, but the researchers were certain the data did not exist and were convinced of the project's value. They therefore redesigned their project and formalized the collection process to comply with Institutional Review Board (IRB) policy.

In the beginning, there was some confusion over which institution's compliance office would need to approve the project before distributing the survey because the researchers represented two institutions and had not engaged in collaborative, evidence-based research before. After discussing the issue with compliance officers at both the University of Arkansas and the University of Tennessee, the researchers concluded that the project could move forward by designating Perez as the principal researcher and Campbell and Collins as co-researchers. The IRB application was, thus, submitted and approved by the University of Arkansas. The University of Tennessee's compliance office simply requested copies of the application and approval letter.

In April 2009, after receiving IRB approval, a letter of informed consent was distributed, along with the survey instrument, to approximately ninety current and former residency program participants. The letter and survey were sent via e-mail to various online discussion lists, directly to individuals identified in the previous project, and to program coordinators. The researchers also distributed the letter and survey to members of the Facebook group, "Academic Library Residents and Fellows." Third, known program coordinators were contacted via direct e-mail asking them to forward the survey URL to their current and former program participants. Finally, on May 19, the research team issued a final call for participation and closed the survey on May 26 to allow for analysis of the data.

The instrument consists of twenty-five questions and includes a combination of open-ended and closed-ended questions regarding basic demography (age, gender, and ethnicity), degree(s) held, and program information (salary, title/rank, and host institution). The target population was limited to those individuals who have participated or are currently in a post-MLS residency program as defined by ALISE (Brewer 1997). The researchers were careful to note in their letter of consent, however, that individuals who had participated in a "residency," "fellowship," or "internship" that complies with this definition are welcome to participate in the study.

FINDINGS AND RESULTS

The instrument asked specific questions regarding resident demographics, degree information, and program information.

Residents' Demographic Information

Age

Our survey pool was predominately in the twenty-five to twenty-nine (28 percent) age range, followed by thirty to thirty-four (26 percent). Overall, the number of survey participants decreased as age increased. The third largest group (15 percent) was in the thirty-five to thirty-nine age range. Two age ranges (forty to forty-four and older than fifty-four) tied for 9 percent of the population. Eight percent of our survey population fell in the fifty to fifty-four age range, and 5 percent were in the forty-five to forty-nine age range (see Table 8.1).

Table 8.1 Age range

	Frequency	%
Younger than 24	0	0
25–29	11	28
30–34	10	26
35–39	6	15
40–44	4	9
45–49	2	5
50–54	3	8
Older than 54	4	9
Total	40	100

Gender

Of the forty respondents, the distribution between female and male resident librarians mirrored closely that of the library profession as a whole. Seventy-eight percent of survey respondents were female and only 22 percent were male (see Table 8.2). On its website, the American Library Association reports that, as of September 2009, its membership remains predominantly female (80.9 percent female and 19.1 percent male). During the 2008–2009 reporting period, Bland stated "the ARL university library workforce consisted of 63 percent females, with males comprising 37 percent" (Bland 2009, 18).

Table 8.2 Gender

	Residents	ALA	ARL
Female	78%	80.9%	63%
Male	22%	19.1%	37%

ALA = American Library Association; ARL = Association of Research Libraries.

Race/Ethnicity

In terms of race and ethnicity, the resident population surveyed was predominately Black (35 percent) followed by Caucasian (33 percent), and then Hispanic (20 percent). Two individual respondents chose Asian or Pacific Islander (5 percent), and Other (5 percent), which represents multiracial and/or biracial residents. It should be noted that ARL does not keep records for this category. The fewest respondents were among the American Indian/Alaskan Native ethnic group (2 percent). The 2008–2009 ARL Annual Salary Survey conducted by Bland (2009) reports a total of 14.1 percent of professional staff in ARL libraries, excluding Canadian ARL libraries, belong to a traditionally underrepresented group (see Table 8.3).

Table 8.3 Race/ethnicity of residents and Association of Research Libraries (ARL) professionals

	Residents (2009)	ARL (2008–2009)*
American Indian or Alaskan Native	2%	<1%
Asian or Pacific Islander	5%	6%
Black	35%	5%
Hispanic	20%	3%
Caucasian	33%	86%
Other**	5%	

* Rounded to nearest whole value for ease of comparison.
** Includes multiracial and biracial residents. ARL does not keep records for this category.

Degree Information

Degree Type

Table 8.4 shows an overwhelming percent of residents received their degree in Library Science (84.6 percent) as opposed to Information Science (15.4 percent). These figures are slightly different than the proportion of Information Science and Library Science degrees awarded in the fifty-six schools reporting to ALISE. In the academic year 2003–2004, 94.9 percent of degrees awarded were masters of library science degrees from ALA-accredited schools, and only 5.1 percent of degrees went to master's of information science students (see Table 8.5).

Table 8.4 Degree held by resident (as of 2009)

	Frequency	%
Master's Information Science	6	15.4
Master's Library Science	33	84.6
Total	39	100

Table 8.5 Degree awarded totals from the Association for Library and Information Science Education (2003–2004)

	Frequency	%
Master's Information Science	321	5.1
Master's Library Science	5,951	94.9
Total	6,272	100

Degree-Granting Institution

The residents who responded to this survey received their degree from every region of the United States—from Massachusetts to California—and up into the Canadian provinces of Alberta and Ontario as well. In all, twenty-five schools are represented in this pool, the most frequent being the University of Alberta and the University of Pittsburgh, which each had four respondents (see Table 8.6).

Table 8.6 Degree-granting institution

Institution	Frequency*	%**
University of Alberta, University of Pittsburgh	4	10.5
Dominican University, University of California—Los Angeles, University of North Carolina—Chapel Hill, University of Arizona, University of Kentucky, University of Michigan, Wayne State University	2	5.3
Florida State University, Indiana University, Kent State University, North Carolina Central University, San Jose State University, Simmons, SUNY Buffalo, University of Alabama, University of Illinois—Urbana Champaign, University of Iowa, University of Maryland—College Park, University of North Texas, University of Rhode Island, University of Texas—Austin, University of Toronto, University of Washington	1	2.6
Total ($N = 38$)		100.0

* Frequency per institution.
** Percentage of total respondents.

Graduation Year

Most of the respondents received their degree in 2006 (six respondents), followed by 2003 and 2008 each of which had five respondents. Four respondents received their degree in 2005 and in 2007, and three received their degree in 1999. There was only one response for all other years dating back to 1983. This variation by year may be a reflection of the number of residency positions available in those years. It is possible there were more active residency programs in 2006 than in other years.

Program Information

The "status" of residents may have had an influence on the results of subsequent questions, particularly those regarding age and satisfaction. The authors thus determined it important to know the "status" of the respondents: were they currently in a residency program, or had they completed a program? Former residents accounted for 79 percent (31 of 39) of respondents, and 21 percent (8 of 39) were current residents (see Table 8.7). Given that more than three-fourths of respondents are former residents, certain response totals or frequencies may favor the perceptions and activities of former residents.

Table 8.7 Status

	Frequency	%
Current	8	21
Former	31	79
Total (N = 39)		100

Salary Comparisons

Thirty-nine respondents provided an answer regarding salary. Approximately 31 percent reported their salary ranged between $40,000 and $42,499. Eighteen percent reported their salary was less than $30,000 per year (see Table 8.8).

Table 8.8 Self-reported salary ranges of residents

	Frequency	%
Less than $30,000	7	17.9
$30,000–$32,499	3	7.7
$32,500–$34,999	1	2.6
$35,000–$37,499	3	7.7
$37,500–$39,999	6	15.4
$40,000–$42,499	12	30.8
$42,500–$44,999	2	5.1
$47,500–$49,999	3	7.7
$50,000 or more	2	5.1
Total (N = 39)		100

According to the ALA website, the 2007 Academic Mean Beginning Librarian's Salary is $48,365. The difference between the highest end of the mode salary range for residents and the Beginning Librarian's Salary is more than $5,000. More recent data from ARL reports the median Beginning Professional Salaries (BPS) for both academic and nonacademic librarians rose from $41,125 in 2007–2008 to $44,000 in 2008–2009 (Bland 2009).

Postresidency Employment

Survey participants were asked whether they remained at their host institution or found employment with a different institution after the completion of their program. Twenty-one (70 percent) respondents indicated they remained at their host institution. Seven (23.3 percent) respondents found employment at another institution, and two other respondents pursued additional graduate education (see Table 8.9).

Table 8.9 Post- residency employment activities

	Frequency	%
Remained at host institution	21	70.0
Employed at another institution	7	23.3
Pursued additional graduate education	2	6.7
Total ($N=30$)		100

Of these seven who found employment elsewhere, five now hold upper-level positions. Currently there are deans, the head of a social work library, a director of special collections, and a chair of instructional services.

Host Institution

Thirty-eight respondents identified their host institution. A clear majority (21.1 percent) of respondents participated in the program at Miami University. Cornell, the University of Alberta, the University of Minnesota, and the University Notre Dame each hosted three of the respondents (8 percent). Four other institutions hosted two of the survey's respondents, and ten other programs each hosted one respondent. See Table 8.10 for a full list of all institutions.

Table 8.10 Host institution

Institution	Frequency[*]	%[**]
Miami University (Ohio)	8	21.1
Cornell University, University of Alberta, University of Minnesota, University of Notre Dame	3	7.9
NCSU Libraries (North Carolina), Purdue University, Ohio State University, University at Buffalo-SUNY	2	5.3
Auburn University, Georgetown University Law Library, University of California, University of Delaware, University of Michigan, University of New Mexico, University of North Carolina—Greensboro, University of Pittsburgh, University of Tennessee—Knoxville, University of Winnipeg	1	2.6
Total ($N = 38$)		100.0

[*] Frequency per institution.
[**] Percentage of total respondents.

Title and Rank

At the time of residence, program participants held a variety of academic positions. These included at least thirteen titles and at least five ranks (see Table 8.11).

Table 8.11 Titles and ranks

Titles	Ranks
Academic Library Intern	Assistant Research Professor
Academic Resident Librarian	Visiting Assistant Professor of Libraries
Assistant Librarian	Visiting Assistant Professor of Library Science
Diversity Fellow	Visiting Lecturer III
Diversity Resident Librarian	Visiting Librarian
Library Resident in Research and Instruction	
Libraries Fellow	
Librarian	
Librarian-In-Residence	
Minority Librarian Intern	
Minority Resident Librarian	
Public Services Librarian	
Resident Librarian	

Not all respondents listed rank in addition to title. Of those that did, "Librarian I" was a frequently mentioned rank. The other ranks listed were reported only once each. The most frequently used title was "Assistant Librarian," which was reported seven times. "Academic Resident Librarian" was another frequently reported title, but deeper analysis showed survey participants who provided this response were from the same program. For example, five of six respondents who listed "Academic Resident Librarian" as their title participated in the program at Miami University.

Residency Period

Thirty-nine respondents provided an answer to the question, "During which year or years were/are you a resident?" Table 8.12 shows the largest group of residents who answered this question (six of thirty-nine) participated in their program during the years 2008–2010. The next most frequent periods were 2007–2009, 2007–2008, 2006, 2006–2008, 2005–2007, and 1995–1996 (two of thirty-nine responses for each period). Other residency periods dating back to 1983 had only one response. The data also indicate variations in duration. Some participants were residents for one year, others for two years.

Rotations Through Departments

In many programs, residents are given the opportunity to rotate through several departments within a library, or different *libraries* within a larger library system. Fifty-five percent of our respondents indicated they rotated, while 43 percent did not rotate through multiple areas of the library. When combined, the respondents worked in nearly every area of a library imaginable: reference/instruction, cataloging and technical services, special collections, collection development, and government documents. They also worked in the areas of systems, administration, serials, electronic resources, interlibrary loan, and digital initiatives. In terms of libraries within a larger system, respondents indicated they worked in a variety of different unit libraries including science, engineering, law, business, area studies, map, and even the health sciences.

Table 8.12 Residency years

Period	Frequency	%
1983–1985, 1985–1986, 1991–1993, 1993–1995, 1997–1998, 1997–1999, 1999–2000, 1999–2001, 2000–2001, 2001–2003, 2002–2003, 2002–2004, 2003–2004, 2003–2005, 2003–2006, 2004–2005, 2004–2006, 2005–2006, 2006–2007, 2007, 2008–2009	1	2.6
1995–1996, 2005–2007, 2006, 2006–2008, 2007–2008, 2007–2009	2	5.1
2008–2010	6	15.4
Total	39	100.0

Special Projects and Assignments

In addition to an opportunity to rotate, residents are also frequently assigned to or chosen for special projects to supplement the residency work experience. These can be understood as extended assignments lasting longer than a typical rotation or as projects given to residents in addition to the regular work responsibilities within a rotation. Eighty-five percent of our respondents indicated they were involved with special projects or assignments like this. The list of specialized tasks the respondents described covered a wide range of subjects, including work in web design, marketing and promotion, and digital projects, along with outreach and presentations to multicultural groups, statistical analysis, and collection analysis.

Professional Associations and Memberships

Survey participants held memberships in an extremely wide variety of international, national, state, and local associations, divisions, and organizations. The most frequently listed organization was ALA, with more than half of the respondents noting their membership. The second most frequently listed association was the ACRL. Other associations mentioned included the Special Libraries Association (SLA), Library Association of Alberta, REFORMA, and the Library Leadership and Management Association (LLAMA).

The third most frequently mentioned association, however, after ALA and ACRL, was the Canadian Library Association (CLA). In fact, although two respondents indicated they were members of the International Federation of Library Associations (IFLA), membership across various Canadian associations is strongly represented in the overall pool of respondents. Besides CLA, respondents indicated they also held memberships in the Canadian Association of College and Research Libraries (CARL), the Library Association of Alberta, and the Canadian Health Libraries Association.

In addition to the major associations, divisions and round tables of ALA are also represented in the results. Respondents indicated they held memberships in the Reference & User Services Association (RUSA), the Library and Information Technology Association (LITA), and the Association for Library Collections and Technical Services (ALCTS). Round-table memberships included Library Instruction Round Table (LIRT), the Intellectual Freedom Round Table (IFRT), the Map and Geography Round Table (MAGERT), the Government Documents Round Table (GODORT), the Social Responsibilities Round Table (SRRT), and the International Relations Round Table (IRRT).

State associations included the states of Texas, Indiana, Ohio, North Carolina, Alabama, Michigan, Oregon, and Minnesota. Respondents also held memberships in associations with a specialized subject focus such as the Seminar on the Acquisition of Latin American Library Materials (SALALM), the Society of Photographic Education, the International Society of Philosophical Enquiry, and the American Association for the Advancement of Slavic Studies (AAASS).

Finally, there were memberships in several caucuses dedicated to issues regarding race, ethnicity, and gay, lesbian, bisexual, and transgender studies. Survey participants indicated participation in the Black Caucus of the American Library Association (BCALA); the Chinese American Library Association (CALA); the American Indian Library Association (AILA); the Gay, Lesbian, Bisexual, and Transgendered Round Table (GLBTRT); and the Ethnic and Multicultural Information Exchange Round Table (EMIERT).

Choosing a Program

A unique selling proposition for residency programs often lies with a multifaceted approach to providing entry-level library and information science graduates with opportunities for professional development, firsthand and full-time work experiences, and library-specific skill sets to empower and shape the early years of their careers. Resident participants represent a microcosm of new librarians' needs and desires at the beginning of their careers. The question, "Why did you choose a residency program?" gave the research team insight into what makes such programs worthwhile ventures.

The predominant theme throughout respondents' answers to this question was the desire to obtain general and specific, guided experience into the various aspects of academic librarianship. Exposure to multiple departments of the library environment was cited as a main objective for new professionals uncertain of their career path and in search of more in-depth knowledge regarding the profession. Respondents also listed goals to pursue during their residency. This range of goals included competency building, preparation for leadership/management positions, chances to learn on the job, and opportunities to network with future colleagues.

For other respondents, the decision to choose a residency position was simply a matter of logistics: it was the first professional job offer or it paid well. Competition for entry-level positions, recession, and career changes were also cited as motives for seeking a residency program. One respondent described residency programs as "a good opportunity to just explore without the need for a long range commitment." Although many residency programs are, on average, temporary, two-year appointments, responses suggested the short-term commitment to the host institution may result in subsequent long-term opportunities, such as a full-time appointment, a national committee appointment, or the discovery of a research interest that can develop over the course of one's career into a more detailed study suitable for publication.

Sources of Residency Vacancy Announcements

A variety of resources were utilized to find residency positions. Electronic discussion lists were the most frequently used resources. The second most commonly used resource was a combination of professional and personal contacts—for example, networking. Internet sites were the third most popular resource for finding residency positions, followed by professional publications and other sources such as leadership institutes, library and information science faculty, a visit with an ARL scholar, and contact with more experienced librarians. University Career Services ranked last as a starting place for seeking out residency openings (see Table 8.13).

Table 8.13 Sources of residency vacancies

	Frequency	%
Email discussion lists	19	30.6
Professional/Personal Contacts	18	29.0
Internet Sites	10	16.1
Professional Publications	7	11.3
University Career Services	1	1.6
Other	7	11.3
Total ($N = 40$)		99.9

Resident Satisfaction

Each individual resident had his or her own story, perception, perspective, and opinion regarding the residency experience. Fifty percent of the respondents were "very satisfied" with the experience. Another 37 percent were "extremely satisfied." Despite an 87 percent positive satisfaction rate, there is a 13 percent negative consideration. One respondent was "extremely dissatisfied" with the experience. This respondent described the experience as overwhelming and identified a need for project and time management workshops at the beginning of the program as a suggestion for improvement. Other respondents, specifically those who were "neutral" or "not very satisfied" with the experience, offered suggestions for improvement. These included a need to guide existing employees to view residents as competent professionals and to include training in subject areas (see Table 8.14).

Table 8.14 Overall satisfaction

	Frequency	%
Extremely satisfied	14	36.8
Very satisfied	19	50.0
Neutral	3	7.9
Not very satisfied	1	2.6
Extremely dissatisfied	1	2.6
Total ($N = 38$)		99.9

Further suggestions for improvement taken from the survey include the following:

1. Respect each resident in a cohort as an individual by maintaining awareness of the different personalities and needs from the program.
2. Understand that direction and a sufficient level of work assignments are a necessity.
3. The residency program should be three years to build leadership competencies.
4. Supervisors should be familiar with the residency program and capable of providing proper guidance.

5. Understand the difference between a professional residency program and an internship. Provide a professional title for the resident librarian.

6. One-on-one mentoring, assessment during the residency program, and rotations of interest to the resident are beneficial.

7. More institutions should have residency programs and offer full-time positions with the host institution post residency.

8. Place less emphasis on the resident being responsible for "diversity initiatives" and more emphasis on "inclusion" of all librarians to play a part in diversity initiatives.

9. Foster a greater understanding of why the residency exists and its purposes at the host institution.

10. The library as a whole, not just the fellowship program, could use a more structured orientation, training, and professional development process and a greater emphasis on diversity for all new hires. The program and the role of the fellow (as a full assistant librarian with the same responsibilities as any new hire) also need to be better understood within the library.

Experiences, Skills, and Abilities

The respondents who were satisfied with their residency program reported on the skills and experiences they attribute to their success as a resident (see Table 8.15).

Table 8.15 Skills and experiences

	Frequency
Oral/written communication skills	9
People skills	6
Flexibility	6
Working across the organization	5
Technical skills	5
Project management	3
Knowledge of organizational culture	3
Time management	3
Learning to be a self-starter	3

Other experiences, skills, and abilities mentioned by the respondents and reported as valuable, include specific, departmental work experience such as cataloging and digital projects, the opportunity to build presentation and public speaking skills, and working collaboratively with both librarians and staff so as to provide new and fresh ideas. Mentoring was also an experience respondents attributed to their success.

128 \ The New Graduate Experience

Advice for Future Residents

Finally, survey participants were solicited for advice for the next generation of residency program participants. The respondents were generous in their replies and included suggestions ranging from service-oriented advice (join professional associations and organizations; participate in committee membership) to academic workplace advice (value and share thoughts and opinions just like any other faculty member; interact with all levels of faculty and staff). Former residents also suggested the following:

- Know your goals
- Work hard
- Learn to balance multiple responsibilities and projects
- Take advantage of learning opportunities (webinars, reading, workshops, courses, etc.)
- Ask questions and ask for help
- Utilize mentorship to network
- Use prior experience as a professional to benefit your host institution
- Prepare for the unexpected and remain flexible and adaptable
- Learn to say no and not spread yourself thin
- Have a sense of humor

SIGNIFICANT FINDINGS AND DISCUSSION

The purpose of *The Residents Report* is to collect, analyze, and synthesize information specific to library residents into one coherent report. More specifically, it is written to inform program managers of the design and practice of other programs, to assist institutions who are considering implementing a program, and to provide library and information science students with a centralized source of information regarding program and resident activity. We hope this work can be continued on an annual basis, enabling the development of deeper, longitudinal studies.

Who will do this work and continue this service to the residency community? One possibility is that members of the Association of Colleges and Research Libraries' Residency Interest Group take up this charge. More specifically, the residents who are members of the group may take on the project in fulfillment of any research requirements their program may include. This will call for release time for scholarship, which can only be given from supervisors and program coordinators. A project such as this, however, can offer the resident an opportunity to gain valuable, firsthand experience conducting evidence-based research under the tutelage of a more experienced practitioner.

Although the findings of certain sections of this survey are consistent with popular conceptions of residency programs (range of rotations, projects, and committee memberships, for example), there are nevertheless several other findings here. First, the residents' demographic characteristics closely mirror those of a typical class of students enrolled in library and information science programs in three important respects: age, gender, and race and or ethnicity. The largest group of respondents is in the twenty-five to twenty-nine age group. Seventy-eight percent of residents are female. Surprisingly, and despite the majority of residency programs' intention to recruit from traditionally underrepresented groups, Caucasians make up a substantial percentage of residents: 33 percent. Although this number is low when compared with the percentage of Caucasians in ARL libraries (86 percent), it is high among residents. In fact, it is the second largest group of residents behind those who identified themselves as Black: 35 percent.

These demographics are important when considering the purpose of many residency programs is to recruit and introduce traditionally underrepresented groups to academic librarianship and to help the profession develop staff that will mirror the demographic characteristics of the people it serves. The largest group of library and information science students and residents are twenty-five to twenty-nine years old. Seventy-eight percent of residents are female, whereas 81 percent of ALA members overall are female. Should these demographics remain relatively stable in the near future, residency programs may need to adjust their recruitment focus to be effective strategies in diversifying library staff with respect to age and gender.

Second, with respect to degree-granting institutions, of the sixty-two ALA accredited schools of library and information science, residents received their degree from only twenty-five schools. Data such as this has not been identified through the literature. Future surveys, therefore, should gather this specific information for longitudinal comparison. Are residents all coming from the same schools? If so, then why? Do some schools promote residency programs better than others? Do some programs target certain schools more than others?

These are important questions that have implications for future recruitment efforts, particularly during times of reduced conference attendance and budgetary constraints. On-site visits may no longer be feasible as a recruitment tactic. Virtual presentations should be explored as an alternative. Recruitment videos can be made. Better websites with FAQ sections can be developed. Live podcasts with Q&A sessions can be performed and recorded for future access. Only future research, however, can provide answers to these questions and help determine which of these new tactics is most desirable.

Another significant finding regarding recruitment is the source of residency vacancies. Thirty-one percent of residents discovered a vacancy announcement through online discussion lists. Professional and personal contacts were the second most popular sources of job announcements. A future study may want to discover which discussions lists are used to advertise positions. This would be relatively easy. Program coordinators keep records of lists used for advertisements, and e-mails sent through ALA-managed discussion lists have archives that can be mined.

It would not, however, be easy to determine which e-mail prompted a resident to apply for a position. Some vacancies appear on multiple lists, and to determine which list hosted the announcement ultimately used by the applicant would rely on applicant memory. Some human resources documentation asks how an applicant learned about a position, but, again, the veracity of this response is dependent on the applicant's memory. Knowing which specific list or lists have the highest impact would be valuable for future recruiting purposes but extremely difficult to measure.

The residents' self-reported salaries are also significant when compared with both the mean Beginning Librarian's Salary (BLS) as reported by ALA, and the Beginning Professional Salaries (BPS) reported by ARL. The largest group of survey participants (approximately 31 percent) reported their salary ranged from $40,000 to $42,499. Eighteen percent (18 percent), the third largest group of respondents, indicated their salary was less than $30,000. The difference between the BLS ($48,365), and the maximum amount of the mode salary range for residents ($42,499) is approaching $6,000 ($5,866 to be exact). The difference between the median BPS in 2008–2009 ($44,000) and the maximum amount of the mode ($42,499) is much lower ($1,501).

One explanation for this could be that most of the residents' host institutions are members of ARL. It would stand to reason, therefore, that the salaries of residents', as beginning professionals and as employees of ARL libraries, are closer to the ARL BPS than to ALA's BLS. Another explanation for this variation may regard a limitation of the researcher's instrument. The residents' reported salaries are aggregate figures and are not parsed out by year like the ALA and ARL publications, which surveyed a one-year period. Residents' reported salaries were not adjusted for inflation, and averages calculated using both 1980s figures and 2000s figures may have some effect on the data. However, given that 73 percent of the respondents completed their residency in the decade following 2000 and that only two respondents completed their residency in the 1980s, the effect on the data is slight.

Miami University hosted 21 percent of the survey participants, the largest of this response group. Other host institutions had far less representation even if they selected a single or multiple residents each year. For instance, the Libraries Fellows Program at North Carolina State University (NCSU), for example, has admitted more than one resident each year. On its website, the Fellows Program states that a total of twenty-four librarians have been or currently are NCSU Libraries Fellows. Yet only two survey respondents indicated they were part of the NCSU program.

The programs at Cornell, Purdue, and SUNY—Buffalo have also had multiple residents, yet their residents' response rate is also low in proportion to the number of residents who completed their program. One reason for this may involve distribution of the survey instrument. Some programs may maintain closer contact with their former residents, allowing for direct forwarding of the instrument. Others may have had stronger rapport with the programs' residents, thus encouraging proactive participation. Regardless, this is an anomaly worthy of further exploration.

LIMITATIONS

There are four distinct factors limiting this study. First, the data was self-reported. Such measures in survey research are prone to error, leading to inaccurate or imprecise responses. The instrument required survey participants to provide responses based on memory that may have faded over time further contributing to reporting errors. Further, the survey participants represented a wide date range of program participation. For example, one survey participant completed a program as many as twenty-six years ago, and nearly one-third of all respondents were residents more than ten years ago. This gap between the time of survey completion and participation in a program may have exacerbated the problem of basing responses on faded memories.

Second, some valuable data may not have been captured due to self-exclusion. As previously discussed, the number of responses from residents in programs with higher numbers of participants was comparatively low. Participation in this study was voluntary. Potential respondents may have excluded themselves from the study simply by not responding. After all, incentives were not offered to respondents.

Additionally, there is the possibility of self-exclusion. Confusion over survey terminology, for example, may have deterred some potential participants from responding. Strictly speaking, and according to the ALISE definitions that guide this research, there are a number of programs that are, in fact, residency programs but that carry the name of "fellow." Participants from these programs may have felt the survey did not address them despite the researchers' best efforts to address this issue in the letter of informed consent which in turn may have limited the results of the data.

Third, the data presented is not separated by resident status, that is, data regarding former residents was not reported separately from that of current residents. Separating the data would allow for deeper analysis into patterns and changes over time regarding salary, degree-granting institutions, resident activities and assignments, rank and title, and professional association members. This is an approach the researchers did not consider when designing the survey instrument. Future surveys should adjust the collection methodology to accommodate this division.

The fourth limiting factor is the absence of a response rate. Currently, there is not a centralized agency that coordinates the different programs found around the United States and Canada. Data regarding the number of programs and the number of residents is not maintained by a single agency, association, or organization. The responsibility for maintaining records of how many residents have been hosted has consequently fallen on the host institutions themselves. These records may or may not be available depending on the institution, the program's history, and current staffing. Some programs simply may not keep such records. Some records may have been lost in transition. Older programs, for example, may have been coordinated by personnel who have since retired or left the original host institution. Therefore, program records that are available may be incomplete or inaccurate.

It should be mentioned that there has not been a centralized effort on the part of program coordinators to share this information across organizational boundaries to help determine a total figure of program participants to date. The exact number of residents both current and former, therefore, is not known. As a consequence, it is not possible to determine a precise response rate, which would allow for an estimate of the reliability and validity of the responses and for a determination of whether the responses are representative of the entire population of residents.

FUTURE RESEARCH

A few topics for future research have been alluded to in the previous section. A study of recruitment practices, for example, is one of these. Which school programs do residents tend to come from each year and why? How can that data be leveraged into actionable items for a program's recruitment efforts? How can recruitment efforts be maintained during times of economic downsizing? How can these efforts be combined with current technology to produce webinars, podcasts, and video and audio files that can be hosted on library websites? Is it feasible to make these projects part of the resident's experience? This is one study that can be performed with relative ease.

Additional studies involve tracking salary and demographic information as well as levels of satisfaction. Overall, these latter issues can be researched if the survey in hand is replicated in the future and administered annually. Only then will longitudinal examination be made possible. Such work will allow for a better-informed understanding of the long-term impact of residency programs with respect to their goals and objectives. Future practitioners will have to repeat this work, however, and the researchers have included their survey to facilitate that process.

CONCLUSION

A review of the literature showed that many sources of library and information science information did not separate out resident data from other aggregate data. Programs may have kept their own data at the host institution, but the data was not shared openly and was not made available to other program coordinators on a regular, consistent basis. Further, such information had not been published in any of the available literature.

The primary aim of this chapter, therefore, is to provide demographic and statistical data regarding residents in a single, unified source and apart from other aggregate data. We hoped to present a model for the publication of a regular, annual report similar to the annual *Employment Report* (Kroll 2007) and the annual ALISE *Statistical Report* (ALISE 2005), but with a specific focus on resident demographics. Toward the satisfaction of that end, the researchers created a twenty-five-question survey instrument that included both open-ended and closed-ended questions regarding basic demography (age, gender, and ethnicity), degree information, and program information (salary, rank, and host institution). The results of that survey were presented and, when appropriate, comparable data from ALA and ARL were juxtaposed with each other. The significant findings and results were discussed in further detail, and suggestions for future research were provided.

The contents herein will be of immediate value to libraries and to librarians who continue to examine the value, use, design, and purpose of residency programs. It will also be of use to residency program coordinators, human resources managers, and personnel officers who have interest in recruitment and retention. Additionally, library and information science faculty teaching courses on diversity and recruitment, and students enrolled in such courses will benefit from the report. Ultimately, the contents will be of use to researchers of strategies for new graduate development, researchers of the history of diversity initiatives in librarianship, and researchers of the recruitment of professional librarians into academia.

REFERENCES

Association for Library and Information Science Education (ALISE). 2005. *Library and information science education statistical report*. Chicago: ALISE.

Bland, L. 2009. ARL salary survey highlights. *Research Library Issues* 266:17–20.

Bragg, J. 2008. Many academic and public librarian positions face wage decline; inflation erodes salary gains for many others. *Library Worklife*. Retrieved from American Library Association website: http://www.ala-apa.org/newsletter/vol5no10/statistics.html

Brewer, J. 1992. *Internship, Residency, and Fellowship Programs in ARL Libraries* (SPEC Kit #188). Washington, DC: Association of Research Libraries.

Kroll, J. 2007. *Employment Report*. University of Michigan, School of Information. http://www.si.umich.edu/careers/placement.htm

APPENDIX 8.1

RESIDENTS REPORT: SURVEY INSTRUMENT

Demographic Information

1. Please supply your age by selecting one of the ranges listed:
   - Younger than 20
   - 20–24
   - 25–29
   - 30–34
   - 35–39
   - 40–44
   - 45–49
   - 50–54
   - Older than 54

2. What is your gender?
   - Female
   - Male

3. What is your ethnic origin? (Categories taken from the U.S. Department of Labor)
   - American Indian or Alaskan Native
   - Asian or Pacific Islander
   - Black, not of Hispanic origin
   - Hispanic
   - White

Degree Information

4. Is your degree in Information Science or Library Science?
   - Information Science
   - Library Science

5. Which institution granted this degree?

6. What year did you graduate with this degree?

Program Information

7. What is your residency status?
   - Current
   - Former

8. **What is/was your salary range as a resident?**
    - o Less than $30,000
    - o $30,000–$32,499
    - o $32,500–$34,999
    - o $35,000–$37,499
    - o $37,500–$39,999
    - o $40,000–$42,499
    - o $42,500–$44,999
    - o More than $50,000

9. **If you are a former resident, what did you do immediately following the conclusion of your residency?**
    - o Remained at host institution
    - o Employed at another institution
    - o Pursued additional graduate education

10. **If you are a former resident employed at another institution, please provide your present employer information and your present title.**

11. **Where did you do/are you doing your residency? (Please provide the name of the institution.)**

12. **What was/is your title during your residency?**

13. **What was/is your rank during your residency? (If applicable.)**

14. **During which year or years were/are you a resident?**

15. **Did/Do you rotate through different departments as a resident?**
    - o Yes
    - o No

16. **If yes, in which departments? Please list.**

17. **Were/will you be involved in any special projects or assignments as a resident?**
    - o Yes
    - o No

18. **If yes, please list and describe.**

19. **Please list your professional associations and memberships.**

20. **Why did you choose a residency program?**

21. **How did you hear about your residency position?**
    - o University Career Services
    - o Professional Publications
    - o E-mail listservs
    - o Internet sites
    - o Professional/Personal Contacts
    - o Other (Please describe)

22. **How many residency positions did you apply for?**
    - o 1
    - o 2
    - o 3
    - o 4
    - o 5 or more

23. **Overall, how satisfied were you with your residency experience?**
    - o Extremely dissatisfied
    - o Not very satisfied
    - o Neutral (neither satisfied nor dissatisfied)
    - o Very satisfied
    - o Extremely satisfied

24. **If dissatisfied with your experience, please offer some suggestions for improvement.**

25. **If satisfied with your experience, please tell us about the skills and experiences that have proven to be important to your success as a resident.**

Chapter 9

Communities of Practice in Residency Programs: The NCSU Libraries Fellows Program

Hyun-Duck Chung and Sandra Littletree

For many of us, the concept of learning immediately conjures up images of classrooms, training sessions, teachers, textbooks, homework, and exercises. Yet, in our experience, learning is an integral part of our everyday lives. It is part of our participation in our communities and organizations (Wenger 2007, 8).

THE SOCIAL CONTEXT OF LEARNING AT WORK

We did not suddenly become librarians when we signed our first post-MLS position contracts. Nor did we complete our learning when library school classes ended. Our competencies and identities toward a professional life have been developing, with support from mentors, peers, and colleagues, over a number of years as we pursued higher education, then advanced degrees, today continuing to evolve through ongoing reflective practice and professional development. Within this process of becoming professionals, our experience in a residency program played a particularly important role in affirming our decision to join the profession and supporting our ability to excel within it.

We met and became colleagues through the North Carolina State University (NCSU) Libraries Fellows program from 2007 to 2009. The NCSU Libraries Fellows Program offers recent MLIS graduates, or those with equivalent degrees, the opportunity to launch their professional careers as fully integrated members of the professional staff. The structure of the fellows program helps new professionals understand and practice what it takes to be a successful academic librarian. Fellows must balance the duties of a core functional area of the library and push forward innovative projects that solve problems in new ways—all while serving on organizational committees and actively contributing to the profession at regional and national levels.

Complementary to this challenging program, an informal and collegial social network provided a rich learning environment. We drew on the concept of Lave and Wenger's community of practice (Wenger 2007) to describe this social context. In this chapter, we describe and reflect on how these two aspects—the formal structure of the fellows program and our participation in an informal community of practice—each played its role in our early career and personal development. In doing so, we offer ideas and best practices toward the design and conceptualization of residency programs at other institutions.

AT WORK IN THE NCSU LIBRARIES FELLOWS PROGRAM

Established in 1999, the NCSU Libraries Fellows Program offers recent graduates the opportunity to begin their professional careers as academic librarians over a two-year period. During this period, fellows are assigned to a "home department" and a "project department" as they join the staff of more than 250 at NCSU Libraries. Home departments are designed to provide an opportunity for fellows to develop the full range of competencies in a particular functional area. Sandy served as a collection manager in her home department. In this role, she managed a collections budget consisting of four subject areas, participated in the beginning of a major collections and journal review process, and helped develop the elementary education and American Indian history collections. Hyun-Duck served as the business reference librarian in her home department, providing instruction and consultation services related to topics in business and management, and developed a liaison relationship with a new campus-wide entrepreneurship initiative.

In their "project departments," fellows are assigned innovative projects of strategic importance to the libraries. In Sandy's case, she reviewed and recommended upgrades to the libraries' core online information literacy tutorial. Hyun-Duck piloted the development of e-learning modules that delivered instructional material in an engaging and reusable multimedia format. In addition to the home and project assignments, fellows also work on smaller, special projects as part of working groups. Serving on interdepartmental library committees provides a way for fellows to meet and work with staff across various departments in the libraries. Sandy served on the diversity committee, and Hyun-Duck was appointed to the digital repository management committee. Finally, fellows also help recruit the next cohort of fellows into the program.

In addition to the duties described above, fellows often engage in many professional activities beyond the libraries. To support this important aspect of career development, each fellow receives a professional development stipend in addition to a competitive salary. The stipend can be used in flexible ways to participate in a variety of training and development programs from leadership institutes to conference presentations and posters at local, regional, and national venues. In this way, the stipend supports the development of expertise in an area of professional interest. For example, Sandy used her stipend to cultivate relationships with communities she was interested in working with as a Native American librarian. Hyun-Duck used her stipend on travel and conference participation activities that were closely tied to her project on developing e-learning modules. Both authors used a portion of their stipends to attend the Minnesota Institute for Early Career Librarians from Traditionally Underrepresented Groups in 2008.

The NCSU Fellows program also incorporates a variety of internal professional development opportunities. The libraries established the fellows advisory committee to help coordinate and guide the professional development of fellows. Charged with facilitating opportunities for the fellows to develop a supportive peer network, the committee plans, coordinates, and delivers programs for this purpose. During our term as fellows, the advisory committee offered sessions on conference presenting, publishing, project management, and getting the most out of our professional development stipend. This committee also conducted tours of other nearby academic libraries, which helped broaden our perspective on academic library work beyond a single institution.

Additionally, the director of libraries hosted a luncheon series at which campus leaders, such as vice-provosts, attended as guests and informally conversed with the fellows. These luncheons provided unique opportunities to gain a broader perspective by discussing campus-wide issues and the role of libraries in higher education. The activities sponsored by the advisory committee and libraries' administration were a valuable asset to our professional development, introducing us to skills that we needed to do our job, and created opportunities to engage in conversations with established professionals in various contexts of higher education. As can be seen from the structure and organized components of the program, fellows are expected to perform well, be highly productive, and learn continuously.

Although some of the programming described here provided important supportive mechanisms, the demands of the program can easily become overwhelming. We often faced a lot of uncertainty, not only as newcomers to the institution but also as new professionals. Furthermore, as in all organizations, priorities can shift or changes in staffing may occur, and fellows can find themselves in the position of having to deal with these complexities in an agile manner. However, we were able to manage the challenges of the program and channel them toward learning and productivity instead of giving way to frustration or burnout. We were able to do so by engaging in an informal community of practice that centered on the fellows program.

SOCIAL CONTEXT OF RESIDENCY PROGRAMS

Complementary to the formal organization of the fellows program, an informal community of practice played a critical role in supporting our professional development as early career librarians. A community of practice is not a new idea. It exists wherever a group of practitioners self-organize and "share a concern, a set of problems, or a passion about a topic . . . [and] deepen their knowledge and expertise in this area by interacting on an ongoing basis" (Wenger, McDermott, and Snyder 2002, 4).

This concept of communities of practice was introduced as a framework to describe learning environments in the workplace (Wenger 2007) and later as a means to manage and harness the knowledge assets of an organization (Wenger, McDermott, and Snyder 2002). The concept has been applied to domains in education, business, and the nonprofit sector. In libraries, it has been used to emphasize the importance of providing a shared, social context for early career librarians from underrepresented backgrounds to develop professionally and remain in the profession (Johnson

2007). It also serves as a framework to assist early career librarians through the process of academic tenure (Henrich and Attebury 2010). In this chapter, we apply the concept to define a rich social context that early career librarians engaged in as part of a residency program.

Defining a community of practice is a complex exercise because, by nature, such communities are informal, have permeable and overlapping boundaries, and are composed of voluntary and unstable membership (Wenger 2007). This model reflects the reality of our experience in that the community we describe did not necessarily include only fellows nor did all fellows engage in the community to the same extent. In fact, the status of any community may change, from being active one year to being latent in others, and in some cases only exist as a potential (Wenger 2007). This instability is likely also true of the community of practice we experienced as fellows. Despite these constraints and limitations, we draw on the vocabulary and framework of communities of practice as a useful way to help convey the rich social learning and working environment we experienced as fellows.

The social environment of the fellows program was rich because it was multilayered and allowed for a natural cycle of renewal among new and more experienced librarians. Although the duration of the fellows program is two years, a new cohort is recruited each fiscal year. This overlap among the first- and second-year fellows allows each new class of fellows to turn to a slightly more senior cohort of colleagues for highly relevant information stemming from their recent experience. In addition to the two cohorts, the library staff includes former fellows who have remained at the libraries in permanent positions in various departments. Although their experiences as fellows were not as recent or directly applicable, their achievements and depth of experience played a distinct yet equally important role in this community.

The Cohort Effect

At the core of the community of practice was our specific year of cohort members, with whom we formed a network of mutual support, information sharing, and collaboration. Our own cohort of fellows started work together at the libraries in July 2007. The cohort of five provided what seemed like an ideal size that allowed us to learn from and with each other simultaneously. The cohort was large enough to offer a diversity of professional interests and personal backgrounds. At the same time, the group size was small enough to allow for cohesion around the common goal of developing our careers though successful contributions to both the organization and the profession.

Initially, we bonded through the shared experiences of relocating to Raleigh, North Carolina, from outside the state. During the first months of our orientation, we exchanged stories about finding places to live, transferring driver's licenses, and becoming acquainted with the city. Although some of the fellows in our cohort already had friends in Raleigh, everyone was open to building new social relationships with each other outside of the work context. Being similar in terms of age and marital status made building these social relationships easier. Over the course of the program, we developed a strong bond, worked toward achieving common goals in learning, and accomplished as much as possible in our work assignments.

Despite working separately in various departments of the libraries, we maintained informal channels of communication to keep abreast of news and share other useful advice that any one of us might have received from our individual supervisors. We also shared information with each other about different types of training opportunities that were available through the distance education office or the information technology department on campus. Such open channels of communication also allowed us to approach each other about questions involving interdepartmental perspectives and to learn more about the everyday workings of other departments. For instance, if Hyun-Duck was working in the Research and Information Services (RIS) department and had a question that involved technical services, she could quickly instant message Kristen Blake, another fellow in our cohort working in that area. If she had a question related to collection management, she could just as easily instant message Sandy to gain some insight about a particular issue.

Informal channels also had the effect of facilitating collaboration among fellows, even though none of the projects or home department assignments required such activities. These lines of open communication, combined with the collegial nature of our cohort, made it easy to work with each other on smaller projects. Hyun-Duck and another fellow, Emily Mazure, collaborated on a video module concerning the use of article databases. Working together on the module allowed us to be accountable to each other and meet and make progress regularly in order to finish the project in a reasonable timeframe. In a related way, but on a broader scale, Sandy scheduled brown-bag lunches for librarians interested in instruction, thereby creating a forum to solicit feedback related to her project on information literacy. This forum had a direct impact on the success of Sandy's project but also allowed each of us to be inspired and motivated to improve our performance while sharing ideas around effective or creative strategies related to our instructional work in general. In these ways, not only did these social contexts make learning and work more enjoyable, they directly resulted in improved performance and outcomes.

Second-Year and Former Fellows

Beyond our core cohort of fellows, our community of practice benefited from the knowledge and experience of second-year and former fellows still employed at NCSU Libraries. Since the beginning of the program more than a decade ago, approximately half of the former fellows remain at the libraries and continue to play an important role in helping successive cohorts foster a supportive micro-culture within the larger organization. Both second-year and former fellows approached our cohort with empathy and honesty, which, in turn, helped to create a culture of trust. In addition, the second-year and former fellows provided models of success and helped us imagine possibilities for the trajectory of our individual careers in both the short and long term.

The empathy of the second-year and former fellows combined with candid honesty in sharing both successes and failures of their experiences helped to establish a considerable amount of trust within the group. Trust plays a critical role in facilitating knowledge among communities and must exist for learning to take place in informal social contexts (Cross, Abrams, and Parker 2004). In our experience, this trust developed out of social interactions in which first-year, second-year, and former fellows all intentionally engaged each other with encouragement, ideas, and advice around the fellows program. Because this social dynamic was built on trust and voluntary membership, interactions proved to be genuine and avoided becoming tedious or threatening.

As knowledgeable peers and more experienced colleagues, the second-year and former fellows advised and encouraged our cohort in a number of ways. They prompted us to reflect on our experiences when they asked us how we were progressing through the program. Former fellows provided safe social venues for current fellows to reflect openly and comfortably on their work experiences with someone who could not only relate but also offer a broader perspective, whether through informal coffee conversations or inviting fellows over to their homes for dinner. Drawing on their past experiences in a candid way, second-year and former fellows offered advice around balancing a demanding workload, relayed relevant aspects of institutional memory, and helped us assess and interpret the organizational culture and our place within it. In this kind of rich social context, the second-year and former fellows not only helped to establish a base of trust in our community, they also served as models of success.

Wenger states that in communities of practice, "more experienced peers are not merely a source of information. They are living testimonies to what is possible, expected, desirable" (Wenger 2007, 156). This characterization accurately portrays our community of practice. Having already attained a year of experience, the second-year fellows offered us very timely and relevant information. As we developed relationships with our more experienced peers, we could anticipate challenges and decisions regarding our careers that we, too, would need to face within a year's time.

While the second-year fellows helped us plan some of our short-term goals, the former fellows offered a sense of possible long-term career paths. Many former fellows hold leadership positions in the library and in the profession at large, with some having been promoted to supervisory roles and departmental managers in the libraries. In recent years, a number of them have also been named as *Library Journal*'s "Movers and Shakers" (LJ Staff 2007, 2008, 2009). The realities of the former fellows' career paths, as well as the habits, attitudes, and competencies that allowed them to achieve success, served as important models and possibilities for each of us to consider, reject, or strive toward.

CONCLUSION

In this chapter, we provided an overview of the formal structure of the NCSU Libraries Fellows Program, including a discussion of our work assignments as fellows, the importance of a professional development travel stipend, and the role of the fellows advisory committee. These aspects are often highlighted as benefits of the fellows program. However, we also emphasized an equally important, but more implicit, aspect of the program: the informal community of practice that can emerge among different cohorts of fellows. Among our cohort members, we easily found a sympathetic ear, suggestions for dealing with unfamiliar scenarios, and mutual support for exploring and discussing the direction of our careers. In addition to these aspects of the community, the second-year and former fellows helped to establish trust and provided models of excellence. All of these factors created a rich social context for learning and provided each of us with greater opportunities to succeed.

Conceptualizing residency programs through the lens of a community of practice allows academic libraries to consider these programs as something more important than merely temporary positions designed for entry-level work. Rather, in serving as the locus for communities of practice to develop and flourish through cohorts and informal channels of support, residency programs have the potential to become an ideal context in which new professionals are encouraged and motivated to continue to excel in this profession.

REFERENCES

Cross, R., L. Abrams, and A. Parker. 2004. A relational view of learning: How who you know affects what you know. In *Creating a Learning Culture: Strategy, Technology, and Practice*, edited by M. L. Conner and J. G. Clawson, pp. 152–168. Cambridge, UK: Cambridge University Press.

Henrich, K. J., and R. Attebury. 2010. Communities of practice at an academic library: A new approach to mentoring at the University of Idaho. *Journal of Academic Librarianship* 36:158–165.

Johnson, P. 2007. Retaining and advancing librarians of color. *College and Research Libraries* 68:405–417.

LJ Staff. 2007, March 17. Energizing Endeca: Emily Lynema, North Carolina State University Libraries. *Library Journal.* http://www.libraryjournal.com/article/CA6423426.html

LJ Staff. 2008, March 18. In context: Hilary Davis, North Carolina State University Libraries. *Library Journal.* http://www.libraryjournal.com/article/CA6535072.html

LJ Staff. 2009. Kim Duckett: Community builders. *Library Journal.* Kim Duckett: Community builders

Wenger, E. 2007. *Communities of Practice: Learning, Meaning, and Identity.* Cambridge, UK: Cambridge University Press.

Wenger, E., R. McDermott, and W. Snyder. 2002. *Cultivating Communities of Practice: A Guide to Managing Knowledge.* Boston: Harvard Business School Press.

Chapter 10

An Intern's Path to Academic Library Administration: 10 Years after the Open Letter

Jon E. Cawthorne

*Thus the task is not so much to see
what no one has yet seen,
but to think what nobody yet has thought
about that which everyone sees.*
—*Arthur Schopenhauer, 1788–1860*

INTRODUCTION

Ten years ago, I wrote an open letter to prospective library residents (Cogell and Gruwell 2001). In the letter, I listed three advantages of a post-MLS residency position over a typical, full-time position: 1) it can be difficult to transition directly from library school into an academic library; 2) residencies offer valuable work experience; and 3) post-master's residency positions are temporary. Since writing the open letter, there have been an increased number of internship and residency programs, and yet these advantages still remain true. Schopenhauer's quote ties together the intent of the open letter and my current passion to encourage anyone interested in administrative roles to think differently about the opportunities right in plain sight. Indeed, we have to be willing to think differently about the possibilities in administrative positions to become leaders in academic libraries.

Internships and residencies in academic libraries allow for unique opportunities to reflect on one's career path in a way few other experiences can match. The open letter included my suggestions for taking advantage of the residency experience. First, you cannot do much about the reputation of the previous intern or resident. Second, respect what you can learn from everyone in the organization. Third, communicate what you want (as a career direction) as much as you can (Cogell and Gruwell 2001). I went on to describe how my residency at Ohio State University Libraries provided me with valuable *time* to think about my future, to see a bigger picture, and to visualize a long-term path for my professional career. More important, the residency program introduced me to all the various facets of academic librarianship, including reference, technical services, collection development, area studies, departmental libraries, and special collections.

As a resident, I had the rare opportunity to observe how information and priorities from the university librarian changed as they were distributed throughout the organization. There seemed to be deep and wide levels of confusion and miscommunication in departments and among staff and librarians. I always thought it was odd that staff and librarians asked me, the resident, numerous questions about library-wide priorities. From the library administration's perspective, the real challenge seemed to be getting all the departments to buy into a collective vision. Now that I work in library administration, and because of my residency experience, I recognize that constant communication among librarians and staff is critical to getting all the library's departments to buy into that vision. In doing so, the library administration can improve the academic library experience for the campus community, students, faculty, and staff.

What are the challenges of the administration of academic library organizations? Are there some people who are more enthusiastic about change than others? How do organizations deal with change? What and how do our leaders communicate? Have you ever been in a library organization where you felt the administration made a decision with which you completely disagreed? Has there been a time when you agreed with the decision to change, but the library administration's implementation left you wondering about the long-term viability and rationale behind the change? There may be more questions, examples, and experiences that inform our perception of library leadership. However, each of these illustrates the challenges faced by administrators to lead, communicate effectively, and build relationships that will sustain significant and lasting change.

I hope my open letter shed light on my observations that what constituted an effective library administrator is the ability to build strong relationships with staff, communicate and translate top university and library decisions effectively, and provide opportunities for professional growth for librarians and staff at all levels. Ten years later, I can see how my perspective has evolved. During the residency, I did not fully understand the challenges faced by administration, but now I have a much better sense of what those are. Here, therefore, I share my experience working toward administrative positions in hope that my insights will encourage us to think differently about that which everyone sees, as Schopenhauer encourages.

This narrative expands on my administrative perspective and offers key areas for consideration for those individuals who are seriously considering competing for leadership positions in academic libraries. First, you should develop a plan of action for yourself and while doing so engage in meaningful self-assessment. Second, embrace calculated risks. Third, once you get into a leadership position (no matter what level), practice shared leadership. Finally, be the mentor you always wanted to have yourself.

While my previous letter focused on getting the most out of a residency in the beginning of one's career, I've progressed in my career to the point that I can answer questions about the opportunities available in library administration. I look forward to sharing the art of library administration with those who are considering administrative and leadership roles in, as Dr. E. J. Josey described to me in a personal message, our "noble profession."

PLANNING AND SELF-ASSESSMENT

My passion for becoming a successful administrator comes from the time when I was in the very early stages of my career, during my residency at Ohio State. As I entered the profession, I thought my aspiration to work at the reference desk was going to put me in a position to help the most people. At the time, top leadership positions seemed out of reach, almost unattainable and, frankly, undesirable. The highest position I could see myself attaining would be head of a reference department. My goals were only as high as I believed I could achieve.

During my residency, I began to ask myself a series of questions. What do I want to accomplish in my career? If I were to work in administration, what type of library would I want to lead? What about library administration interests me? What skills am I missing? Finally, what is my vision for academic libraries and can I articulate it quickly? As I talked to top leaders and observed the behavior of the organization, the more I began to think about long-term possibilities for my career and about the skills I needed to acquire to compete for higher level positions.

On my path to administration, I've had many setbacks, but through it all, I maintained a constant plan for my future by engaging in ongoing self-evaluation and improvement. For example, I decided that I would attend as many leadership institutes as possible before I managed librarians or staff. Although some of the leadership content was repetitive, I developed long-lasting, meaningful relationships over the years with like-minded colleagues. One particular institute that hosted a wide variety of librarians and libraries presented a particularly challenging exercise. Each designated group was asked to come up with a marketing campaign for a library. Time was limited, and we were expected to report our plan to the entire class of participants.

The discussion started off cordially and respectfully but quickly grew tense as each librarian seemed to be advocating for the type of library he or she represented. I'm sure they surmised, as I did, the exercise would be easier if we each made our own campaign for our own specific kind of library. However, there were no concessions made, and the discussion advanced only sparingly. I, like many at the table, grew frustrated with our lack of progress. Because our group could not decide which type of library (academic, public, or special) to market, we had little to report to the larger group.

One of the facilitators of the institute observed our entire discussion and gave us some feedback that has stuck with me to this day. He said the exercise was meant to cause conflict and disagreement but, at the same time, to stimulate change. The facilitators knew we all came from different libraries, but they wanted to see how well we could adapt and work together, recognize the different opportunities we afforded one another, and think beyond our own experiences.

It was anticipated that leaders would emerge from the exercise, including someone to help define a process and get buy-in from the others around the table. When the session was complete, the facilitator who observed our discussion went around our table and asked each of us how we thought we handled the exercise. He talked about how well we exercised our influence to direct the discussion and outcome for our group. He also commented on our nonverbal communication. Each of us was culpable for the lack of progress at our table.

Eventually, he came to me and described why and how my participation was inflexible and not indicative of leadership behavior. He noted how I tried to influence the group, but, in fact, when I didn't get my way, I just checked out and stopped participating in the discussion. Although his assessment was correct, it was uncomfortable for me to hear that criticism. I did learn, however, that even if you believe a group is going in the wrong direction, you have to respect the process and figure out where your leadership strengths fit in.

Collectively, our group was not able to see past our own conflict and disagreement, and I was a big part of why we couldn't move forward. Having realized this, I am now constantly striving to remain flexible, to hear and consider the opinions of others, and to search for common ground that taps into the basis for new thought. Now, as an administrator in an academic library, I reflect on that experience as I work with people in organizations that are in the process of navigating change.

From this anecdote, it's clear we have to be open to different ideas as described by the Arbinger Institute in their work *Leadership and Self-Deception* (Arbinger Institute 2002). In terms of self-assessment, for example, we can help people complete their assessments by showing them how to identify 1) areas in which they create their own problems, 2) areas in which they are in denial about the problems they've created, and 3) areas in which they refuse any attempts to help them stop creating those problems (Arbinger Institute 2002). Learning to navigate between these three areas is difficult work, but I believe sharpening one's leadership abilities will remain at the heart of any lasting institutional change.

Although the work is challenging, academic libraries definitely need additional, highly motivated people with long-term vision and desire to influence change within their organizations. Over the years, my self-assessment has led me to books, websites, and, more recently, the pursuit of a PhD in Managerial Leadership in the Information Professions from Simmons College. Even though I have recently transitioned into a leadership position, it is still important for me, as an administrator, to take stock of what skills I have and identify where I need to improve.

EMBRACING CALCULATED RISKS

In addition to conducting meaningful self-assessment, another challenge for aspiring library leaders and administrators is to understand that, at times, the role may require some experimentation and risk. As my journey continues, I am reminded by Meg Wheatley's suggestion that we do not experiment enough:

> Many of us have created lives and organizations that give very little support for experimentation. We believe that answers already exist out there, independent of us. We don't need to experiment to find what works; we just need to find the answer. We are dedicated detectives, tracking down solutions, attempting to pin them on ourselves and our organizations. (Wheatley and Kellner-Rogers 1996)

How will you acquire the skills to compete professionally for top leadership positions? Are you, for example, willing to relocate? These kinds of questions frame opportunities for calculated risk taking. My decision to move my family from Eugene, Oregon, to Detroit, Michigan, was not a popular idea at home or at work. However, at this point in my career, I didn't have management experience, and this necessitated the move, a calculated risk that proved to be an important decision in my career.

As Coordinator for Reference and Outreach Services at the University of Oregon, I supervised twelve students from a donor gift of $25,000. When I became the Director of Main Library in Detroit, I was responsible for 154 people in 17 departments and a collection development budget of $3.4 million. (The entire staff was also represented by seven different unions.) The University of Oregon and Main Library in Detroit had different demographics, different cultures, and, of course, the libraries were different. I recall people asking, "How can you move to management in a public library?" Then, they would say, "Well, given academic library culture, you will not be able to return to academic libraries if you leave!" It had the potential to take me outside of academic libraries for good, but it was a calculated risk I was willing to make.

Once I arrived in Detroit, I had many setbacks. With just about every decision I made came a grievance filed by the staff and or the librarians. I felt like I had entered an administrative boot camp. It took me a while to fully understand how to accomplish anything in the library's well-established, seven-union culture. In that position, I learned important management and leadership lessons that helped me succeed and that remain with me to this day. After the first seven months at Main Library in Detroit, the grievances subsided, in part, because of these lessons.

One of these lessons, taken from the first leadership institute I attended, focused on patience and flexibility. When making a change, it is extremely important to considering timing. Some of the largest candidates for organizational or personal change can't happen right away. I had to look at the bigger picture and dissect each change into smaller, more manageable pieces. In addition, I needed to be willing to wait for these changes to take place over time, on a schedule I could not determine alone, and I had to be flexible with my own expectations for these changes.

Second, and very important, I learned to listen. People at all levels of the organization will tell you a great deal, even give you creative solutions, if they believe you are really listening. Third, I internalized the need for and importance of good communication. Often, large academic libraries experience difficulties communicating their mission and vision along with maintaining open lines of discussion between the administration and staff. Yet this is a vital part of any well-managed organization. Good communication allows for transparency in the workplace and is integral to building trust and productivity. These are insights that can be attained over time and can help anyone interested in leadership positions. As I look back, the management experiences were valuable, and there were always surprises; but it was absolutely the right decision for me to leave Oregon for Detroit. Luckily, on a personal level, my family also bought into the calculated risk, and, ultimately, they all thrived in Detroit.

Before moving to Detroit, I was looking for positions that gave me the experience I needed to compete for leadership positions in libraries. Ultimately I made the decision to leave academic libraries to gain management experience. While in Detroit, I was able to use my management experience as the Director of Main Library to revisit my potential career trajectory back into academic libraries. My experiences are somewhat unique but demonstrate that it is possible to move between academic and public libraries.

After gaining the management experience I sought, I said, "Maybe now I can look at where I want to live." This shift allowed me to look for positions in San Diego, California, and Portland, Oregon. I was fortunate to find a job at San Diego State University as the Associate University Librarian responsible for Information and Collections. I was ready for the challenge of academic library administration only because I made the decision to leave it for an opportunity to earn management-level work experience. The changes in my career, together with the support of my family, kneaded me into the person I am today. Only time will tell what the future holds, but I look forward to connecting and supporting people in large organizations at the highest levels of our profession while pursuing emerging research trends.

PRACTICING SHARED LEADERSHIP

As I've moved into administrative positions, it was clear that one person could not effectively begin, sustain, and institutionalize all the changes required of the twenty-first century academic library. To create academic library organizations, top leaders (deans, university librarians, etc.) must rely on the involvement of individuals throughout the organization. Shared leadership is an emerging theory that focuses on the leadership influence of individuals at all levels of the organization.

Current leadership research reveals new models that should be applied for the future success of academic libraries. In fact, the library field is just beginning to understand the extent to which leaders throughout the organization influence organizational change. If library administration becomes a career path, the profession will need people willing to recognize both formal and informal leaders in the organization. My success has depended on seeking out these leaders and building useful and invigorating relationships during this time of severe economic downturn, technological changes, and pending retirements. As a result of all these factors, leadership has grown in importance. The more I have learned about the nuances of management and leadership, the more I believe in practicing shared leadership.

BECOMING THE MENTOR

I've been fortunate to work in academic, public, and special libraries. Many mentors, friends, and colleagues helped me along the way. My high expectations for myself and my tremendous optimism are simply a reflection of their belief in me. People I've looked up to professionally like Robert Wedgeworth, Dr. E. J. Josey, Sylvia Sprinkle-Hamlin, Dr. Maurice Wheeler, Edythe O. Cawthorne, William D. Cunningham, Dr. Peggy Sullivan, Dr. Miles Jackson, and the late Dr. John C. Tyson would expect me to pass on their insights to the next generation of library leaders. In fact, I now understand we are merely stewards of this great profession, and it is a personal pleasure to see others succeed in their leadership aspirations.

I remember one conversation with one of my mentors quite vividly. At a time in my career when I served in a senior-level administrative position at Detroit Public Library, I still felt I needed to find additional mentors to emulate. I ran into Peggy Sullivan at an American Library Association (ALA) conference in 2001. Peggy Sullivan worked in libraries for well over fifty years and made significant contributions as a leader in both public and academic institutions. In the early '90s she served as the Executive Director of the ALA. She knew my grandmother, Edythe O. Cawthorne, who worked for twenty-five years as a children's librarian in Prince Georges' County Public Library system. Peggy and I met frequently, and eventually, we became friends. About once a year, Peggy and I would run into one another at an annual conference. We'd have a little time to chat about her travels, my job, the family, and what was going on in the profession.

When I ran into Peggy in 2001, she had been retired for several years. As always, we chatted about her travels and my job. Just before we parted, I asked her for names of people who might serve as good mentors. She looked at me and said, "Well, Jon, I think it is time for you to find people to mentor." That short conversation changed my entire professional perspective and focus. I was striving to find additional mentors, and Peggy made a simple statement that revealed a new opportunity for me. The conversation ushered in a new role for me as mentor. I realized that becoming a good mentor was the best way to thank the people who helped me. This is an important lesson for anyone in our profession, and it is particularly relevant for emerging leaders.

Mentoring is about sharing one's perspective. In the best-case scenarios, mentors serve as role models and partner with those being mentored (Servais and Sanders 2006). Mentoring can be most effective when it informs our choices and opportunities of what is possible. Sometimes the act of mentoring takes a great deal of patience, but in the end, you have helped people expand their internal and external perspectives related to future possibilities. I believe mentoring is a significant part of my overall contribution to leading the academic library of the future and to fostering leadership potential in others.

CONCLUSION

Like others, there are days when I feel less sure about my own influence and feel that progress toward change is moving too slowly in our profession. I sometimes ask, "Why am I here?" Why don't I ever see the significant change in people or institutions I hope for? And yet, the answer usually comes quickly, unexpectedly, and from the course of my daily life.

My son, Micah, is nine years old. Like most nine year olds, Micah asks large and small questions to help him define his world: Dad, how many stars are there? Who is going to take me to school tomorrow? Recently, he started to combine ideas and ask more thoughtful questions. I arrived home after a rather difficult day. Micah was ready and waiting with one of his questions: "Dad, if you were stranded on an island, what would you eat first, your thumbs or your toes?" I just looked at him, and, of course, he was serious.

With a very steady voice, I responded, "Son, have you considered all the options?" What were all the options? We went through them. What was the thinking that went into his question in the first place? We talked a long time. I gave him advice, encouragement, and praise. If nothing else, I acknowledged his desire to solve a problem given a very difficult set of circumstances. As I was able to give him some alternatives and help him think about his particular situation and his future, I was reminded why I love and have a passion for administration: I enjoy facilitating change in academic library organizations through the development of people.

Ten years after writing about my residency experience, I still have a long way to go. There are many people for me to meet, and there is more for me to accomplish. When I look ahead to the end of my career, I'd want my professional colleagues to say, "He loved his work, cared about people, and understood the art of leadership." I also hope people whom I've mentored express their gratitude for our relationship by investing in the development of our future leaders. In the future, my accomplishments will not rest solely on sound fiscal management; the building of new, innovative collaborations; and raising funds through development, but on how many people I helped successfully ascend to academic library leadership positions.

I believe my story is a good example of someone who stuck to a plan while continuing rigorous self-assessment, took some calculated risks, and now continues to strive to become a mentor in the spirit of those who mentored me. Planning for the future by methodically gathering all the necessary skills and abilities to become the leader this profession needs will be the greatest, most enduring contribution an individual can make to it.

SELECTED READINGS

Arbinger Institute. 1998. *The Choice: Suppose Everything in Life Depended on One Decision*. Salt Lake City, UT: Arbinger Institute.

Arbinger Institute. 2002. *Leadership and Self-Deception: Getting Out of the Box*. San Francisco: Berrett Koehler.

Bennis, W. G. 1989. *On Becoming a Leader*. Reading, MA: Addison-Wesley.

Bolman, L. G., and T. E. Deal. 2008. *Reframing Organizations: Artistry, Choice, and Leadership*. San Francisco: John Wiley & Sons.

Boyatzis, R. E., and A. McKee. 2005. *Resonant Leadership: Renewing Yourself and Connecting with Others through Mindfulness, Hope, and Compassion*. Boston: Harvard Business School Press.

Conger, J. A. 1998. *Winning 'Em Over: A New Model for Management in the Age of Persuasion*. New York: Simon & Schuster.

Depree, M. 2008. *Leadership Is an Art*. Studio City, CA: Phoenix Audio.

Goleman, D. 1998. *Working with Emotional Intelligence*. New York: Bantam Books

Jaworski, J., and B. S. Flowers. 1996. *Synchronicity: The Inner Path of Leadership*. San Francisco: Berrett-Koehler.

Kahane, A. 2004. *Solving Tough Problems: An Open Way of Talking, Listening, and Creating New Realities*. San Francisco: Berrett-Koehler.

Kouzes, J. M., and B. Z. Posner. 2002. *The Leadership Challenge*. San Francisco: Jossey-Bass.

Phillips, D. T. 1993. *Lincoln on Leadership: Executive Strategies for Tough Times*. New York: Warner Books.

Rath, T. 2007. *Strengths Finder 2.0*. New York: Gallup Press.

Schwartz, P. 1996. *The Art of the Long View: Planning for the Future in an Uncertain World*. New York: Currency Doubleday.

Senge, P. M. 2004. *Presence: Human Purpose and the Field of the Future*. Cambridge, MA: SoL.

Wheatley, M. J. 1999. *Leadership and the New Science: Discovering Order in a Chaotic World*. San Francisco: Berrett-Koehler.

Wheatley, M. J., and M. Kellner-Rogers. 1998. *A Simpler Way*. San Francisco: Berrett-Koehler.

Zander, R., and S. B. Zander. 2000. *The Art of Possibility*. Boston: Harvard Business School Press.

REFERENCES

Arbinger Institute. 2002. *Leadership and Self-Deception: Getting Out of the Box*. San Francisco: Berrett-Koehler.

Cawthorne, J. 2001. An open letter to prospective library interns. In *Diversity in Libraries: Academic Residency Programs*, edited by R. V. Cogell and C. A. Gruwell, pp. 125–130. Westport, CT: Greenwood Press.

Servais, K., and K. Saunders. 2006. *The Courage to Lead: Choosing the Road Less Traveled*. Lanham, MD: Rowman & Littlefield Education.

Wheatley, M. J., and M. Kellner-Rogers. 1996. *A Simpler Way*. San Francisco: Berrett-Koehler.

Chapter 11

Fires, Floods, and Residents, Oh My! The Residency Program at the University of New Mexico Libraries

Sarah Stohr

A LITTLE BACKGROUND

If you had asked me at any point during my first three years of undergraduate studies which career path I was headed down, without a doubt, I would have said something profound, along the lines of: "um" or "uh". . . or just stared blankly at you. Librarianship was not on my radar. I was an English major and loved to read but was pragmatic about the types of jobs often held by those who chose to spend their college years reading made-up stories instead of learning how to program computers or cure diseases. I presumed my career opportunities would be limited to proofreading copy or shuffling papers behind an office desk, and all I hoped for was that I could proof those copies in an office where I liked my coworkers and where there would never, ever, be screaming children around. And perhaps there would be cake.

That all changed after my junior year of college when I watched the movie *Party Girl*. While it would certainly be less embarrassing to say that I chose my career path based on words of wisdom from a trusted mentor or because I spent my childhood dreaming of how great it would be to instill a love of reading in others, it would be untrue. I totally became a librarian because of a movie about a raver-girl-gone-wild who changes her ways after working in a library. Parker Posey starred as the main character in the film, and I love Parker Posey. According to my logic at the time, if Parker Posey liked working in a library, it stood to reason that I would, too. While my logic was flawed, my hunch turned out to be right.

Fast-forward three or four years. I'd graduated from college and worked in the children's department at a public library and spent time as an elementary school librarian (so much for my no screaming children plan). It was when I was working as a school librarian in Santa Fe, New Mexico, that I decided if I wanted to really make a career out of librarianship, I needed to get my MLS. In August 2004, I moved across the country to attend school at the University of Kentucky.

In graduate school, though, I felt the same sense of confusion I had felt during my undergraduate years whenever anyone would ask me what my career plans were, only in this case, the question was always, "So what type of library do you want to work in?" I didn't have that answer. I knew I wanted to be involved in public services, but I didn't feel like I knew enough about various libraries to commit to saying I was interested in academic or public librarianship.

During graduate school, I had an assistantship working in the reference department of the main library at the University of Kentucky. My experiences there, though, were limited to working on the reference desk and attending training sessions. I never got to see how academic libraries really worked as a whole.

When it came time to start looking for a "real" job after graduate school, I focused my search on reference positions in public and academic libraries. What I found, though, was that I didn't have the experience most academic libraries were looking for, even in positions that seemed like they were entry level. It was at the point that I had almost given up on finding an academic library job when I saw the announcement for the library resident position at the University of New Mexico (UNM). The job seemed too good to be true. Applicants didn't need to have prior professional experience and would be encouraged to explore different departments and aspects of the library system at UNM. That was exactly what I was looking for—a chance to figure out which aspect of librarianship truly interested me and to have health insurance while doing it!

Unlike many residency programs, the University of New Mexico's program was open to any recent graduate. Applicants did not have to belong to an underrepresented group to apply but did need to have a demonstrated record of interest in or experience with issues of diversity in librarianship. Knowing that I wanted to return to New Mexico after getting my MSLS, I made the decision to focus all of my graduate research on library issues in Hispanic and Native American communities. This interest translated seamlessly to the University of New Mexico, where Hispanic and Native American students comprise a large portion of the student body.

GETTING THE JOB

The application process for the residency position was like none that I'd ever experienced. I was used to applying for a job, waiting a few days to hear back, and then going for an interview. Not so with the residency position. I sent my application in January 2006 and didn't hear a word from UNM until April when they asked to set up a telephone interview. A date was chosen, and as it approached, I grew more and more apprehensive. This would be my first interview with an academic library, and I didn't know what to expect. All of my previous interviews were conducted in person and never involved more than a single face-to-face meeting.

With just a few days to go before my interview, I was reading the Santa Fe newspaper online and noticed a tiny little story headline: Fire at UNM's Zimmerman Library. "That's not good," I thought. I tried to find more information, but there really wasn't much to find, just a few vague sentences in the newspaper. That night, I checked my e-mail and found that my telephone interview had been postponed; I was convinced that the library had burned down and the search would be cancelled.

When I finally had my telephone interview, it went much better than I had imagined. Being semi-neurotic, I'd written down possible questions I might be asked and their answers on 3 x 5 cards, which I had strewn about me as I spoke with the committee members on the phone. The questions they asked were all directly related to the job description, so nothing came as a surprise. I'd prepared a few questions to ask the committee members, but when the time came for me to unleash them, the only thing that came out of my mouth was: "So what's up with the fire?"

It was at that point that I knew the committee liked me—they began telling me the story of what had happened and how they were coping, and soon we were chatting like old friends. At that time, the committee didn't have any information about what had caused the fire, which collections had been damaged, or how long the building would be closed. They sounded hopeful that everything would be back to normal in the near future. It would turn out that the fire and its ramifications would become central to my entire experience as a UNM resident.

Although I felt good about my phone interview, over a month went by before UNM contacted me to set up an in-person interview. During that month, I had convinced myself that I was never going to get a real job, so I was quite relieved to find out that they wanted to hear more from me. The bad news was that they wanted to hear more from me in just a little more than a week's time. I frantically prepared for the interview. I was asked to give a thirty-minute presentation on the roles of a resident in an academic library. Having never been a resident or knowing what a resident actually does, I spent the next week trying to find out as much as I could about resident programs. At the time, there really wasn't much information to be found. I relied on *Diversity in Libraries: Academic Residency Programs* (Cogell and Gruwell 2001) and the few articles I could find to give me a better understanding of how resident programs work.

At last, I arrived in Albuquerque, ready to interview but extremely nervous about the whole process. My interview began with my presentation, which was a relief, as public speaking makes me anxious and I wanted to get that portion of the process over with as soon as possible. My presentation slides consisted of nothing but cartoons from *The New Yorker,* a decision I'd been second-guessing ever since I'd initially made it. It turned out to be a good choice, and the audience seemed engaged and interested during my presentation. The rest of the interview day went pretty smoothly, although it was overwhelming to meet so many people and hear about so many different aspects of the library.

The best part of the interview process was having some time to speak with Evangela Oates, the resident hired the previous year. Evangela and I did not have any scheduled one-on-one time to speak together during my day on campus, so I cornered her during lunchtime and tried to get in as many questions about the program as I possibly could. She provided a wealth of information about the program, the University Libraries, and UNM itself. During the interview, I learned that Evangela would be continuing as a resident for one more year, meaning there would be two residents working alongside one another. This came as a very welcome surprise to me; it would be so much easier to transition to the program with someone who had gone through the same thing just a year earlier.

I went back to Kentucky after the interview, and several long weeks passed before I received a call from UNM offering me the position. In all, it took seven months between the time I initially applied and when I was offered the position. I accepted immediately, and within a few weeks I drove across the country to New Mexico to start the residency program. I was excited at the prospect of learning all that I could about how an academic library works without having all of the pressure of being a permanent tenure-track faculty member.

ORGANIZATION OF THE RESIDENCY PROGRAM

Dr. Teresa Y. Neely, Director of UNM's Zimmerman Library, spearheaded the organization of the resident program at UNM, which initially began with the hiring of Evangela in the summer of 2005. Dr. Neely created a program that was highly organized and carefully planned, yet also gave residents the opportunity to explore and specialize in areas of librarianship that held their interest. The residency program comprised several parts: an initial orientation to the entire library system at the University of New Mexico, an ongoing contribution to the reference and instruction departments at Zimmerman Library, resident projects, and, of course, "other duties as assigned." I should have foreseen that a library that had just experienced a devastating fire four months before my date of hire would be full of interesting and very unexpected "other duties."

ORIENTATION

The first part of the program consisted of a detailed orientation to the University Libraries. During the first twelve weeks of the program, it was my job to meet with almost every single employee in the library to attain a thorough understanding of how the organization was run. My first few days of work were filled with learning calendar systems and making appointments (and cancelling a few, too, because I'd messed up the calendar system). Over the course of three months, I met with almost all of the libraries' 180 employees, including the interim dean, the directors of all of our branch libraries, as well as the law and medical school library directors, the map librarian, and the mail clerk. Most of the people with whom I met were incredibly kind and generous, encouraging me to ask questions and taking the time to provide thoughtful and detailed answers whenever needed. The majority of employees walked me through a typical workday for them, showing me various aspects of their work, such as how they cataloged e-books, ran reports in our cataloging system, or digitized archives.

It was interesting to talk to people about their jobs and to see how the library system comprised so many parts. I found myself fascinated by all of the activities that people were doing at UNM, and almost every day I would think about how perhaps I wanted to switch gears and become a science librarian, a map librarian, or work in special collections. I was exposed to many facets of librarianship that I hadn't previously considered. I realized that if I'd taken an entry-level job in a reference department instead of pursuing the resident program at UNM, I would have missed out on this opportunity to learn about what it means to be a part of a large library system. Observing the ins-and-outs of so many jobs gave me a breadth of knowledge about libraries that I don't think I could have received anywhere else. It was my job to learn as much as I could about the roles of the people in the library and I embraced it whole-heartedly.

As part of my in-depth orientation, I also attended at least one meeting in each department within the library and shadowed employees at every public service point. As I attended these meetings, I learned about different management styles and various team projects. I went from knowing virtually nothing about how an academic library works as a whole to having a pretty in-depth knowledge of how one operates, all within the span of a few short months. Looking back, I can't imagine beginning a residency program without this period of involved orientation. The orientation allowed me to explore and think about which aspects of librarianship really interested me. It reaffirmed my interest in public services yet made me begin to think more specifically about what goals I wanted to set for myself as a librarian.

REFERENCE AND INSTRUCTION

Residents were required to participate in providing reference and instruction at Zimmerman Library (the humanities, social sciences, and education library at UNM). Although I had experience working in the reference department at the University of Kentucky, I spent my first few months at UNM shadowing librarians at the reference desk several times per week. The student population, research interests, and even the library resources were quite different at UNM and it was invaluable to have the opportunity to learn about all of it before working at the desk by myself.

Once the spring semester began, I was assigned to regular reference desk shifts, working alongside another librarian. I received training on databases to which we subscribed and made it a point to attend training sessions at our branch libraries so that I would know how to help students looking for information that didn't fall within Zimmerman Library's purview. After the spring semester was over, I was allowed to work solo on the reference desk and also signed up to take one of the regular evening shifts.

Providing library instruction was the one duty I found quite intimidating. Public speaking has never come easy to me and, although I had taken an instruction course during graduate school, I always felt like my strength as an instructor came from my ability to put together amusing PowerPoint slides rather than to actually discuss the material the slides covered. I quickly learned that this would have to change at UNM.

The library instruction program for students enrolled in the basic English composition course at UNM was in need of more librarians to teach the fifty-minute sessions. Similar to my time shadowing at the reference desk, I spent numerous hours observing instruction sessions. I probably watched fifteen instructors present to students on the same basic topic, and I quickly figured out what worked and what didn't, which tactics interested students, and which bored them to death. When, a few months later, it was time for me to begin teaching sessions on my own, I felt like I was well prepared if still anxious.

My experience in the instruction department was one of the most unexpected and positive opportunities that came my way during the residency program. The more instruction sessions I conducted, the better I felt, and soon I was able to stand up in the front of the room and feel confident in my ability to engage students as I taught them what they needed to know about the library in the limited time we had together. Eventually, I was asked to become the interim library instructor for the English department at UNM, conducting library instruction sessions for upper and graduate-level English courses in addition to the basic composition classes. I built relationships with faculty members outside of the library and learned how to successfully design relevant sessions for students of a variety of abilities.

As a resident, I had the unique opportunity to take my time to explore the fundamentals of library instruction. I was encouraged to think about what it means to be a good teacher and to try to understand the needs of the students we are serving. I came into my own as an instructor at UNM and learned how to be comfortable with and excited about library instruction.

RESIDENT PROJECTS

Dr. Neely devised a means of encouraging library-wide participation in the resident program by soliciting departments within the library to submit resident project proposals to her for consideration. On my first day at UNM, Dr. Neely and I met and looked over the half dozen or so project proposals that had already been submitted. With one exception, it was my decision as to which projects I selected. Project proposals were submitted by departments throughout the entire program so when I completed one project I would look at the proposals and select another. Many of the project proposals that were submitted came about after my rotations through a department. If someone was working on a project that I found interesting, I would encourage him or her to submit a proposal.

The projects I selected were varied, and each was chosen because I thought I would learn a valuable new skill. The first project that I took on, however, was assigned by Dr. Neely. It involved reviewing every serial item housed in Zimmerman Library's reference collection. I had to find out which funds had purchased each item, track its purchasing data for the past five years, and see whether there were any other copies of the item within the entire library's collection.

Initially this project didn't interest me, but as time progressed, I realized I actually enjoyed it. I learned a great deal about using Millennium, UNM's integrated library system (which manages most of the circulation, cataloging, serials, and reports for the library), and discovered just how much it costs to put together a reference collection. The final report that I prepared was given to Dr. Neely, who used the data to inform subsequent cancellation discussions.

Another project I worked on was creating online tutorials with our distance services librarian. This project grew out of my initial meeting with the distance services librarian during my orientation to the library. I thought her job was interesting and that I'd like to learn more about what she does, so we discussed potential projects. Since I had experience creating tutorials with Captivate, we decided that would be the best place to begin. Eventually, I created five tutorials for our online students, honing my instructional design skills tremendously in the process.

When I'd first been asked by Dr. Neely to think about what type of proposals I might like to work on, a grant-writing project was the first thing to come to mind. I had not worked on grants in the past, and I knew that it would be great experience for me to see how the process worked. The Center for Southwest Research (UNM's special collections department) was very receptive to my working with them on such a project, but it took almost a year for us to flush out the details. We decided that, under the supervision of the Center's Director, Michael Kelly, I would help write a proposal to the National Historical Publications and Records Commission (NHPRC) to get funding to have the LaDonna Harris and Americans for Indian Opportunities papers processed.

LaDonna Harris, the ex-wife of former U.S. Senator Fred Harris, is a Comanche woman who has worked to promote the rights of indigenous people in the United States and across the world. Her papers, and the papers of the organization she founded, Americans for Indian Opportunities, document her efforts in promoting equality and accountability. After studying LaDonna, her organization, and the collection, I wrote the narrative of the grant, and Michael Kelly and Kathleen Ferris edited and compiled the necessary financial and institutional data. The proposal was submitted to the NHPRC in October 2008. In May 2009, we received notification that the grant would be funded for more than $50,000.

UNIQUE SUPPORT SYSTEM

There was never a time during my residency when I felt like I had to navigate the program or academic librarianship alone. Dr. Neely was a tremendous source of support. On my first day of work, we sat down to discuss her expectations for me as a resident. She let me know that if I needed or had any questions about anything, she would be there to help, and throughout my two years in the program, she backed up that claim on countless occasions.

We set up weekly meetings so that she could check in with me regularly to make sure I was progressing through the program. These meetings also gave me the opportunity to discuss what I was experiencing as a new professional and to ask her any questions I might have. Dr. Neely also received countless question-filled e-mails from me during the time between our meetings; she was always patient and answered my questions honestly and thoroughly. She was very protective of the residents, whom she referred to as her "Baby Librarians," and throughout the program she demonstrated her commitment to our success.

Dr. Neely also encouraged Evangela and I to set up regular meetings with one another. Although we would eventually share an office, Evangela and I did not have the opportunity to spend much time together during my first semester at UNM. The fire had forced Evangela (and countless other employees) to seek office space elsewhere, and my orientation duties kept my schedule quite full. Our regular meetings were a time when I could debrief with Evangela and talk openly about my experiences in the program. As the "senior" resident, Evangela was a constant source of knowledge, encouragement, and inspiration. She had already gone through her first year of the resident program and was able to share her firsthand knowledge and experiences. I never felt embarrassed to ask Evangela questions; if there was an issue going on within the library faculty or if I had a question about a procedure or a policy, Evangela was always there to share what she knew with me. It was Evangela who encouraged me to apply to the American Library Association's Emerging Leaders program (to which I was accepted as a member of the 2008 cohort).

When Evangela's two years in the program were over, I was able to find the same sense of camaraderie with the next resident, Megan Beard. As the "senior" resident, it felt good to be able to offer her my own support and advice when she needed it during the initial stages of her time in the program. I could remember how it felt, just a year earlier, to be new to UNM and starting my first professional librarian position. Luckily, I'd had Evangela there to help me navigate that first year. The support system that was created by having two residents at a time was an advantage that I had not foreseen when I accepted the position. The University Libraries, of course, benefitted from having two new and eager librarians each year; I don't know that the UL had anticipated how much the residents would appreciate having a peer with whom they could share the experience. For me, it was one of the most beneficial aspects of the program.

UNIQUE OPPORTUNITIES

My two years in the residency program provided many opportunities that I'd never even considered as possibilities. The fire at Zimmerman Library was a truly devastating event that caused more than $18 million in damages. It ravaged portions of the library's journal collections and forced Zimmerman Library to remove most of the remaining journal collection for close to two full years. In addition, much of the reference collection was inaccessible for almost a year.

During my time as a resident, I watched the library system grapple with all of the issues created by the disaster. I saw how students and researchers were affected by the loss and how the library system tried to accommodate them as much as possible. I learned how departments and workgroups that were displaced from their offices because of the fire resolved workflow and space issues. In fact, I learned this firsthand during the initial months of my residency when I, seven other reference staff and librarians, and our desks were all housed in the circulation area. Despite these challenges, I was privileged to see how the library took advantage of the devastation to redesign spaces and rethink how to provide services to students.

As part of the restoration efforts, Dr. Neely and several other members of the reference department were deeply involved in what was called the "pack-back." It was a process of trying to *pack* the books *back* into the library—books that had been removed for cleaning almost two years earlier. There were days when it felt inconceivable that the library would be able to complete the recovery process within the deadline stipulated by the administration. When semitrailer trucks full of books began to return to the library, it was amazing to see how quickly and efficiently the library came back to life. The military-style precision and planning that went into the pack-back was inspiring, and I learned valuable lessons about post-disaster recovery.

In addition to learning about recovery processes, I was able to contribute to the effort in several areas. I helped reshelve books when our reference collection was returned and signed up for additional reference and instruction duties so that others could be free to handle the pack-back. My most significant contribution consisted of taking over the task of scheduling the reference and information desks. The person in charge of scheduling was a critical contributor to the pack-back effort and needed to devote all of his time to making sure everything went as planned. As a result, I was given the opportunity during my second year as a resident to provide relief by assuming responsibility for scheduling both desks.

A second, substantial opportunity presented itself in the midst of our fire recovery efforts. Before the library's services and collections were completely restored, Zimmerman fell victim to a large flood. I learned about the flood while working at the reference desk and immediately experienced firsthand what it is like to evacuate a large academic library during the busiest time of the day. The library's basement flooded, and everyone needed to be ushered out of the building as quickly as possible. This was not an experience I'd anticipated being a part of when I signed my resident contract. The flood turned out to be a devastating setback to the fire-recovery efforts. The University Libraries' staff, however, was now old hands at recovering from disasters, and the situation was handled smoothly and effectively.

In addition to my other duties, I served on several committees during my time as a resident. I was a member of the marketing committee and represented the library at outreach program events such as New Student Orientation days. I served as an honorary member of an RFP (request for proposal) committee that was formed to find a new electronic journal management service for the libraries. Like many other residency program participants, I was also a part of the search committee for the next resident at UNM, a first for me and quite an eye-opener. I was able to participate in the entire process of hiring an academic librarian. This was probably one of the most helpful and practical experiences of my entire residency because I will be able to use the knowledge I gleaned from the process each time I apply for a new position.

CONCLUSION

Participating in a residency program was undoubtedly the best early career move I could have made. The residency experience highlighted just how little I knew about academic librarianship and how the world of academia works. Luckily, I learned the ropes of academic librarianship in an environment where my inexperience was welcomed and embraced. I credit the staff of the University Libraries for creating an environment where I felt constantly encouraged to learn as much as possible. If the UL staff had not been so supportive, I doubt my time in the residency program would have been as fruitful and rewarding—their commitment to the residents was the reason I was able to emerge from the program as a much more capable and confident librarian.

The most important thing I learned as I participated in this residency program was that the manner in which the program unfolds is really in the resident's hands. Even though UNM's program was highly structured, there was sufficient flexibility for me to engage in other activities. If there was a project I was interested in or a skill I wanted to develop, for example, all I had to do was share my interest to be given an opportunity to participate. I felt like I had the freedom to explore every single aspect of librarianship that I was interested in—and, in many cases, experiences that I'd never imagined as possibilities. In fact, one of the projects I'd worked on even helped me secure a position at UNM when my residency program was over. In June 2008, I was hired to be a distance services librarian at UNM; my experiences creating online tutorials for the library during my residency helped support my application for the position.

The opportunities that came my way during the program went well beyond my expectations, and the professional relationships that I built are ones that I will continue to value for years to come. My journey through the resident program was not one that I took by myself, and I will always consider Dr. Neely, Evangela Oates, and Megan Beard as especially important to my growth in the profession. I am grateful that the program provided the opportunity to work so closely with them, and with the staff members of the University Libraries who so graciously took me under their wings.

REFERENCE

Cogell, R. V., and C. A. Gruwell, eds. 2001. *Diversity in Libraries: Academic Residency Programs.* Westport, CT: Greenwood.

Chapter 12

Meeting the Challenge: My Experience in a Residency Program (and a little advice for others who might be thinking about entering one)

Asher Jackson

In 2006, I was offered the position of Pauline A. Young Resident at the University of Delaware for a two-year term. Prior to receiving this offer, I submitted customized résumés and cover letters for sixty jobs over a two-month period, fifty-six of which yielded the dreaded "don't call us, we'll call you" response. Having just gone through an extremely frustrating job search, I was very happy to be offered a position specifically designed to give me an opportunity to gain the work experience that I so obviously lacked as a brand-new librarian. I accepted the residency offer, relocated to Delaware, and began my time at the library filled with a renewed sense of enthusiasm for the opportunities that the position would allow me to explore.

The unique structure of the University of Delaware program allows residents to develop a breadth and depth of both work-related skills and professional perspective that serves participants well throughout the balance of their careers. Residents are treated exactly the same as tenure-track librarians and are expected to participate in the same professional activities that all other librarians undertake. In the first year, residents rotate through three departments, spending roughly four months in each location. During my first year, I worked in the Special Collections, Public Services, and Technical Services departments. Rotations are built around specific assignments with self-assessments and supervisor evaluations submitted upon completion of each rotation.

In the second year, residents work with supervisors to create an assignment in the department they find most interesting. This allows residents time to develop more in-depth skills in a particular area of librarianship. In addition to my residency assignments, I also served on local and national committees, attended conferences and helped create and present poster sessions. I also assisted with a user study for the University of Delaware Library website home page and lobbied Delaware legislators for additional funding for public, K–12, and university library projects statewide. The position was every bit as challenging—and also deeply satisfying—as I had hoped that it would be.

Acclimating yourself to an entirely new profession adds an additional layer of complexity because professional service outside of the library is an expected part of working life in most academic settings. For example, as a member of the American Library Association's (ALA) New Members Round Table, I helped design materials for first-time conference attendees for the 2008 Annual Conference in Anaheim, California. I also worked with the Delaware Library Association (DLA), first as a volunteer lobbyist, then as a member of the DLA Legislative Day Organizing Committee.

Attendance at conferences is also an expected part of professional librarianship in academic libraries. Between September 2006 and August 2007—my first year as a resident—I attended seven conferences, including the Joint Conference of Librarians of Color (JCLC), two DLA conferences, the ALA Annual and Midwinter Meetings, the Association of College and Research Libraries (ACRL) biannual conference, and the ACRL Rare Books and Manuscripts ALA preconference. These conferences presented opportunities to connect with other professionals, gain further education directly related to my residency assignments, and consider my own areas of interest or concern related to professional librarianship such as minority recruitment and intellectual freedom. Both professional service and continuing education allowed me to develop relationships with librarians outside of my normal work environment, and those connections have provided a valuable support network as I continue my post-residency career.

Fortunately, most residency programs are designed to account for the series of adjustments that are a part of the professional development process. My residency coordinator, Julie Brewer, was valuable both as a point of contact and as a mentor. Through her, I was able to take advantage of opportunities that were available to me early on in my residency, such as scholarships for conferences. During this time, I had to find my way through the complicated series of local, regional, and national organizations; round tables; interest groups; and committees, which were difficult to comprehend during my first few months. Without her assistance, I might have missed these opportunities.

As time went by, I was able to communicate my own emerging professional interests, which led to an incredibly rich, rewarding array of options that I could pursue. When recalling my residency period and relating my experiences to others, I found that the functional aspects of the job and the professional opportunities that I enjoyed during my time in residence were not its most significant. Instead, two major elements still stand out in my mind: getting the chance to develop an insider's view of librarianship as a professional and using the experiences that I had to help me position myself within the broad spectrum of professional pursuits that are available to every new librarian.

With those two elements in mind, I would like to offer the following advice to anyone who is either starting a residency or who might be wondering what a residency can do for them. *First, your professional training isn't over just because you have a library degree.* Almost all of us have heard, from a professor, mentor, or colleague, that your degree really only prepares you to be an "entry-level" librarian. This statement is true of most professions. Experience develops as a result of the time and effort that you invest not only in your academic credentials, but also the time and effort that you put into your professional qualifications as well. A residency is an excellent opportunity to consider what kind of expertise you would like to build on while at the same time soliciting advice from others who are already a part the profession.

Participation in conferences, workshops and professional seminars also provides opportunities for continuing your professional education. Find out whether your institution offers funding for attending events such as those sponsored by ALA, the Association of College and Research Libraries or the Society of American Archivists; if they do, take advantage of it. If they do not offer financial support, ask your supervisor, residency coordinator, or department head to offer support for scholarship or grant applications to attend events within your area of interest. Most professional library associations offer funding for new professionals to attend their annual conferences.

In addition, there are often special funding opportunities and events available for members of minority groups, such as the Minnesota Institute for Early Career Librarians from Traditionally Underrepresented Groups (Minnesota Institute) or the Joint Conference of Librarians of Color. There are also funding opportunities at nearly every conference for librarians who are interested in producing relevant research for an association in an emerging professional area, such as preserving digital materials or creating online collaborative learning spaces for university students and scholars.

Second, take advantage of as many opportunities as you can. Most residency programs give you the chance to experience numerous professional "firsts": these include research studies, poster sessions, publication opportunities, and service on local, regional, and national committees. Because of the seemingly endless array of developments that represent the ongoing evolution of both information-related technologies and the accompanying user behaviors, there are many opportunities for ground-floor work in developing areas of librarianship. The technical skills and specializations that you, as new librarians, bring with you when you are hired (or the skills that you learn while on the job) meld well with "localized" experiences.

Look for opportunities to collaborate with more experienced colleagues on research projects, presentations, and committees. Very often in these situations, both you and your coworkers will be surprised at how many interesting, relevant, workable ideas you are able to generate, as well as the talents that you display when helping to implement them. Of course, the level of new professional knowledge you gain from being a part of any first-time experience is truly immeasurable and will lead to many more positive experiences down the line. Remember that librarianship is a constantly evolving profession. Try to maintain a certain level of flexibility with regard to your professional goals and interests.

Third, look for opportunities that don't fit your original plans. You never know what the experience might lead to. Residency programs generally afford participants an enormous amount of professional freedom. There is a level of flexibility built into most programs that you are not likely to have again once your residency comes to an end. Some residents take advantage of this to adapt their residency to their interests in unique ways: creating an "ideal position" for themselves in a specific department, choosing a dual assignment across two departments, retaining an affiliation with a specific department after a rotation period ends (thereby continuing to build certain skills throughout the entire residency), or working as a liaison between the library and an academic department or specific group of scholars.

Whatever you choose, remember to look for things that present an interesting challenge, an unexpected opportunity, or an experience in an area where you have none. Even seemingly minor experiences will give you a chance to develop and display your unique set of capabilities and will help you develop rapport with other members of the profession. At the very least, keeping yourself open to having experiences that you had not planned will deepen your understanding of librarianship as a whole. In the best situations, you will create a unique, valuable area of specialization for yourself that may make a major contribution to both your institution and the entire library profession.

Of course, there are always some opportunities that end up being central to your residency experience and prove to be of immeasurable value. For example, I was accepted to the 2008 Minnesota Institute for Early Career Librarians from Traditionally Underrepresented Groups (Minnesota Institute). This is a major biannual event specifically tailored to minority librarians who work in academic libraries and have no more than three years worth of professional experience.

The Institute lasts for one week and is an intensive, small-group environment. Although the seminars and workshops that serve as the core of the institute are valuable on their own, the unplanned interactions between participants—many of which developed into long-term professional relationships—elevated the experience to a truly invaluable level. These interactions also give participants the rare chance to voice their concerns about subjects varying from professional research methods to career advancement, as well as share issues and insights, in a comfortable professional space outside of their respective daily work environments.

Fourth, learn where and how to focus your energies and look for opportunities for advancement in those areas. Given the advice about keeping your options open offered earlier, this point might seem counterintuitive, or even downright contradictory. However, there is a difference between allowing for new experiences and being overwhelmed by them. An overabundance of possible options, sometimes known as "death-by-opportunity," can create major issues. These can manifest themselves as either personal (stress, mental and physical exhaustion) or public (missed deadlines, incomplete or shoddy work) problems, or both. In addition, work-related issues, balancing a new career with personal interests, relationships, and family demands can become quite a challenge. Often, residents aren't certain what to say "yes" to and what options should be explored at a later date, or possibly passed up altogether.

Keeping in regular contact with your residency coordinator, mentor, or other trusted colleagues will help you to know when you have enough on your plate. Another good technique is to keep a journal, rough-draft CV, or other types of documentation available either on your real-world desk or on your computer's virtual desktop. Refer to it often and update it as necessary. Every once in a while, review it and see whether you can spot a narrative thread that points toward some kind of consistency within the experiences that you are having during your residency. Most programs require that residents submit a periodic review of some sort. Your documentation will serve an important purpose, as well as give you the opportunity to discuss where and how to focus your efforts with your coordinator, mentor or supervisors.

Last, library residents represent both the immediate and long-term future of librarianship. Use what you have learned to help other people understand our value as professionals. Keep in mind that you are training for a profession, not just a job position. It is important not only to learn how to be a professional librarian in the day-to-day sense but also how to participate in the profession on a larger scale. This is one of the ways in which a residency program can give you an excellent head start when it comes to your professional life. In addition to the different types of professional involvement mentioned earlier, learning how the organizational structure works within an academic setting is a major part of this period of exploration. Dealing with administrative issues such as personnel and project management eventually become a part of every librarian's job. As your future unfolds, you will need to be prepared to assume the mantle of leadership.

As your career progresses from a residency to a permanent or tenure-track position, expect major changes not only in your professional life but in your personal life as well. Learning to deal with work obligations outside of "normal" business hours, continuing education opportunities, research-related projects, recruitment efforts, library advocacy, and outreach (both inside and outside of your academic institution) are all a part of the everyday world of librarianship.

As a profession, librarianship is often not well understood by those on the outside. College or university administrators often question the necessity of employing such a large number of highly trained and, by extension, well-paid professionals within one unit, especially since the library itself is almost never a revenue-generating operation. Students may underestimate the wealth of information and professional assistance available in the library, preferring the "ease" of performing perfunctory research. The built-in transience and open-all-hours usability afforded by a wireless connection, a Web browser, and the simplest possible search interface help enable this preference.

Faculty members and other scholars, who are often overextended and don't have time to make frequent trips to the library, may resort to creating de facto libraries within their own departments. They may not realize that they are duplicating efforts to answer a set of needs—sometimes poorly and far less in-depth—that the library itself has already addressed. In addition, librarianship is often perceived as an isolated, monastic profession that does not have a strong connection to the larger academic world and nothing to contribute to the rapidly maturing technological landscape represented by the continuing development of the Web. It is vital that, from your residency onward, you learn to address these issues directly, succinctly, and in a way that generates interest in the library, as well as an understanding of its relevance to the scholarly life of the overall academic institution.

When considering all of the factors mentioned here, it is fairly clear that there is a huge learning curve for new librarians entering the profession, and it won't always be easy. However, taking full advantage of the opportunities offered during a residency can help you create a rewarding experience that will equip you to meet the professional challenges that await you, both now and well into your professional future. When my residency ended, I realized there was much more that I wanted to accomplish, especially when I considered the possibilities for archival collections on the Web.

I discovered that I wanted to teach and do research that would help library and archives professionals to meet the challenging, but nonetheless powerful, opportunities presented by the speed, flexibility and interoperability of the online universe. I believe that the library profession is in a unique position to provide insight and experience into the organization, distribution, use, and preservation of online information. I decided that my professional future lay in advocating for the continued relevance of librarianship in the digital age through teaching, research, and collaboration with other professional fields like computer science, human-computer interaction, and information technology.

After further exploration, it became clear that working toward a doctorate in library and information science was the best avenue for me to pursue my plans for the future. I realized that the additional training and education I would receive would place me in a position to help me to have an impact on the future direction of the profession overall. I would learn how to formulate theories, develop research questions, conduct scientific investigations, and write scholarly articles. All of these activities, I concluded, would help me work toward my goals regarding teaching, research, and collaboration.

About the time that I began to consider returning to school, the ALA Spectrum program announced that they were accepting applications for individuals interested in entering doctoral studies programs in library and information science. Since I was already considering getting a Ph.D. by then, I knew that I needed to take advantage of the opportunity while it was being offered. I earned my Master of Library Science degree from Simmons College and had worked closely with the archives management faculty, so I decided to apply to the Ph.D. program there. I was admitted and began the process of studying and doing research on digital curatorship for archival materials. The experience has been as enriching and rewarding as I had hoped.

Digital curatorship is the study of every aspect of the archival process as it relates to the Web: accessioning, organization, preservation, and information retrieval are all elements of a fairly broad area where librarians and archivists will have a significant presence online well into the foreseeable future. Understanding this broad-based perspective would have been much more difficult if I had not been a part of a residency program where exposure to multiple areas of librarianship (in my case, special collections, public services, and access services) is central to the overall experience.

Questions emerged during my residency. What knowledge can archivists share with Web-based organizations regarding the preservation of digital documents and other objects? Can catalogers help information retrieval specialists understand the value of controlled vocabularies and taxonomies? How can reference librarians' experiences with the informational needs and search habits of their users be marshaled to help build better online search tools? All of these put me on a path that I hope will allow me to find new, innovative answers that will help place librarianship on the leading edge of the informational universe. Whether I ultimately become a scholar, administrator, or practitioner, I am grateful that my residency allowed me both to ask questions and to use the skills that I developed to help answer them.

Chapter 13

A Law Library Residency: My Georgetown University Law Library Experience

Yasmin Morais

INTRODUCTION

The Georgetown University Law Library is the fifth largest academic law library in the United States. It comprises two distinct libraries: the Edward Bennett Williams Law Library (Williams), with a collection focused on U.S. legal resources, and the John Wolff International and Comparative Law Library (Wolff), which contains international legal resources.

The Georgetown Law Library Resident Program began in 1999 and was created to encourage candidates from underrepresented groups to pursue a career in law librarianship. The program also aims to contribute to the growth and development of newer law librarians and facilitate their contribution to the Law Center's academic life. To my knowledge, it may be the only law library residency program at this time. I was the fifth Resident Librarian hired, and my two-year residency period was July 2007 to June 2009. A sixth Resident Librarian started on July 1, 2009. Two of the five alumni of the Georgetown Residency Program are currently working in law libraries, two are in general academic libraries, and one is believed to be working with a private company.

MY ROAD TO LIBRARIANSHIP

Librarianship is my second career. In December 1999, I moved to Toronto, Canada, as a self-sponsored immigrant from Jamaica, convinced that my master's degree in international relations, fluency in Spanish, and nine years of project management experience with the United Nations Development Program would open many employment doors for me. They did not. Underemployed and frustrated, I stumbled upon the University of Toronto's master's program in information studies while searching for doctoral programs in political science. I was intrigued by the program description. I had never considered librarianship, but libraries had always been a welcoming space for me. I decided to enroll in the program in September 2004, first on a part-time basis, and was later allowed to switch to full time to complete the program quickly.

I had many serendipitous experiences at the University of Toronto, which, looking back, paved the way for some of my successes as a library student, and later during my residency program at the Georgetown Law Library. Among the first was an announcement via the faculty's listserv, which described the Association of Research Libraries' (ARL) Initiative to Recruit a Diverse Workforce (IRDW). As a Canadian citizen, I was not sure if I could apply for the scholarship. My early inquiries to the former coordinator of the program, Jerome Offord, led to my application for, and receipt of, a scholarship which not only afforded me financial support, but also leadership training, networking opportunities, mentorship, and a visit to an academic library.

I was the first University of Toronto library student to participate in the IRDW program. My status as an ARL Diversity Scholar broadened my network and opportunities to meet Diversity Scholars like myself. I met many of these scholars at a leadership seminar, held in conjunction with the American Library Association Midwinter meeting in San Antonio, Texas as well as an introduction to an academic library during a four-day symposium at Purdue University Libraries. I have remained in contact with many of the ARL scholars and have developed close friendships with some.

I knew from the beginning of my program that I wanted to work in an academic library. By my second year, however, I was certain that I wanted to pursue a residency program. My mentor, aware of this interest, recommended a book that she had coedited, *In Our Own Voices: The Changing Face of Librarianship* (another eye-opener for me), and I read with keen interest the residency experiences of the librarians in this publication. Having had no library experience before my library school program, I was convinced that I would benefit from a program that provided an opportunity to see the library in its totality. In addition, I would be able to explore a variety of interests that might not be possible while in a permanent, full-time job. I also felt that a residency program would allow me to determine whether academia was where I truly wanted to be.

In the final year of my program, I took a course on legal librarianship. This was to prove advantageous in my application to the Georgetown Law Library Residency Program. I had worked in a law firm in Jamaica, as well as completed a course in international law as a requirement of my master's in international relations, so the legal field was familiar to me. The legal librarianship course, however, was from a different perspective and provided me with a foundation in the organization of legal information, research, and writing. This course also provided exposure to legal databases such as Westlaw and Lexis and class discussions about careers in law librarianship.

THE JOB SEARCH

My job-searching experience was more positive and less stressful than I imagined it would be. Holding a full-time job at the time helped and afforded me the opportunity to search at my own pace. I also kept an open mind about relocating, so I cast a wide geographic net. Of my three applications (University of Calgary, University of New Mexico, and the Georgetown University Law Library), Georgetown was the only one that not only extended an opportunity for an interview but also offered me the two-year Resident Librarian position.

The Georgetown vacancy announcement came via my faculty's listserv, midway during my legal librarianship course. How fortuitous was that?! In addition to the cover letter and resume, the application process required submission of my library school transcript, and a personal statement. One important point here for future residents who may be interested in law librarianship is to not discount or omit previous related activities or courses. For example, I had omitted from the first draft of my personal statement to Georgetown my experience working in a law firm, as well as the Law of the Sea course I had taken, and then realized these were relevant. I was extremely overwhelmed and grateful to be offered an interview at such a prestigious university, and my interview followed my first ACRL conference in Baltimore, Maryland, in March 2007. I was also fortunate that my job offer was made a month before the completion of my library program. I was better able to focus on the completion and presentation of my projects and my final exams without the added stress of job hunting.

THE RESIDENCY

My open approach to relocating made my move from Toronto to Washington, DC, fairly smooth. I decided to reside in Maryland, a fairly easy commute to the Georgetown Law Library, and I had approximately three weeks to spare before my start date of July 1, 2007.

The Georgetown Law Library Residency Program is well structured, with an institutional commitment to the program. In year one, the resident must complete the reference and cataloging rotations. During the second year, the resident can choose from rotations in Collection Services, Special Collections, Administration, or International Law with ongoing participation in reference shifts, a feature of the residency. At the end of each rotation, the resident completes a self-assessment, and a performance evaluation is then completed by the department head. During the final year, the resident must also complete a project which can be instructional or research in nature.

I credit my smooth transition and great start in the program to the work of the Residency Committee. The chair of the Residency Committee remained in constant contact with me following the formal job offer and provided me with useful information and links regarding relocation as well as upcoming orientation and conference registrations. I therefore felt well prepared and informed on my first day on the job.

It should be noted that the residency committee consists of eight members, two of whom were added after my first year. In the second year of the residency, the Resident Librarian serves as an ex-officio member, extending total membership to nine. The Resident's participation on this committee includes being a part of the search committee for the incoming Resident Librarian.

Throughout my two-year residency, this committee served as a resource for me with respect to any issues related to my rotations, evaluation, mentorship, professional development, and any other concerns related to my residency. The committee meetings were always a welcoming space for me to seek guidance concerning the residency and to raise any concerns. I was also assigned a mentor who was not a part of the committee itself. This allowed me to bond with an experienced librarian, who provided guidance throughout my residency on professional development opportunities, the job search, and any other professional or personal issues I wanted to discuss.

YEAR ONE: LEARNING THE ROPES

The Reference Rotation

The structure of the two-year residency allows for continuous participation in the reference shifts, and therefore the Reference Department could be described as the resident's home department. The resident's first rotation starts in reference and lasts for approximately six months. Initially, I had an orientation session with the Head of Reference and was allowed to sit with experienced reference librarians at the reference desk before being scheduled for shifts on my own. During the busy fall semester, reference is double staffed, so I was able to work at the second reference desk alongside an experienced librarian.

The Georgetown Law Library's reference department is an extremely busy one, serving the research and reference needs of students, faculty, alumni, and members of its public patron program. Faculty and students at the Georgetown University main campus who are conducting legal research or pursuing law courses are also served. The public patron program provides access to the library's onsite collection as well as reference service through an annual membership for government agencies, law firms, nonprofit institutions, and other organizations. In addition to its full-time Juris Doctor (JD) program, the Law Center also has a fairly large part-time program and offers a number of advanced degrees such as the Master of Law (LLM), Master of Studies in Law (MSL), which is aimed specifically at working journalists, and the Doctor of Juridical Science (SJD). The Law Center also offers a paralegal program.

Reference services are provided via the reference desk, telephone, e-mail, and virtual (chat) reference. Shift rotations include staffing both the Williams and Wolff reference desks. My reference duties during my first year involved working evenings and weekends. During the second year of the program, the resident does not work weekend shifts. This policy was established a few years after the program started, based on the suggestions of previous residents to allow for more time to be available for residents to focus on completing the final project. Some of my early assignments in the reference department included the updating of state research guides, which allowed me to become familiar with state codes and key print and electronic resources for researching state laws.

The learning curve was a fairly steep one. The supportive environment, however, made learning easy. The library's commitment to the professional development of the resident allowed me to carve out time for conference attendance, research, and publication. At the very start of my residency, for example, I was given the opportunity to attend my first annual American Association of Law Libraries (AALL) conference in New Orleans in July 2007.

One of the features of this conference is the segment devoted to newer law librarians, called the Conference of Newer Law Librarians (CONELL). CONELL can be described as a conference within a conference, and its aim is to welcome new members of AALL and to introduce them to the association and its leadership. Another objective of CONELL is to allow newer law librarians to meet each other in an informal setting, which it is hoped will lead to the establishment of lasting connections. At this session, I was able to network with my peers while learning about their paths to law librarianship and their experiences in their respective libraries.

In addition to the introduction to AALL, the library paid for my membership in the Law Librarians Society of Washington, DC (LLSDC). This is an active organization of law librarians in the DC area, and I benefitted from their professional development initiatives, as well as opportunities to meet other librarians at social events sponsored by the association. Later in my residency, I also had the opportunity to contribute an article on my residency experience in the association's journal (Morais 2008b).

The first year of my residency was a productive one for research and publication. I was asked to create two new research guides, Native American Law, and Gender and the Law, both of which were my first in-house publications on the library's website (Georgetown University Law Library). Reflecting on my residency, the many opportunities to publish stand out. Following on the publication of the guides described earlier, I took advantage of my professional development time and created a guide to the Caribbean Court of Justice (Morais 2008a). I was aware of this new court but realized there were no current guides especially in light of recent developments related to the court and Caribbean jurisprudence, specifically regarding the role of the United Kingdom Privy Council as a court of last resort. I approached the editor of an online journal about the idea, and there was instant interest, which lead to the publication of the guide.

To current or future residents, I would like to stress that you should never be hesitant to approach editors about ideas you may have for articles. From my experience, editors are always interested in ideas for their journals and welcome your suggestions for relevant content. I was motivated by the publication of my article to conduct even further research, while gaining the confidence to continue writing for publication. We are all aware how important publication is for tenure track librarians.

Librarians at the Georgetown Law Library have faculty status, and as such, teaching was another responsibility I picked up during my first rotation, which, as mentioned earlier, was in reference. I was given the opportunity to conduct training labs on the Westlaw and Lexis legal databases, as a part of the Legal Research and Writing component which first year law students must complete. This experience was quite beneficial to me, as it strengthened my own knowledge of these databases and allowed me to be even more proficient in my searching at the reference desk.

Cataloging Department Rotation

At the end of my six months in the reference department, I moved on to my rotation in the Cataloging Department. I was actually very excited about this rotation for a number of reasons. In my library program, I had to take a compulsory course on cataloging. This course turned out to be strictly theoretical and did not allow for any practical exposure to cataloging. I was, therefore, looking forward to being able to see the practical applications of the theoretical knowledge I had learned in the cataloging course. Another reason had to do with my growing interest and desire to obtain a job that would allow me to perform both cataloging and reference duties after my residency, a rare combination in a lot of libraries.

The cataloging rotation turned out to be one of my favorites in the two-year residency. I was pleasantly surprised at how much I liked cataloging, and my colleagues at Georgetown were surprised as well. They commented that I was the first resident to exhibit such a keen interest in technical services. During this rotation, I acquired a greater understanding of AACR2, Library of Congress subject headings, MARC 21, and OCLC searching. I became proficient in copy cataloging and also had some opportunities to attempt upgrades and original cataloging.

During this rotation, I also attended an in-house workshop on cataloging rare books and other special collections resources. I must also point out that a good foundation was laid for my cataloging rotation in that the Head of Cataloging actually identified a number of workshops offered by the OCLC CAPCON Service Center in Washington, DC, prior to the start of my rotation. I also collaborated with Marylin Raisch, the Associate Law Librarian for International and Foreign Law, to compile the most significant foreign, comparative, and international law articles of the past one hundred years, on behalf of the Foreign, Comparative and International Law Special Interest Section (Morais and Raisch 2008). This compilation commemorated the *Law Library Journal*'s

100th anniversary in 2008. My interest in and satisfaction with the rotation led to a personal request to extend my rotation two additional months, making my total time in the department eight months.

Special Collections

My next rotation was in the Special Collections Department. The Georgetown Law Library has a strong and extensive rare books and manuscripts collection, primarily in American and British resources. I was enthusiastic about this rotation because of several U.S. History, Latin American History, and Development of Civilizations history courses I had completed as an undergraduate. In library school, I had also wanted to take a course called Rare Books and Manuscripts, but because of its popularity, there was always a long wait list, and I was never able to enroll. My duties included assisting patrons at the Special Collections reference desk, reshelving, reviewing rare book catalogs and cross-checking our catalog for items, scanning, and, my biggest project of all, the creation of a research guide on Scottish Legal History, a topic I personally chose.

The Scottish Legal History guide was an exciting project for me, with my interest stemming from a brief visit to Scotland and a fascination with its history. During the course of my research for the guide, I discovered that Georgetown actually has a large collection of rare Scottish legal materials. I created a comprehensive guide tracing the early development of Scots Law, and highlighted the print and electronic resources available to scholars of Scottish legal history. I also approached an editor about the possibility of publishing a version of the guide, and my suggestion was enthusiastically received by the editor, who later published the article in the online legal journal *Globalex* (Morais 2008c). The department head also suggested that I attempt the library's first online exhibit and along with the Electronic Resources Librarian and Special Collections Assistant, I produced an online exhibit, "Early Modern Famous Scottish Trials."

This rotation turned out to be a busy and productive one for me, and I was pleased with what I learned about special collections and the projects mentioned earlier. The rotation also sharpened my reference skills because it made me more aware of the print and electronic sources available to assist patrons with historical legal research.

YEAR TWO: TOWARD PROFICIENCY

Collection Services

In my final year of the residency, I started my last rotation in Collection Services. I chose this rotation because I had completed a collection development course in library school and felt that this was an area that would round out my experience. I was also aware that several job advertisements were stressing experience in collection development and I wanted exposure to current issues in this area. This rotation turned out to be very satisfying. I worked on an exhibit and conducted a collection analysis of the library's DVD collection, comparing our collection with that of four other law libraries. I also worked on an assessment of our DVDs on professional responsibility, in response to a faculty member's request for updated DVDs in this area. In addition, I identified resources for new selectors, attended selection committee meetings, and became more familiar with OCLC tools for collection analysis.

My Final Project

Throughout my second year, my reference duties continued and a large part of my time was also occupied with the identification and completion of my research project. At the start of my residency, I was intrigued by the chat reference service, because I had never used it prior to my Georgetown residency. I decided to look at how chat reference was being utilized by students, faculty, and alumni over a one-year period.

For this project, I retrieved chat transcripts for the period covering January to December 2008 and coded them based on the user and the specific type of reference query being asked. The Head of Reference, Sara Sampson, was enthusiastic about the project, because the chat service had not been evaluated since implementation in 2005. A small team, including Sara, assisted me with the coding of the transcripts.

At the end of the coding and cross-checking, I entered the data into an Excel spreadsheet and analyzed the findings. The exciting results gave us a greater understanding of how the service was being utilized along with descriptions of the users' queries. We also attained deeper insight about the types of resources that were in demand and what faculty and students were researching. I made two presentations of my findings to library staff. Upon completion of the project, Sara and I collaborated on an article, "A Content Analysis of Chat Transcripts in the Georgetown Law Library" (Morais and Sampson 2010). In addition the project was also submitted to and accepted by the AALL for its July 2009 annual conference, which would serve as my first conference presentation.

Professional Development Support

Professional development support continued in my second year, and instead of the AALL conference, I opted to attend my first American Library Association annual conference, held in Anaheim, California, in June 2008. Georgetown provided one hundred percent of the support for my conference attendance. I was also able to benefit from a newly instituted two-week mini-sabbatical, approved by the Scholarly Writing Committee, which facilitated my completion of the draft article on the findings of the chat research project. This two-week scholarly leave was tremendously beneficial, because the time allowed me to focus on the completion of the article.

The Residency Search Committee and My Own Job Search

My second year proved to be both exciting and stressful with my project, committee meetings, reference desk rotations, collection development rotation, and conference attendance, in addition to telephone and on-site interviews related to my own job search. As the residency drew to a close, I became very involved in the search committee work for the recruitment of a new Resident Librarian. This was an interesting experience for me, because I was conducting my personal job search. I had never been on a search committee before, so the experience provided me with great insight on what search committees look for in a candidate, as well as the interview and selection process.

One of the main lessons learned from my involvement with the search committee was how to be objective in narrowing candidates from an extremely large pool. I had to review many resumes and therefore had to focus on the specific qualifications and attributes that the committee required for a short list. I also had to conduct reference checks as well as arrange and attend luncheons with candidates.

Throughout this time, my own mentor worked hard to assist me with identifying jobs, fine-tuning my resume, and posing some mock interview questions to me. My mentor was exceptional in that she invested a great deal of her personal time in assisting me in my search. She was actually my second mentor; my first had accepted a new position in a law library in North Carolina about six months after I started. Both of my mentors were initially approached by the Chair of the Residency Committee to serve as mentors, and they both willingly accepted the role.

Although I wanted to remain in a law library, with the possibility of performing both cataloging and reference duties, I remained open to general academic library positions. In the end, I received two telephone interviews and was invited to four on-site interviews. Two such interview offers were from law libraries—one for a Reference Librarian, and the other for a Cataloging Librarian. After careful consideration of my personal circumstances and my professional preference, I chose to remain in the Washington, DC, area and was pleased to accept the Cataloging Librarian position at the David A. Clarke School of Law Library at the University of the District of Columbia. In addition to my core cataloging functions, this position involves participation in reference rotations, some collection development duties, as well as faculty liaison responsibilities to two of the law professors.

CONCLUSION

My residency at the Georgetown Law Library was an extremely rewarding one. It allowed me to hone my skills in reference, teaching, cataloging, special collections, and collection development. In my two years there, I published six articles, made two internal library presentations, and gave my first conference presentation. I was also a part of a three-member team to create a treatise finder, which helps first-year students locate legal treatises. My learning environment was stimulating as well as nurturing. Seasoned librarians took me under their wings and taught me so much, and to them I am grateful.

I viewed all of my rotations as learning labs and was so eager for knowledge that I soaked up everything like a sponge. I looked for ways to challenge myself and to explore opportunities for growth and development. Along the way, my personal network and library connections grew, and I gained some personal friends and lifelong colleagues. I would certainly recommend the Georgetown Law Library Residency program for people who are interested in law librarianship or may have taken legal courses but are unsure of the demands and challenges of working in a law library.

For those interested in technical services, there is the opportunity to gain competence in cataloging legal resources whether they are general in nature or rare/special collections. For people with an interest in public services, there is the possibility of reference and teaching, particularly for librarians who also hold the JD qualification.

Law librarianship is an interesting specialization for librarians, and one that is growing, given the importance of the law in all aspects of our lives and emerging legal issues. Although it is a specialized area of librarianship, within this specialization, there is also room for even further subspecialization. Law librarians work in academic, court, county, and law firm libraries. They also work with vendors as catalogers or marketing and support specialists. The residency opened my eyes to the range of career possibilities, and it also allowed me to find my own niche as a professional librarian. One of the memorable highlights of my time at Georgetown was being presented with a certificate on the completion of my residency by the dean of our law school.

It is my hope that this essay will provide inspiration and guidance for current or future residents, particularly those who may be considering a career in law librarianship. Early on in my residency, I decided that I was going to take ownership of it and try to acquire as much experience as I could. Although a good program structure was in place, I was responsible for my own learning. Not all residencies are created equal, and being a part of the ACRL Residency Interest Group has revealed a variety of residency structures and experiences.

Having a positive attitude and a proactive approach, however, can go a long way in making your residency experience worthwhile. Don't be afraid to take on challenges. Ask many questions and own your residency. I knew, for example, that I would benefit from two more months in the Cataloging Department. I asked for the extension and got it. Take advantage of any opportunities for mentorship. Although I had two very special mentors, I always felt that every colleague at Georgetown was my mentor and had something to teach me—and they did. I feel fortunate to have participated in a post-MLS residency program after graduation; if I had to do it all over again, I would definitely opt for a residency program.

REFERENCES

Morais, Y. 2008a. The Caribbean court of justice: A research guide. *LLRX.com* (February 27). http://www.llrx.com/features/caribbeancourtofjustice.htm

Morais, Y. 2008b. Learning the ropes: A resident librarian reflects on law librarianship. *Law Library Lights* Summer: 9–11.

Morais, Y. 2008c. Scottish legal history: A research guide. *Globalex* (Nov/Dec 2008). http://www.nyulawglobal.org/globalex/Scottish_Legal_History.htm

Morais, Y. 2009. Down the up escalator: Finding worklife balance. *AALL Spectrum* 13:20–21.

Morais, Y., and M. Raisch. 2008. Foreign, comparative and international law SIS. *Law Library Journal* 100:714–725.

Morais, Y., and S. Sampson. 2009. Chat 2:0: Renovating virtual reference. Paper presented at the annual meeting of the American Association of Law Libraries, Washington, DC, July 25–28, 2009.

Morais, Y., and S. Sampson. 2010. A content analysis of chat transcripts in the Georgetown Law Library. *Legal Reference Services Quarterly* 29:165–168.

Neely, T. Y., and K. A. Khafre, eds. 1996. *In Our Own Voices: The Changing Face of Librarianship*. Lanham, MD: Scarecrow Press.

Chapter 14

Recollections of a Resident

Patrick José Dawson

The United States is a diverse nation—diverse in geography, climate, and population. According to a May 2008 Census Bureau Report covering estimates for 2007, slightly more than one-third of the population of the United States claimed "minority" racial or ethnic heritage (America.gov). Compare that with the 2000 census in which the Caucasian population composed 77.1 percent of the total population (U.S. Census Bureau). In only seven years, the Caucasian population has declined to 66 percent of the total population.

The fastest growing population in the United States is Latino/Hispanic. This population already comprises the highest proportion of the total population in the state of New Mexico. By midcentury, the highest proportion of the total population in the states of California and Texas will also be Latino/Hispanic. One of the problems in higher education today is that the population of students in higher education does not reflect the diversity of the population of the United States. According to the U.S. Department of Education, National Center for Education Statistics' website, underrepresented minorities (URMs) compose 34 percent of the U.S. population, while URMs compose only 22 percent of the undergraduate student population. However, only 9 percent of the faculty at institutions of higher education represent underrepresented minorities. For libraries, the numbers are similar.

The My SA News website reports that in 1990, there were approximately 200,881 professional librarians defined as those holding master's degrees compared with 190,255 in 2000, a 5.3 percent decline. Minorities made up a fraction of the 1990 total number: African Americans (15,500), American Indian/Alaska natives (904), Asian and Pacific Islanders (6,787), and Latino/Hispanics

(6,164). In 1990, approximately 171,470 were Caucasian. Only Latino/Hispanics are increasing their numbers in libraries, and not by much. There were 206 more Latino/Hispanic librarians in 2000 than in 1990.

In 2007, the Association of College and Research Libraries (ACRL) released a white paper, coauthored by Teresa Neely, Director of the University of New Mexico's Zimmerman Library, and Lorna Peterson, Associate Professor of Library and Information Studies at the University of Buffalo (Neely and Peterson 2007). *Library Journal*'s website highlights some of the paper's suggestions for achieving diversity:

- Develop a comprehensive, collaborative recruitment and public awareness campaign for recruitment, eliminating duplication and channeling all efforts through one resource. The nursing profession, which also suffers from a chronic staffing shortage, provides a "fully developed, functional, and proven successful model" with discovernursing.com, a project of various national nurses' organizations and Johnson & Johnson. The proposed clearinghouse of information should be accompanied by print, radio, and TV recruitment ads.

- Retain minority librarians by creating a welcoming and flexible environment that considers work culture issues, honors employee values and opinions, offers compensation and rewards, provides good management, and recognizes the need for work-life balance. All hires benefit from such an environment, the report notes, but it is "especially significant for retention of minority hires" because those staffers often lack a built-in support network.

- Advance minority hires to management positions. As the authors note, this is one topic an earlier ACRL white paper on recruitment and retention did not address (ACRL 2002). Ways to groom minority staff for leadership roles include providing opportunities for mentoring and shadowing leaders, soliciting nominations for awards and recognition, doing job rotations, and providing support for participation in fellowships and institutes. The report also recommends tracking openings for top jobs and the "available leadership pool" of minority candidates and developing subsequent data reports. The goal is to create "a system of accountability regarding the retention and advancement of underrepresented groups in libraries."

We are all aware of these problems and of the fact that we need to recruit this population actively into the library profession. Yet at the same time, it is our responsibility to mentor and help these librarians become successful and develop into library leaders. In this chapter, I want to relate how I became Dean of Libraries at Northern Illinois University as a sort of lesson on what can be done to help diversify the ranks of professional librarians and move underrepresented librarians into leadership roles.

In September 1985, I was a newly minted librarian having just received my Masters of Library Science degree from the University of Arizona. I was fortunate that my library education was funded from a Higher Education Act Title II-B grant administered through the University of Arizona. This grant funding was a spin-off from the Graduate Library Institute for Spanish-Speaking Americans (GLISSA), established at the University of Arizona Graduate Library School (as it was known in the 1970s) by Dr. Arnulfo Trejo in 1975. Funding for GLISSA was provided by a U.S. Department of Education grant.

Although GLISSA only lasted four years, it was a visionary, innovative program and many current librarians benefited from GLISSA including colleagues such as Salvador Güereña, a former REFORMA (the National Association to Promote Library & Information Services to Latinos and the Spanish Speaking) president. The University of Arizona continued to secure Title II-B funding to educate members of underrepresented groups in Library Science and continues to do so now through its Knowledge River program.

When I decided to pursue a degree in library science, I did my share of shopping for programs with available funding for students. I was pleased that I was accepted at Arizona and was sure that the graduate program would benefit me in the future when it came time to secure employment. The program at Arizona was a very good one, covering aspects of librarianship that were new to me. The faculty was up-to-date on the latest trends in libraries and also well versed in the fundamentals of librarianship, such as cataloging and classification. Although the program lasted only a calendar year for me, a lot was packed into that year.

When I entered the job market, I was mobile and willing to consider employment at any location. So I began my quest to become an employed professional librarian. Because I am a native of New Mexico, I initially hoped to stay in the Southwest, but I decided to work in an academic library. My options, consequently, were limited for that geographic area. The job prospects in 1985 were encouraging, yet most advertised positions in academic libraries asked for previous experience. I had paraprofessional experience, but no professional, post-MLS library experience.

This was before the Internet, so webinars and search engines were not available to learn about available work experiences. Also, this was before employment blogs, online lists, and commercial e-mail notices. I was dependent on the job announcements that came to the University of Arizona and the ads in the *Chronicle of Higher Education* and *American Libraries*. What I had at my disposal were the telephone, print job notices, campus job placement centers, and the U.S. Postal Service, all of which I fully utilized.

About one month before graduation, Dr. Margaret Maxwell, then acting director of the Graduate School of Library Science (as it was known in the 1980s), called me into her office. I was concerned our meeting may be related to my coursework, academic standing, or ability to complete my degree. The meeting had nothing to do with these concerns. Rather, Dr. Maxwell informed me of an interesting new program for which I might qualify and benefit. The University of California at Santa Barbara (UCSB) had created a minority internship program, and the University Librarian at the time, Dr. Joseph Boissé, was notifying the various graduate programs in library science of the new UCSB Internship program.

This sounded intriguing; I saw it would be a way to obtain professional experience, and it was also an entry-level professional position. I contacted the library at UCSB, and they requested a statement of purpose, my transcripts, and a resume. When I sent the required documentation, I was interviewed by telephone by Dr. Boissé and the search committee. A few days later (which at the time seemed like weeks), I received a call informing me that I was one of two candidates selected to be the first interns at UCSB. Martha Henderson from Kent State University was the other intern selected. We were both to start on September 16, 1985.

To be honest, librarianship was not my first career choice; it was something that circumstances brought me into. Like many with a bachelor's degree in the social sciences, job prospects were slim in the late 1970s, and, like many with a degree in the social sciences, I believed my prospects for employment would be enhanced by obtaining a graduate degree. I therefore entered graduate school at the University of New Mexico (UNM) and completed my master's degree in history in 1980. By the time I received my MA, I sorely needed full-time employment.

I was able to obtain a position in the Acquisitions Department of the Zimmerman Library at the University of New Mexico, which opened up the world of academic libraries to me. Granted, as an undergraduate and graduate student, I had been a regular library user and asked my share of questions when seeking help for assignments and research, but I really had no idea how libraries actually worked. The behind-the-scenes perspective of a library is very different for those seeking information than for those who deliver information. Now I was beginning to learn about acquiring, classifying, and delivering information, not simply consuming it. Over time, I became interested in library work and decided to try for another position in the library that would allow me to use my language skills.

The University of New Mexico has a Latin American and Iberian Studies Program and Institute, and an extensive library collection of Iberian and Latin American materials. When the position became available in 1981, my ability to read both Spanish and Portuguese made it possible for me to become a copy cataloger. I enjoyed working with these library materials and especially enjoyed being part of the university community and environment. After about a year and a half, the head of the Cataloging Department at UNM and my supervisor talked to me about obtaining a graduate degree in library science, something that up to that time I had not considered. The fact that the profession needed diversification was a plus and piqued my interested in pursuing an education in library science.

After this mini-recruitment session, there was, coincidently, a visit to the UNM library by recruiters—one from the UCLA Library Science Program and another from the University of Arizona's Library School. Things were coming together, and the time was right to get serious about an education in library science. All of this started the chain of events from shopping for a library school, to securing funding for the education, and to becoming a librarian. The next step was to become an employed librarian, and that is where the UCSB program came in.

The advantage of being the first in a new internship program was that Martha Henderson, the other intern, and I were able to influence the design of the program and its outcomes. On the other hand, that also meant there would be a series of trials and errors in the mechanics of the program. One of the first changes made was the length of the appointment in the program. Because both Ms. Henderson and I were given a one-year appointment, we were applying for permanent positions halfway into the year, and that became more important than our learning experiences.

This problem was recognized by the administration, and currently the internship is a two-year appointment. This decision was based on our experiences and applied to the intern that followed us in 1986. The other change that was made is that candidates are now brought on campus and interviewed by a committee rather than relying solely on a telephone interview. This change was made to acquaint the candidates with the interview processes that they would most likely go through in their future.

The UCSB program focused on promoting and recruiting librarians of color into academic libraries. This would allow program participants to gain professional work experience, build their skills and resume, and make them more employable when seeking a permanent professional position. The interns were expected to learn and manage the job requirements of a professional librarian. They earned the same salary as an entry-level academic librarian, but they were also expected to contribute on the same level as permanent professionals.

During the program year, we spent the first four months working on the reference desk to gain public service experience. We were also paired with a librarian to present bibliographic instruction classes. Later, a second pairing was made with a subject specialist to learn about collection development and management of collection budgets. Two components of the UCSB internship I very much appreciated were excellent professional development support and opportunities to network with other professional librarians and teaching faculty. For example, the head of the library committed to funding conference registration, travel expenses, and a per diem for us. As new librarians living in Santa Barbara, California, one of the more expensive housing markets in California, neither Ms. Henderson nor I had much in the way of disposable income so this support was invaluable.

The other component was networking. Dr. Boissé introduced both of us to other library administrators in the University of California system and his colleagues in the American Library Association (ALA). Through these contacts, we were both able to secure memberships on ALA committees. This assistance was sincerely appreciated. A second practical application and benefit of this networking component was the ability to meet teaching faculty through the subject specialist librarians and learn about faculty expectations of the library. At the same time, we developed inroads and insight into the workings of the university community.

Often, new librarians, who themselves were recently graduate students, can be intimidated by the prospect of talking to faculty about teaching and research. Having a mentor available to introduce us to their colleagues made the transition of student to professional much smoother and less intimidating. In most academic libraries, librarians, whether faculty or academic employees, are reviewed in a manner similar to the teaching faculty. It was useful to be able to talk to other librarians and faculty about the review process.

The UCSB program has the interns go through a review cycle after their first year. It is consistent with the timetable for assistant librarians and helps prepare the interns for future reviews. University service is weighed in the review process as well, and the ability to become involved early in one's career helped pave the way for future involvement in local, state, and national committee activities.

When Ms. Henderson and I arrived at UCSB, we were as new as the internship program. Many members of the staff had no idea what we were supposed to do or how they were to interact with us. We were librarians but not in permanent positions. Some thought we were still students in a student intern position, and others thought we were window dressing. Dr. Boissé made sure that the staff of the library engaged with us on a professional level. We met with him quarterly and interacted with our mentors on a consistent basis as Dr. Boissé was committed to the success of this program as well as our individual success as librarians.

How, then, did the UCSB program originate? In 1984, Raymond Sawyer, then Vice Chancellor for Academic Affairs, wanted to promote diversity in hiring and retention on the Santa Barbara campus. To achieve this goal, he was willing to provide financial assistance. Dr. Boissé, recently hired as the University Librarian at UCSB, decided to act on this offer, and thus the UCSB internship was conceived.

Initially, funding for salaries and professional development were provided from three sources: the Office of Vice Chancellor for Academic Affairs, the Office of Affirmative Action (as it was known then), and the UCSB Libraries. In subsequent years, and for a number of reasons, funding for the internship from sources other than the library began to diminish. Rather than let the internship wither, Dr. Boissé made funding for the program a permanent part of the library budget.

Over the course of my career, I have seen the issue of diversity addressed and promptly forgotten, for diversity is often addressed as a one-time "feel good" program. It would have been easy to start the UCSB internship program, run it for a year or two, use the justification that there was no funding available to let the internship fade away, and then claim we did something for diversity. However, diversity is not a short-term project, it is a lifelong commitment. To the credit of the UCSB Library, there have been two University Librarians since Dr. Boissé retired, and both have been committed to continuing the program.

Because of the success of the UCSB program, the University of California, through the Office of the President, started a system-wide internship program for diversifying the librarian population in 1990. This program would place newly graduated librarians at a University of California (UC) campus in the northern and southern part of the state. The dividing line between north and south campuses for the University of California is between UC Santa Barbara and UC Santa Cruz. Salaries and benefits would come from the Office of the President. To qualify for the program, a campus simply needed to accept and accommodate the intern and to offer him or her professional development support.

During 1990, UC Santa Cruz and UC Irvine each accepted an intern. Despite the success of the program and of the interns, I find it disappointing that this program was terminated in 1992 because of "financial constraints." It is curious that, of the ten UC campuses, UCSB remains the only one that still supports this type of program.

In 1986, both Martha and I completed our internships and moved on to permanent positions. Ms. Henderson moved on to a career at Temple University, and I remained with the University of California. I first moved on to an original cataloguer position at the Riverside campus and then on to a reference position at the Irvine campus. Throughout these moves, I maintained my relationship with the internship at UCSB. When the next intern arrived in 1986, I went to Santa Barbara to orient and assist the intern in whatever way I could. The new intern and I would talk often about goals and expectations, along with the experiences of both myself and Ms. Henderson. I did not expect at the time that I would return to UCSB in the future.

To date, fifteen individuals have completed the UCSB Internship, including myself and Ms. Henderson, and there is currently an intern working there. I believe that the program is successful because of the accomplishments of all who have completed the program. The UCSB Internship "graduates" hold positions at Texas A&M University as the head of Collection Development, the University of Michigan as the Romance Languages and Literatures Librarian, Northeastern University as a Subject Specialist Librarian, Stanford University as Latin American and Chicana/o Studies Librarian, and at other institutions in the state of California and beyond.

Despite these successes, the UCSB Internship has gone through challenging times as well. The original name in 1985 was the Minority Internship Program. In 1992, it was changed to the Minority Fellowship Program to reflect the fact that participants had already earned their graduate degree and the term "fellow" better reflected this than "intern." In 1996, California voters passed Proposition 209, the proposal of the then University of California Regent Ward Connerly. This proposition amended the California State Constitution to prohibit public institutions from considering race, sex, or ethnicity in admission and hiring.

The term "minority," therefore, had to be dropped from the program title, and it is now known as the UCSB Library Fellowship Program. Proposition 209 was reflective of a mood shift against affirmative action that has long been a threat to programs such as the UCSB Library Fellowship Program. In 1978, the Supreme Court ruled on the *Regents of the University of California v. Bakke*, which held that whereas affirmative action systems are constitutional, a quota system based on race is unconstitutional (*Regents v. Bakke*). This has been an issue that has challenged programs that are intent on diversifying populations and encouraging equality.

I returned to UCSB in 1993 to become head of the Colección Tloque Nahuaque (Chicano Studies Collection) and remained active and involved with the internship program until I departed California in 2008. During that time, I was involved in the selection, training, and mentoring of interns. This has been rewarding and fulfilling work, through which I have met wonderful colleagues.

Besides the UCSB program, another program I became associated with that is not a residency program but that has been beneficial is the Association of Research Libraries (ARL) Leadership and Career Development Program (LCDP). I was fortunate to be in the first class of participants in 1998. The program is an 18-month, intensive study for midcareer librarians from underrepresented racial and ethnic groups who show promise in assuming leadership roles in ARL libraries. The ARL, ALA, and ACRL have all demonstrated a firm commitment to diversifying the population of professional librarians through various initiatives including the ALA Spectrum Initiative and the ARL Initiative to Recruit a Diverse Workforce.

Currently, I am Dean of Libraries at Northern Illinois University. I believe my success in becoming a library director can be attributed to the internship program at UCSB and to the ARL LCDP program. These programs, and the generous time and effort of the many individuals who have mentored and coached me during my career, have had a direct influence on my success and achievements. Currently, I am working with the administration of Northern Illinois University to develop a residency program and to continue the effort to attract, retain, and promote diversity in the academic library community.

What, then, are some lessons to be learned from all of this? The first lesson regards the power of recruitment. Keeping my own recruitment at UNM in mind, I have often talked to student and library employees about becoming a librarian. It is up to all of us, as librarians, to recruit the underrepresented into the library profession. We, as librarians, have a pool of students and staff to recruit from in all of our libraries.

Second is the power of funding. We, as librarians, need to ensure that programs such as Title II-B funding are continued. The Library Education and Human Resource Development Program, Title II-B of the Higher Education Act of 1965, is authorized to make awards for fellowships, institutes, and traineeships for the study of library and information science. And don't forget that we can personally contribute to scholarships at institutions that have graduate programs in library science or scholarships offered through ALA.

Third is the power of residency programs. I have recounted how the UCSB program has benefited my development in the field of professional librarianship. There are other successes at other institutions that have residency programs as well. Librarians need to encourage our own, as well as other institutions, to develop and/or maintain residency programs as these programs are a proven way to advance the careers of underrepresented groups into the profession. Consequently, I can say that the experience of the UCSB internship cemented my commitment to diversifying the population of professional librarians and began my long-term involvement with internship, residency, and other diversity programs.

Fourth is the power in mentoring and coaching. We, the librarians with experience in the profession, should mentor new librarians, introduce them to colleagues, and get them involved in the profession so that they may be successful. Last is the need to support diversity programs. ALA, ACRL, and ARL have all committed resources to diversifying the population of librarians. We need to support these initiatives and become involved to nurture the effort. As stated earlier, working for diversity is not a one-time effort, but rather a lifelong commitment.

REFERENCES

America.gov. U.S. minority population continues to grow. http://www.america.gov/st/diversity-english/2008/May/20080513175840zjsredna0.1815607.html

Association of College and Research Libraries' (ACRL) Ad Hoc Task Force on Recruitment and Retention Issues. 2002. *Recruitment, Retention, and Restructuring: Human Resources in Academic Libraries* [white paper]. Chicago: ACRL.

Neely, T. Y., and L. Peterson. 2007. *Achieving Racial and Ethnicity Diversity among Academic and Research Libraries: The Recruitment, Retention, and Advancement of Librarians of Color* [white paper]. Chicago: Association of College and Research Libraries.

Regents of the University of California v. Bakke 438 U.S. 265 (1978).

U.S. Census Bureau, Population Estimates Program. Population by sex, race and Hispanic origin. http://www.census.gov/popest/estimates.html

Chapter 15

Welcome to the Ozarks: The Making of Crickets, Mandalas, and Monographs

Megan Zoe Perez

"You should go back to working in a library," she said. "That's all you ever talk about." She was right, too, although I never realized it until then. At the time, I was working for New York City's Department of Public Safety as an investigator for the Civilian Complaint Review Board (CCRB). As an investigator, I was responsible for fielding allegations of police misconduct. My responsibilities included collecting evidence such as police documents, medical records, 911 recordings, and witness testimony to help piece together the events of the police-civilian encounter. I would then process this evidence, author a report that rendered a judgment regarding the alleged misconduct, and forward the report to the executive board for review.

My fellow investigators and I were issued badges, the power of subpoena, and commissioner of deeds' rights. We interviewed accused police officers in our offices. We barged our way into secure areas of emergency rooms using our badges, and we issued subpoenas for telephone records and court documents. We were all very impressed with ourselves. My work at the CCRB, however, was not a career. It was a job. So as I sat at my desk one afternoon, thinking about my professional future and she said to me, "You should go back to working in a library. That's all you ever talk about," I knew I'd be combing the stacks again, and soon.

Prior to working for the CCRB, I had a few years of experience working in and around the book industry. As an undergraduate, I worked in the collection development department of my alma mater, Southwestern University in Georgetown, Texas. I also worked in the periodicals department while in graduate school at Boston College. My appointment there, however, was only valid during the school year, so during the summer and holiday, I worked at a bookstore. After two years of coursework, serials binding, and gift wrapping I left school and the bookstore and went to work full time for Time Warner Trade Publishing in downtown Boston. I began working there in 1998, but it wasn't until late in the summer of 2001 that my experiences in and around books, both personal and professional, began to point toward a potential career path.

I remember sitting at my desk at the CCRB thinking about my future, my life, and my career. Then, literally, it just hit me. "A library! Why not work in a library? Now there's an idea. Who do I know who works…. Deb! Deb works in a library!" I first met Deb through a mutual friend while working for Time Warner. Deb and I immediately became friends and continue to remain close to this day. At that time, we were in similar situations: in our late 20s, wondering about the future, and willing to relocate, if necessary. Despite our shared circumstances and interests, Deb left Boston in the early summer of 2000 for a job in Ithaca, New York. While I was playing cops and robbers in the outer boroughs of the City, she was on her way to a career in librarianship working as a reference assistant in the Olin Library at Cornell University.

In the summer of 2001, while plotting a way out of the CCRB, I picked up the phone on an impulse and called Deb. I was done visiting jails and detention centers. I'd had my fill of police car ride-a-longs and officer interviews. I was ready for another change and decided I should give librarianship a try. It seemed like a potential match for me, so I called Deb to ask if the library was hiring. It was. Someone had just been promoted out of an assistant position, and Olin Library was looking for a new reference assistant. Two weeks later, I was in Ithaca interviewing for a job. A week after that, I was crossing the Delaware Water Gap and moving into my new apartment right across the street from my old friend, Deb Raftus, who would later move on to her current position as the Romance Languages and Literatures Librarian at the University of Washington.

I approached my new position at Cornell as a litmus test. Despite having previous library experience, this was my first time working in a library *full time*, and I accepted the position knowing I was going to use the experience to determine whether I would pursue librarianship as a career. During the second year of my employment at Cornell, Deb began her studies at the University of Washington's Information School. Finally, after three years of working as an assistant and enduring the long, brutal winters of upstate New York, I decided I, too, wanted to earn my degree in library science and pursue librarianship as a career. In December 2004, I submitted my application for admission to the School of Information and Library Science at the University of North Carolina at Chapel Hill (UNC-CH). Eight months later, I began my studies.

IN PURSUIT OF THE DEGREE

UNC-CH was more than generous in supporting my matriculation with both a Carolina Academic Library Associate (CALA) position and a Margaret Ellen Kalp Fellowship. These awards included monetary support, a twenty-hour per week assistantship in a campus library, and professional development workshops. I was also fortunate to receive a Spectrum Scholarship from the American Library Association (ALA), a MENSA Education and Research Foundation Scholarship, and support from the Association of Research Libraries' (ARL) Initiative to Recruit a Diverse Workforce (IRDW). These latter awards also included training institutes and professional development opportunities as integral parts of the programs.

The IRDW, for example, hosted a preconference institute for all of the program participants prior to ALA's Midwinter Conference in 2006. It also provided for a four-day workshop in April of that same year hosted by Purdue University. The Spectrum Scholarship program hosted an institute of its own for its scholarship recipients: the Spectrum Leadership Institute. This institute took place during the summer of 2006 just before ALA's Annual Conference in New Orleans, Louisiana.

The influence the Leadership Institute had on my career development is inestimable. Prior to attending the institute and during my time as a student at UNC, my professional interests focused on public services, particularly government documents. In fact, my assistantship required me to work on the reference desk for ten hours each week and to work in the government documents department for another ten hours each week. When I wasn't on the desk, I could be found climbing the shelves of the basement stacks quietly stalking oversized World War II posters and catalogs of drawings by E.E. Cummings.

During my first year of school, I had daydreams of working for the Library of Congress, the National Archives and Records Administration, or the Smithsonian. This wasn't a surprise to me considering my school sponsored a fall field trip to the Library of Congress, the Smithsonian, and to the headquarters of National Public Radio. The Spectrum Leadership Institute, however, altered those interests away from public services and government documents and toward something completely different; that *did* surprise me.

The 2006 institute was both professionally and personally noteworthy for at least two distinct reasons. First, it was held just days prior to ALA's Annual Conference in New Orleans. This event holds special significance as ALA was the first national association to hold a major conference in New Orleans after hurricanes Katrina and Rita. Second, the Spectrum Scholars were there days before the regular conference attendees. This tenuous distinction was not lost on any of us.

The downtown area was clear of any sign of natural disaster, but the specter of recovery still lingered in the air. It did not take much prompting for restaurant staff, for example, to sit down at our table and discuss with us their thoughts on the past, present, and future of New Orleans, and they were more than grateful to have so many librarians as guests of the city. On its website, Global Experience Specialists (GES), the official services contractor of ALA's Annual Conference that year, indicated that the city benefitted from the conference both emotionally and economically. Gene Poche, GES general manager said, "Because ALA is the largest trade show since Hurricane Katrina, these loyal and dedicated workers were eager to be part of this very important conference and the return of major trade shows in their city" (Global Experience Specialists).

Economically, the event generated millions of dollars for the city. According to GES industry reports, each conference attendee generates $1,500 in economic impact during a meeting or convention. That year, nearly 17,000 librarians, exhibitors, and supporters attended. "The success of the ALA Annual Conference," said Stephen Perry, CEO of the New Orleans Metropolitan Convention Bureau, "sends a resounding message that the New Orleans experience that visitors know and love is not only intact, but thriving" (Global Experience Specialists).

Second, the institute provided exposure to a completely different professional world. At this stage in my career development, I had already worked in and around libraries for at least six years, but I had never been surrounded by so many creative, eager, energetic, and curious-minded people of color all in one room, all yearning to be information professionals. Granted, we each had different interests within the profession, but simply being in the same space, sharing joint learning experiences, and fostering new friendships and future professional contacts is an effect of the institute that is difficult to recreate, let alone describe. There were sixty-seven Spectrum Scholars that year, and I cannot speak for the other participants, but I know the Institute changed me.

When I returned to North Carolina that summer, I had a different energy, and I had different needs. My professional interests shifted away from public services and government documents and toward issues of organizational development, new graduate recruitment and retention, human resources, and, perhaps most important, issues of diversity in academic librarianship. These subjects would not have been introduced to me in library school, and I would not have known that they were missing from the curriculum had it not been for both the Spectrum Institute and the IRDW.

Before my second year of classes resumed, and after the institute, I realized I was missing a sense of meaning and purpose to my decision to become a librarian. While at Cornell, my decision to go into librarianship was a practical one: I enjoyed the work, it was a relatively stable industry, and benefits for academic librarians were comparable, if not better than, perquisites in other professions. After the institute, I was wistful for a connection between the personal and the professional. I was confused, so I asked myself a series of questions: "How can I, knowing what I now know and seeing what I've now seen, go back to academic life as it was before? How can I use the privileges I was being afforded for the benefit of others? How could I give back to my peers, to my supporters, and to my colleagues?" These are questions I struggled with for weeks, and I think it was just blind chance that I began to regard residency programs as a possible answer to these questions.

I cannot tell you when my interest in residency programs was initially piqued, but I do remember two distinct moments from that summer that set in motion a long series of events, including the publication of this book. First, I remember reviewing my program materials from the Spectrum Institute and the IRDW workshops. I noticed there were a couple of presentations on residency programs that I simply overlooked and failed to attend. I remember thinking, "How could I have missed these?" In one case, I am quite certain I opted instead to attend a panel session on earning a doctorate. The most likely explanation for missing those sessions, however, is that I, like many other students in the middle of their first year of library school, simply didn't know what a residency program was.

The second distinct recollection I have about the summer of 2006 is that I made a conscious and deliberate decision to turn the subject of residency programs into my master's paper topic. Of this, I was certain, and I was aggressive. The semester had not yet begun, but, by mid-August, I had nearly completed my review of the literature, designed a survey, and outlined ideas for a series of independent studies to complete the project.

At the end of the 2006 fall semester, my literature review was complete, as was the design of my survey instrument. By March 2007, I completed an internship at Duke University Libraries and two independent studies, distributed the survey instrument, collected and analyzed the data, and finalized my report. Ultimately, I earned the Dean's Achievement Award, which is given out each year by UNC-CH's School of Information and Library Science to the top two master's papers in each graduating class. After completing the remainder of my requirements for graduation, I received my degree in May 2007. I then had to turn my attention to my future after library school.

AFTER THE DEGREE

After spending several months reviewing the literature and talking to residents, fellows, and coordinators, I had a pretty firm understanding of what the residency experience was like for others and how it helped, in most cases, advance one's career. I was convinced, then, that actually *participating* in a program would be the next logical step in my career development. All I had to do at that point was identify programs that were accepting applications for new residents and to start the application process itself.

The Job Search

In the fall of 2006, my second year of school, I had an informal meeting with two staff members from North Carolina State University (NCSU) to talk about their Libraries Fellows Program. We talked for approximately 20 minutes and discussed the program structure, my interest in the program, my professional goals, and the formal application process. Shortly thereafter, I submitted my resume and cover letter, but, ultimately, I was not selected for an on-site interview nor was I offered a position as a fellow at NCSU.

The second program I applied to was Cornell's Library Fellows Program. I had worked in the reference department for four years before enrolling in library school. I also recalled the director of human resources encouraging me to apply for the IRDW program, and the university librarian supporting my ACRL support staff scholarship application in the fall of 2004. Given this history with the institution, I felt I had an advantage over the rest of the applicants. I was familiar with the system and the organizational culture of the libraries there, so I submitted my resume and cover letter in the summer of 2007. I was later invited for an on-campus interview.

The interview lasted for an entire day. I did not have to give a presentation, but I did have to answer *lots* of questions, including some surprise questions—"Who is your library hero?" for example. Later that morning, I met with the search committee, which included a former resident, the current coordinator of the program, and the director of human resources. They listened as I expressed my interest in continuing to work on diversity issues as a resident. I presented my strategy to contribute to the university's diversity plan, to coordinate diversity-related programs for the academic community, to establish a standing library diversity committee, and to work on this book project.

During the remainder of the morning, I met with still other department heads and had lunch with a group of librarians from various unit libraries around campus. One of those meetings included a short, informal "coffee break"–style meeting with one of the managers from human resources. I again explained my interest in diversity issues and my desire to include those issues in the library's strategic plan. I was told that Cornell had a campus-wide policy of inclusion, that everyone was valued, and that diversity created "silos" separating individuals from the rest of the community campus. This was a shock to me. UNC had a diversity plan and a library diversity committee. Duke had a diversity plan and a standing diversity working group. For the first time that year, I faced the reality that not every institution has the same approach when it comes to diversity issues in libraries, and it was becoming clear that my diversity plans were a hard sell.

At the end of the day, I was debriefed by the director of human resources. We talked about a timetable for hiring the new residents, compensation, benefits, relocation expenses, and my final thoughts on the day. It was beneficial to have a final debriefing session at the end of a long day. I couldn't handle answering many more questions, so it was a relief to be on the receiving end of a conversation for a change; it also gave me an opportunity to ask some questions that came up throughout the course of the day. It took several weeks to receive notification from Cornell that two other candidates were selected as that year's residents. By this time, it was early September. I had graduated from school in May. My assistantship was over. The lease on my apartment was expiring. I was stressed out, plain and simple. Prospects were not looking hopeful. In addition to these two residency positions, I applied for two other jobs, but those applications met with similar results. These obstacles were not part of the plan. From my conversations with previous residents, however, this seems to be a somewhat common resident experience. It's almost a rite of passage.

After some time, I saw an advertisement for a new residency program opening at the University of Arkansas Libraries. The description of the residency program at the University of Arkansas was typical in some respects. It was intended as a broad-based opportunity for an entry-level librarian interested in beginning a career in academic librarianship. The program allowed the resident to rotate through multiple functional areas in the first year of the program and to specialize in another during the second. The requirements and compensation for the position were also typical: recent graduate of an ALA-accredited master's degree program, strong interest in academic librarianship and a commitment to service work. The duration of the appointment was for twelve months at a time, renewable after an annual review. Perquisites included health and dental insurance, a retirement plan, annual leave, and additional benefits such as a professional travel allowance and assigned time for scholarship.

There were, however, two unique features of the program at Arkansas that attracted me. First, the program offered an optional third year in which the resident could continue to specialize in one area of librarianship and complete a capstone project suitable for publication. I had never come across a program that offered a third year, and I was interested in the idea of a final research year to conclude a program. Second, the vacancy announcement listed "demonstrated commitment to diversity" as a preferred qualification of the applicant. This was also new to me. In all of the research I had done on programs up to this point, I had not seen one that had either of these two components. Some might encourage members of underrepresented groups to apply, but I could not recall ever coming across another program that listed demonstrable experience with diversity as a preferred qualification. I found these facets intriguing.

Thus, in the fall of 2007, I submitted my application to the University of Arkansas, and, later that month, I had a telephone interview with the search committee. Very soon after that, I had an interview on campus. The on-site interview was longer than most: one and a half days, and I was required to do a presentation on the value of diversity in academic libraries.

Over the course of that day and a half, I met with the dean, all of the associate deans and directors, members of the administration, the technical and public services departments, the staff and faculty concerns committees, the electronic resources division, and the subject specialists. There were some breaks and lunches as well as a dinner, but the only people I can think of that I did not meet with were the archivists. Aside from the department of special collections, I met with everyone in the library from top to bottom. After lunch on the second day, I was escorted to the airport and flew back home.

Shortly after returning to North Carolina, I received a phone call from the associate dean of the libraries offering me the position as the first University of Arkansas Librarian-In-Residence. I enthusiastically accepted, arrived in Fayetteville, Arkansas, on November 5, and began my position on November 13, 2007.

The University of Arkansas Librarian-In-Residence Program

My first two weeks on the job were spent attending committee and department meetings and meeting with the heads of library systems, cataloging, acquisitions, the performing arts and media center, the David Pryor Center, library facilities, serials, and public services. At the time, the Libraries' Human Resources Director position was vacant. At the end of November, one of the candidates for the position, Jeff Banks, gave a presentation on the value of diversity in academic librarianship. During his presentation, he suggested the library create a standing diversity committee to incorporate the university's diversity plans into the library strategic plan. I was seated next to our dean during Banks's presentation, and when he mentioned "library diversity committee," I gave her two little elbow bumps and looked at her with raised eyebrows. "Fine," she said, "set it up, and you can chair it." Just like that, the libraries' diversity committee was established, and I was named its first chair.

This new role inaugurated a dual appointment for me. Fifty percent of my time was to be spent as the librarian-in-residence, rotating through different departments and getting a broad-based introduction to the world of academic librarianship. The other 50 percent was to be spent working as the libraries' diversity officer. Both of these positions were brand new to me, and to the libraries. I was intimidated. I was frightened. And I felt pressured. Within a few weeks of beginning my tenure at the libraries, I was reporting directly to the dean and carving out the roles and responsibilities for two newly minted positions. At the same time, however, I knew I had few alternatives. After all, I was the one who lobbied for these.

Rotations

During that first year, and in my capacity as a resident, I completed two rotations, one in web services and one in special collections. In the former, I acted as curator for an online exhibit of government documents celebrating the libraries' centennial anniversary of its status as a member of the Federal Depository Library Program (FDLP). I also created and managed a variety of websites, including a central portal of digital collections for all of the state of Arkansas' research library members.

While working with the archivists in special collections, I worked under the head of the manuscripts division. In that rotation, I processed manuscript collections and created finding aids for these and other collections, provided assistance to student workers creating their own finding aids, and visited potential donors off campus. I was also afforded some specialized training during this rotation. My supervisor and I participated in a four-day Amigos Library Services online training seminar on encoded archival description. My favorite part of my rotation in special collections, however, was creating an inventory of the collected materials of Laurence Luckenbill.

Luckenbill is a University of Arkansas alumnus, but he is better known for his role as Sybok, Spock's brother in the movie *Star Trek V: The Final Frontier*. He is also married to Lucie Arnaz, the daughter of Desi Arnaz and Lucille Ball. Luckenbill travelled the country, frequently staging a series of one-man plays, often portraying political figures like Lyndon Johnson and Theodore Roosevelt. His collection, consequently, is substantial and included his play publicity photos, videos, press clippings, contact sheets, screenplays, drafts of plays, and more. There were also boxes of props and set ornaments from these plays. To my delight, one of these boxes was filled with nothing but teddy bears, clearly taken from his play on Roosevelt.

My second year in the program was rather unique for me in a number of ways. First, the location was atypical. Toward the conclusion of my first year, I decided to rotate through human resources. Residents do not often choose to rotate through this department. Most seem to work in reference and instruction, technical services and cataloging, and collection development with a bit of archival or digital work mixed in.

The work I did in this rotation also was atypical. Instead of learning about human resources directly through self-study or guided learning experiences, my rotation supervisor and I decided to assemble a human resources training module for future residents. My job, as a resident, was to put together a type of curricular learning model that would include topics for instruction, methods of instruction, and methods of evaluation and assessment.

On the one hand, the purpose of this was to give me an introduction to the themes and issues involved in the study of human resources. On the other hand, however, the purpose of this rotation was to create a training platform or training module that could be used by other departments in the training and development of future residents. People often regard the subject of human resources as involving issues of compensation, benefits, and recruitment only. Through my work on this module, however, I learned that human resources deals with much more than just these topics, and I learned from an administrative, formal, and legal point of view what it means to be a professional.

An understanding of Equal Employment Opportunity law, workplace safety, job analysis, employee development, performance management, and promotion and tenure were all topics I had heard about in passing, but I never realized how these issues affected employees at all levels of the organizational chart, including the residents. Being able to discuss the elements of job analysis and various methods for designing a job offered me some tools and questions to use as a resident when examining future positions. Is my current position well designed? Can anything be different? What are its shortcomings? What are its advantages? These are also some of the questions I can consider and answer when I review future vacancy announcements.

I enjoyed this rotation so much that, upon its conclusion, I recommended to Banks that all future residents begin their appointment with a rotation in human resources. He concurred and added that if it is not used as a starting point, it should at least be a requirement of the program. We agreed that this kind of training would give them a solid understanding of what their roles, responsibilities, and expectations would be as an employee regardless of which area they ultimately choose to work in. They would become aware of their legal rights as an employee, know the limits of an employer's expectations, and gain an awareness of the processes, policies, and ethical issues involved in resolving any conflict between the two parties.

Libraries' Diversity Officer

Overall, my first year as a resident was a positive experience. I learned new skills. I was given funding to travel to four professional conferences, and I was permitted to work on projects I expressed interest in. Some of my most memorable experiences from the program at the University of Arkansas, however, came from the other half of my appointment as the libraries' diversity officer. My work in this capacity did not take shape until the second year of my program, and even though I struggled with the lack of guidance for such a position, I am more than pleased with the outcome.

Diversity Collection Enhancement Grant

The first task I set for myself as diversity officer was to found and chair the libraries' first, permanent diversity committee. Members of the committee were appointed by the administration, but I was also given permission to invite other members to serve on the committee, members whose skill and/or experience would fill specific gaps in the committee's existing capabilities. For example, the committee's plan to enhance the libraries' collection of monographic, diversity-related titles required someone with experience in the area of collection development. Therefore, we invited the head of acquisitions to join the committee based on her collection expertise.

Together, the committee members created a mission and vision statement, and I designed a website to publicize the libraries' diversity activities by making the website more visible to the university community. As the chair, I was also responsible for incorporating the university's diversity plan into the libraries' strategic plan. Creating a strategy for this was fairly easy. I used the university's plan as my guide, listed its main objectives, and then created actionable items for the library committee in support of each of these objectives. For example, one of the university's objectives was to ensure that varied perspectives of a diverse community are reflected in the university's curriculum (University of Arkansas Diversity Task Force, 2002). To support this, I wrote a monographic collections grant for titles relating specifically to the areas of lesbian, gay, bisexual, transgender, and queer studies; race relations; religious studies, particularly those of the East and Middle East; workplace diversity; and disability studies.

Originally, the grant was a small, internal proposal created for our director of collection management. It was titled the Diversity Collection Enhancement Grant (DCEG) and requested a mere $2,000. The proposal was forwarded up the organizational chart to the Dean of Libraries, who asked me to rewrite parts of it and resubmit it to her. This was a year in which our acquisitions budget was frozen. We maintained our subscriptions to electronic resources, but we didn't have funds for monographic acquisitions. We even suspended our approval plan. Even though the amount I requested was small, I was confident it would not be awarded because the acquisitions budget was so tight. When it came time for me to rewrite the proposal then, I asked for four times the original amount. What did I have to lose, right?

To my surprise, the proposal was approved for two years as a pilot program and fully funded by the Office of the Provost and the Associate Vice Chancellor for Institutional Diversity and Education, Dr. Carmen Coustaut. The DCEG idea was underway, and the diversity committee was making strides toward satisfying one of the objectives of the university's diversity plan. To date, the committee has acquired approximately two hundred titles through this grant, and the libraries' diversity website has been reworked to highlight each of these titles in a rotator on the site sidebar. Each time the site is visited, a new title will appear in the sidebar showing an image of the cover and basic bibliographic information, including the call number.

The real joy in working as the libraries' diversity officer, however, lay not in collection development and managing the DCEG fund, but in satisfying a different university objective: building an inclusive, affirming, learning culture for all members of the University of Arkansas community (University of Arkansas Diversity Task Force 2002). In support of this objective, I partnered with other campus units to create two cocurricular programs for the students, faculty, staff, and surrounding community: a documentary film screening and a Tibetan mandala project.

A Cricket in the Court of Akbar

In the fall of 2008, I invited Andrew Mendelson to campus to screen his new movie, *A Cricket in the Court of Akbar*. Andrew is a musician and documentary filmmaker. His specific instrument of choice is the sitar, and he recently travelled to India to participate in the Sri Mahendra Bhatt Music Competition, the largest music competition in the state of Rajasthan, India. He was the first white, American student to participate in this prestigious contest. *Cricket* documents his travel to India, the tension between his Western identity and the Indian musical community, and the relationship between master musician and learner.

Although Andrew and I were roommates in college, we parted ways after graduation. We met again, by chance, in the lobby of the CCRB building in New York City. He happened to be working in the same building for a nonprofit a few floors above my office. We kept in touch with one another after that chance encounter and, while in library school some four or five years later, I learned about the film. I immediately thought it would make a fantastic diversity program, so I "put it in my pocket," so to speak, and kept it as an idea to put into action once I had a permanent position. When I was appointed at the University of Arkansas, and once I was named chair of the diversity committee, I finally had an opportunity to make this program idea a reality.

Andrew and I planned this event for several months in collaboration with the music and journalism departments and the multicultural center. After securing a venue for the screening, travel funds, and identifying available times to visit with classes and students, we decided that the best time for Andrew to visit would be early in November 2008. This was a difficult task for me as I was also co-coordinating a postconference with Julie Brewer, program coordinator at the University of Delaware, for the 2008 National Diversity in Libraries Conference in late October of that same year.

On November 3, 2008, however, Andrew finally came to visit campus, performed for a variety of music classes, met with graduate students, interviewed with the campus and local papers, and screened his film. It was a highly successful event, and Andrew has since been busy traveling around the country screening his film at a variety of film festivals and universities. These events included the San Diego Film Festival, the South Asian Film Festival in New York City, and the Asheville Film Festival in Asheville, North Carolina. As an aside, Andrew was part of the music team for Mike Myers's movie, *The Love Guru*. The University of Arkansas, however, has the distinction of being the first campus to screen his film.

The 2009 Tibetan Mandala Project

The second program I planned was a Tibetan mandala and artifacts exhibit in the main library's reading room. A mandala is a complex, geometric design that is intended to represent the universe and our interaction with it. They have been created by a variety of cultures throughout history including Hindu, Navajo, and Chinese, as well as Tibetan. They can be constructed out of sand, glass, thread, butter, and even carved into wood. Depending on the complexity of the design and the number of artists working on its construction, a mandala may take several weeks to complete.

A similar program was held on campus in 2006, but it was in a much smaller space. Visitors had to wait in line to view the mandala and the limited space did not allow for an extensive exhibit. After consulting with Geshe Thupten Dorjee, a native of Tibet and Visiting Assistant Professor in the Fulbright College of Arts and Sciences, and Dr. Sidney Burris, Director of the Fulbright College Honors program, a much larger event was planned to take place inside the library in the spring of 2009. The event was named the 2009 Tibetan Mandala Project, and I was named the chair of its coordinating committee.

For the entire month of March 2009, a quartet of Tibetan Buddhist monks, artists, and scholars visited the campus to create a sand mandala for the university and surrounding campus community and to offer lectures and workshops regarding Tibetan culture. Thangkas (Tibetan silk paintings), sacred statues, stupas (an icon of Buddhist art), and other authentic, Tibetan artifacts were also on display in the reading room to complement the larger mandala exhibit. The event was attended by more than five hundred people, including university students, faculty, and staff; elementary school children from local schools; high school students from area high schools; university administrators; and members of the surrounding northwest Arkansas community. Some visitors came from places as far away as Rapid City, South Dakota, and Naperville, Illinois.

The cost of the program, including fees, materials, housing and travel for the monks, publicity materials, and catering for opening and closing receptions was in excess of $5,000. Despite the project's scale, duration, and expense, it was enthusiastically supported by campus groups including the library administration, the office of university programs, the Fulbright College of Arts and Sciences, the multicultural center, and the Students for a Free Tibet registered student organization. Financial support was also provided by area businesses, community organizations, and private individuals.

The program was a tremendous success and was featured in a large number of media outlets including Fayetteville local newspapers, *The Morning News*, the *Northwest Arkansas Times*, the campus radio station, the campus newspaper, and local television. The overall reception from my colleagues and the university administration was more than positive, and working on such a project with representatives of a culture on the verge of extinction was a remarkable experience both personally and professionally.

Perhaps most significantly, and as an unexpected ancillary benefit, these two programs together helped establish for the libraries a reputation as a keystone in the development, planning, and execution of cocurricular diversity programs on campus. Upon conclusion of the documentary film screening, the director of the multicultural center asked me to meet with him in the spring as he wanted to be sure to earmark some of the center's own funds for library directed programs in the future. During the planning stages of the mandala project, the director of student programs invited me to work with her on future programs that can be funded by her office under the guidance, direction, and coordination of the libraries. Also, in an interview with an area newspaper, the new Vice-Provost for Diversity, Dr. Charles Robinson, recognized the library for having its own diversity plan. Although he praised the diversity-related efforts of the university as a whole, the library was the only specific campus unit he named. This signifies the development of a degree of organizational capital that will go a long way toward providing inroads for future library initiatives.

Service and Scholarship

In addition to fulfilling the duties and responsibilities outlined for me as librarian-in-residence and as diversity officer, I, like many other academic librarians, was expected to engage in a variety of service and scholarship activities.

Service

During my tenure as a resident, I served as a member of several committees both on the local and national level. Locally, I was a member of the web development group, the library human resources advisory council, the programs and marketing task force, and the recently formed library council. Nationally, I was a member of the Library Leadership and Management Association's (LLAMA) Leadership Development Committee. Given my participation in the Spectrum Scholars program, I was invited to serve as a member of the Spectrum Scholars Interest Group and the Spectrum Advisory Committee. Perhaps my most coveted service work, however, involved my participation in the Association of College and Research Libraries' Residency Interest Group (ACRL RIG).

During the annual Diversity Officers Discussion Group at the 2007 ALA Annual Conference, I suggested a working group be created for residents, both past and present, and program coordinators. Julie Brewer seconded the idea, and that same summer, an informal group of residents and coordinators came together to create the Residency Working Group. Initially, this group was supported by the ARL's diversity programs under the direction of Jerome Offord, Jr. Jerome arranged meeting space for the group at the following ALA Midwinter Conference and facilitated the creation and management of an electronic discussion list hosted on ARL's server.

The following year, however, ACRL announced a measure to amend their bylaws allowing for the creation of interest groups alongside sections and discussion groups. The purpose of the measure was to allow association members to create a "home" within ACRL for areas of interest, scholarship, and study that were not already represented by existing sections or discussion groups. By the summer of 2008, the measure passed, and I initiated the migration of the ARL RWG into an official interest group within ACRL.

The process took several months. A proposal and a petition, which required twenty-five signatures of current ACRL members, were prepared. Once the initial proposal and petition were submitted, secondary documentation needed to be completed, including a Board of Directors Action Form indicating the manner in which this interest group would support the strategic goals of the association. The paperwork was completed and submitted in August 2008, and in late October of that year, we were approved and the Residency Working Group became the ACRL Residency Interest Group. The group now had a formal home with a higher degree of visibility, access to server space on ALA's website for a website of its own, an open, easier to locate electronic discussion list, a small allowance for program support at conferences, and representation on ACRL's newly formed Communities of Practice Assembly. This was the first interest group to be approved by the ACRL Board of Directors, and as a result of my efforts, I was named ACRL's Member of the Week early in November 2008.

Scholarship

In addition to these service activities, I also involved myself in a variety of scholarly endeavors. Prior to my arrival at the University of Arkansas, I had a small amount of experience with writing for publication. The master's paper I wrote during library school earned the Dean's Achievement Award. I also wrote two short pieces that were featured in online newsletters, one for *C&RL News* online and one for an ARL newsletter (Perez 2005, 2007a). After I arrived in Arkansas, however, I became involved with the Social Responsibilities Round Table (SRRT) of ALA. SRRT's newsletter features book reviews in each issue and, through my membership with the round table, I was given opportunities to write reviews of my own. I wrote two separate reviews for SRRT, and each was accepted and published (Perez 2007b, 2008a).

A much larger scholarship project I took on was the coordination of a postconference workshop on residency programs for the National Diversity in Libraries Conference (NDLC) in Louisville, Kentucky, in October 2008. The idea for the post-conference was developed by Jerome Offord and, with the assistance of Julie Brewer, the three of us coordinated an all-day, postconference workshop to take place at the conclusion of the NDLC. We hosted presentations from both residents and coordinators, had breakout sessions for each of those groups, and coordinated a panel discussion facilitated by Deborah Nolan from Towson University. In addition to co-coordinating the program, I was the keynote speaker and delivered a talk titled "Practicing Proficiency: The Past, Present, and Future of Library Residency Programs" (Perez 2008b). This was my first time delivering a talk of my own in front of an audience of seasoned professionals, but the evaluation form I put together indicated the overall workshop was a positive experience, and my talk received approving comments.

Another scholarship effort I took on during my residency was a presentation at ACRL's 14th National Conference in Seattle, Washington. One of the audience members of my presentation at the NDLC, Trevor Dawes, Circulation Services Director at Princeton University, e-mailed me after the conclusion of the postconference. At the time, he was cochair of ACRL's Seattle Panels Selection Component Committee and charged with securing one or two "hot topic" presentations for the conference. As a result of my talk at the NDLC, Trevor invited me to submit a proposal for one of the two "hot topic" presentation slots.

A substantial portion of the talk I gave at the NDLC was based on the work of one particular individual: Dr. Sylvia Hall-Ellis from the Morgridge College of Education at the University of Denver. After receiving the invitation from Trevor, I reached out to Dr. Hall-Ellis and inquired whether she'd be interested in collaborating with me on this project. She readily agreed, and three months later, Dr. Sylvia Hall-Ellis, Dr. Denise Anthony, and I were giving a "hot topic" talk at the

ACRL conference titled "From Novice to Expert: Collaboration for Succession Planning" (Perez, Hall-Ellis, and Anthony 2009).

Last, this book. I had the idea for a book of this nature when I was in library school, but the successful completion of a master's paper was a requirement of my library science program. At that time, the paper took priority over everything else so, like the *Cricket* film project, I put the book idea aside for the time being. I didn't pick it up again until I was interviewing for jobs. When asked about projects I would like to work on as a resident, I described a few functional areas I was interested in such as human resources and archives. I also mentioned that I had an idea for a book and that I'd be interested in working on it as a part of my scholarship work.

While I was in library school, I met Raquel Cogell, coeditor of *Diversity in Libraries* (Cogell and Gruwell 2001). I shared my idea about this book with her, and she was very supportive. After I secured a job at the University of Arkansas, I began making plans. I thought about contributors. I thought about content. And I thought about the book's arrangement.

Around this same time, Ms. Cogell introduced me to her coeditor, Cindy Gruwell. Gratuitously, Ms. Gruwell worked at St. Cloud State University, just up the road from the University of Minnesota where I attended the Minnesota Institute for Early Career Librarians from Traditionally Underrepresented Groups (Minnesota Institute), hosted by the University of Minnesota. While at the Minnesota Institute, Ms. Gruwell and I met to discuss the idea for this book. I presented her with some ideas for contributors and content, and at the conclusion of that meeting, we agreed to work together and submit a prospectus to Libraries Unlimited.

In late July 2008, after returning from the MNIECL, I telephoned Sue Easun, Acquisitions Editor for Libraries Unlimited, and pitched my idea. She said she was sold on the idea, but the decision to proceed with the project was now up to her editorial board. Two weeks later, the board approved the proposal, and in August 2008, Ms. Gruwell and I were awarded the contract for this book.

SUMMARY

My overall experience as librarian-in-residence at the University of Arkansas is difficult to describe. On the one hand, I was afforded substantial and frequent opportunities to learn and to grow into a more competent professional. I was given release time for scholarship. I was not only allowed but encouraged to participate in national-level service activities. I was regularly invited to participate in committee work within the libraries and on the university campus, and I was most generously supported in terms of professional development. In 2008, for example, I attended four conferences: ALA Midwinter, ALA Annual, the Minnesota Institute, and the National Diversity in Libraries Conference, all funded by the libraries. I was also permitted to be creative with my professional interests. This included the mandala and the *Cricket* projects, which enjoyed the support of the university community, the libraries, and my colleagues.

On the other hand, I encountered a variety of struggles and challenges with my experience as well. My years as a resident were full of "firsts." On the local level, I was the first resident in a brand new residency program. I was appointed as the libraries' first diversity officer, and the first chair of the libraries' first standing committee on diversity. I also learned I was the first Hispanic faculty member at the libraries since opening in 1875.

On the national level, I was the first convener of the first ACRL Interest Group. I co-coordinated a national postconference and wrote book reviews for the first time. I gave presentations at conferences in front of librarians much more experienced than myself, and for the first time ever,

I began work on a substantial manuscript. Looking back on my tenure as a resident, I feel I acquired a deeper knowledge of the workings of an academic library, service work, and collaborative programming. At times, I took great pride in engaging in so many professional endeavors for the first time. At the same time, however, these firsts presented unique challenges that often left me feeling alone, isolated, and without local peers. I often felt as though I had to resolve these challenges by myself.

Former residents frequently report this same feeling, particularly in programs where they are the only resident. These same residents also report on the value of mentors and departmental homes in these situations. Unfortunately, I did not have either of these. I did not have a regular department to anchor myself to, nor did I meet with a regular supervisor for the overall program until after the conclusion of my first year. I had supervision when I worked in my various rotations, but they oversaw my work in those departments only.

Although the program did not have a schedule of rotations or an overall program coordinator at the conclusion of my orientation, the dean and library directors worked with me to put some of these support mechanisms in place as quickly as possible. After immediate consultation with the libraries' administrative personnel, my first rotation assignment was arranged just one week after my orientation. Shortly thereafter, a coordinator for the program was put in place and a plan for the remainder of my time as librarian-in-residence was implemented including learning objectives, project assignments, and methods of evaluation.

Despite these adjustments, the duration of my rotations presented a different, unexpected challenge. Because my position was split between resident and diversity officer, my rotation times were cut in half. I would only work in a department for approximately twenty hours per week instead of the customary forty. If I had a six-month rotation in special collections, for example, it was really reduced to less than three months of full-time work. Factoring in holidays, supervisor and resident sick or vacation days, and time off for resident and supervisor conferences, there were almost two additional weeks of rotation time subtracted from the already shortened rotation experience.

These shortened rotation times are a concern for me as I come to the conclusion of my appointment and enter the job market. I have acquired a wide variety of experience in a number of areas. I have some archives experience. I have some web-design experience. I have some research and publication experience, and I have some program planning experience. However, I don't feel as though I have enough experience in any one of these areas to demonstrate the proficiency I assumed I would.

These challenges may have been made less complex if support mechanisms were in place prior to the start of my appointment—mechanisms such as a program coordinator, the assignment of a departmental home, and regular interaction with a mentor. Ongoing and regular communication with one specific individual who would support me, have empathy for my situation as a new learner, as a new faculty member, and as a person of color in a predominantly White culture would have made my experience much less stressful. I found it difficult to support myself through trying moments, and creating my own role and my own objectives took quite an emotional toll.

This is not to say that I was without a mentor. In fact, I was assigned one for the duration of my appointment, but I was *assigned* a mentor. I did not have an opportunity to choose my own mentor, and I was not given an opportunity to offer my own feedback on who would ultimately become my mentor. This was somewhat of a disappointment for me. Rapport and trust are crucial ingredients for a mentor relationship to be successful, and I don't establish these quickly with new people. This is a personal challenge, however, and I recognize it's something I can and should work on as I move forward in my professional relationships.

Knowing this, and realizing it partway through my residency, I developed a strategy for improving my mentor-mentee relationships. I assembled a mini mentor-mentee agreement sheet. In it, I suggested some actions mentors and mentees could think about to facilitate the establishment of rapport between one another and to make the relationship more fruitful. For example, I suggested mentors and mentees plan shared learning activities, create a schedule for regular meetings, establish some objectives at the onset of the pairing, and revisit those objectives later in the relationship. Unfortunately, I developed these too late in my residency to test and implement them, but I do think they are useful tips for future relationships.

CONCLUSION

There are a number of suggestions I have for improving the resident's experience at the Librarian-In-Residence Program at the University of Arkansas, many of which may be useful to other programs. I have documented these suggestions and left them with the libraries' for future reference, but I will mention just a few of them here. Some are familiar and easy to recognize: set up a home department, create learning objectives ahead of time, provide a regular supervisor, and create a schedule for rotations. Other suggestions are not so evident. First, in a situation like mine, I recommend eliminating the split appointment, at least in the first year. Working in two capacities simultaneously is challenging for anyone, especially a new graduate. Instead, a better model might be to have another librarian serve as the diversity officer for one or two years and have the resident shadow the officer. Then, after a year or two of observation, incorporate some of the diversity officer's responsibilities into the resident's regular work responsibilities. This will gently expose the resident to these new activities and duties through firsthand observation. It will also allow the resident to assume some responsibility for this position under the direct supervision, and with guidance from, the former diversity officer.

I also recommend the program be tied to a larger, broader network. Residents are often unique employees in their respective institution. They are recent graduates who are new to the profession, new to the geographic region, and new to the organization. They are also often the only person from an underrepresented group in their new organization and, in many instances, the only resident. What makes residents unique is that they are all of these things at once, and it easily creates feelings of isolation. It is difficult to identify another kind of employee who shares all of these characteristics and all of its attendant experiences.

One idea for resolving this and for creating a community of peers among residents is to take advantage of the technology available to us. Financial resources may not be available for every resident to attend every conference throughout the duration of the appointment. There are other ways, however, to facilitate the introduction of residents to one another across geographical barriers. Simple, freely available, video and teleconference tools can be used to provide residents with shared learning experiences, with a free exchange of ideas and experiences, and with a network of colleagues with whom they can develop together in the years ahead of them.

Unfortunately, the current, nationwide economic situation has necessitated reductions in university budgets across the country. In an effort to parry layoffs, some institutions have implemented hiring freezes, suspended job searches, and left vacant positions open for the remainder of the 2010 fiscal year. This is similar to the situation at the University of Arkansas. The Librarian-In-Residence Program will continue after my departure, but the hiring of a new, second resident will be delayed for a short time. As of this writing, a new search has not yet been initiated, but a new resident is expected to begin the program during the 2011 fiscal year. I hope the works in this book and the local documentation I've left behind will help maintain the program, help it fulfill its objectives, and help it sustain the rapport the libraries' have established with other campus units.

REFERENCES

Cogell, R. V., and C. A. Gruwell, eds. 2001. *Diversity in Libraries: Academic Residency Programs*. Westport, CT: Greenwood Press.

Global Experience Specialists. First major trade show in New Orleans since hurricane Katrina is a success. http://www.ges.com/about/press/press_detail.asp?newsID=142

Perez, M. 2005. Building the future: Attracting students from diverse backgrounds into librarianship. *C&RL News online,* 66(6). http://www.ala.org/ala/mgrps/divs/acrl/publications/crlnews/2005/jun/ntlconfrpts.cfm

Perez, M. 2007a. Professional residencies: Lessons from the healthcare industry. *Synergy: News from ARL Diversity Initiatives*, 2.

Perez, M. 2007b. Review of *Covering: The Hidden Assault on Our Civil Rights*, by Kenji Yoshino, *SRRT Newsletter*, December 2007.

Perez, M. 2008a. Review of *Library Daylight: Tracings of Modern Librarianship, 1874–1922*, by Rory Litwin, *SRRT Newsletter*, June 2008.

Perez, M. 2008b. Practicing proficiency: The past, present, and future of residency programs. Paper presented at the National Diversity in Libraries Conference Post-Conference Workshop on Residency Programs, October 4, 2008, in Louisville, Kentucky.

Perez, M., S. Hall-Ellis, and D. Anthony. 2009. From novice to expert: Collaboration for succession planning. Presentation at the Association of College and Research Libraries' 14th Annual Conference, March 12–15, in Seattle, Washington.

University of Arkansas Diversity Task Force. 2002. *Diversity Plan for the University of Arkansas*. Fayetteville: University of Arkansas.

Conclusion

Cindy Ann Gruwell

In *Diversity in Libraries: Academic Residency Programs* (Cogell and Gruwell 2001), E. J. Josey, a maverick in the field of academic librarianship, pointed out the need to recruit traditionally underrepresented groups into the profession of academic librarianship. In reference to the residents' narratives in the aforementioned book, he stated, "I believe they can make a difference in the effort to increase the number of minorities in academic research libraries specifically as well as increase their numbers in all types of libraries generally" (Cogell and Gruwell 2001, xii). Now, ten years later, this new publication serves as a testament to the perseverance of two unique groups of individuals: program coordinators and entry-level librarians.

Administrators who have maintained, developed, and managed new and continuing residency programs are recruiting a diverse pool of professional librarians to work in academic libraries. Their continued efforts give testimony to their commitment and determination to recruit new graduates into the profession through their respective programs. Through their programs, an ethnically diverse group of entry-level librarians has become engaged in the profession and taken the risk of accepting temporary positions with no guarantee of a permanent job. These individuals have had the opportunity to enter the profession with support and ongoing training that has allowed them to flourish and jump-start their careers. Their varied experiences within the institutions they represent, shared mentorship, and, most of all, the responsibilities we all face in the early years of our careers give them a unique window with which they can view the profession as a whole and academic librarianship in particular.

Throughout this book, we have seen numerous examples of well-established programs such as the Ohio State Mary P. Key Diversity Residency Program and the University of California—Santa Barbara Library Fellowship Program, as well as newer programs like the Librarian-In-Residence program at the University of Arkansas and University of Tennessee Diversity Residency Program. Most have experienced a variety of challenges, including administrative changes, program revisions, and budget shortfalls, to name a few. Each program is unique and varies in quantity of residents, length of program, and structure. Despite these differences, however, they have one important element in common. They all have strong commitments to the recruitment of traditionally underrepresented individuals into the field of academic librarianship through their residency programs. As noted by several authors in this book, librarians have a unique opportunity to pave the way for our new recruits. The development of post-MLS residency programs serves as one example of how current, academic librarians can welcome and mentor newbies in the profession.

There is no doubt that residencies can create a win-win situation for all parties involved. Administrators looking to diversify their pool of professional librarians and others who have specifically developed their programs as a recruitment tool seek out individuals who will benefit professionally while simultaneously fulfilling needs of their host institution. Residents are given the opportunity to explore the academic profession and to test and hone both their skills and knowledge. This unique exposure allows them to see firsthand how librarians perform and attend to their everyday work assignments in areas such as reference, instruction, and special collections, as well as their participation on committees, involvement in professional organizations, and management of both main and branch libraries.

In addition to the narratives describing residencies by administrators and residents, important research delineating various aspects about the residency programs allows us to review and make prognostications for the future. Residency programs have filled a variety of needs for the residents and the institutions alike. This is made clear in various chapters, such as Chapter 11 in which Sarah Stohr describes how she took the lead in scheduling the reference desk during a library crisis, or Chapter 6, in which Jill Keally discusses the case of the University of Tennessee, where the selection of projects and rotations are mutually beneficial to both the resident and the library. By looking at programs from the inside out, we can better understand how residencies serve as a recruitment tool and, at the same time, meet the varied needs of academic libraries. During this time of budget cuts, we as librarians cannot forget the need to plan for our future. Leaders and innovators will be not only needed but expected. The influx of new recruits, especially those from traditionally underrepresented groups, will allow for fresh perspectives and reflect that which academic librarians have become: members of a diverse, vital, changing force who readily acknowledge the changes in our world and who are ready and willing to learn how to serve our academic communities.

Whether written by residents, program coordinators, or administrators, the chapters included in this book describe the application processes, detail the structure of residency programs, and, in several cases, provide candid descriptions of firsthand experiences in residency programs. From the deserts of the Southwest to the Canadian province of Alberta, a substantial number of universities have recognized the importance of recruiting a diverse workforce. Through their efforts, a fair amount of headway has been made. However, in relation to the overall quantity of academic librarians, and especially those of color, there remains much to be done.

What does the future hold? It is well known that librarians are experiencing dramatic changes in both technology and budgetary constraints relative to their libraries in general and the profession overall. This is especially evident in the need to recruit new professionals who have fresh ideas, new skills, and different voices that will support and enhance the work we strive to achieve in academic libraries. With the graying of the profession comes opportunity for new recruits (Steffen and Lietzau 2009). The bigger question looks at what mechanisms are used to encourage individuals to pursue librarianship as a career and, at the same time, highlight the opportunities and possibilities for the immediate and long-range future. Add to these factors the need to diversify the profession to reflect our user base, and it is no wonder that we need to take into the account the manner in which we both recruit and train our new professionals.

> The need to recruit and retain excellent new librarians from diverse backgrounds not only enriches the library experience but also provides support for ensuring campus success in teaching, learning, and research. These librarians bring new perspectives, ideas, and training to jump start the academic library's entry into the twenty-first world of global scholarship, learning methods, and high-tech means of communication. (Dewey and Keally 2008, 629)

Whether the approach is to develop and maintain residency programs, adopt different mentoring models like those described in Chapter 7 on nurse preceptors, or promote communities of practice (see Chapter 9), we must recognize the need to think ahead and plan accordingly.

REFERENCES

Cogell, R. V., and C. A. Gruwell, eds. 2001. *Diversity in Libraries: Academic Residency Programs.* Westport, CT: Greenwood Press.

Dewey, B., and J. Keally. 2008. *Recruiting for diversity: Strategies for twenty-first century research librarianship.* Library Hi Tech 26(4):622–629.

Steffen, N., and Z. Lietzau. 2009. Retirement, Retention, and Recruitment in Colorado Libraries: The 3Rs study revisited. *Library Trends* 58(2):179–191.

Index

ACRL. *See* Association of College and Research Libraries
ACRL-RIG. *See* Association of College and Research Libraries
Agnew, Shantel, 86
ALA. *See* American Library Association
ALISE. *See* Association for Library and Information Science Education
Altier, Mary E., 93
American Association for the Advancement of Slavic Studies (AAASS), 125
American Association of Colleges and Nursing (AACN), 93
American Association of Law Libraries (AALL), 174, 177
American Indian Library Association (AILA), 125
American Libraries, 15, 183
American Library Association (ALA), xii, 5, 31, 34, 54, 84, 93, 115, 118, 132, 150, 172, 177, 184, 190; Black Caucus of, 18, 67, 125; Board of Education for Librarianship, xv; Cultural Development Grant, 85; Emerging Leaders program, 161; New Members Round Table, 84, 166; Office for Diversity, 5; Office for Personnel Resources, 34; Spectrum Advisory Committee, 199; Spectrum Scholars Interest Group, 199; Spectrum Scholars Leadership Institute, 191, 192; Spectrum Scholars program, xvii, 5, 169, 186, 191, 199; Spectrum Scholarship program, 190, 191
Andragogy, 96, 109
Anthony, Denise, 200
Arbinger Institute, 148
ARL. *See* Association of Research Libraries
Arnaz, Desi, 195
Asheville Film Festival, 198
Association for Library Collections and Technical Services (ALCTS), 124
Association of College and Research Libraries (ACRL), xv, xvi, 67, 93, 124, 166, 173, 182, 186, 187, 193, 199, 201; Board of Directors, 200; ClimateQual, 5; Communities of Practice Assembly, 200; cultural competency guidelines, 5; interest groups, xv, 12, 26, 166, 199, 200, 201 ; Racial & Ethnic Diversity Committee, 18; Rare Books and Manuscripts Section, 166; Residency Interest Group (RIG), xv, xvi, xix, 6, 8, 26, 103, 179, 199, 200
Association of Library and Information Science Education (ALISE), xvi, 1, 6, 31, 93, 109, 115, 116, 117, 119, 130, 132
Association of Research Libraries (ARL), xvi, xix, 4, 5, 33, 48, 51, 54, 62, 88, 115, 119, 121, 125, 129, 130, 132, 186, 187; Annual Salary Survey, 119; Diversity Initiative, 66; diversity programs, 199; Diversity Scholar, 172; Initiative to Recruit a Diverse Workforce (IRDW), xvii, 5, 109, 172, 186, 190, 192, 193; Leadership and Career Development Program (LCDP), 186; Leadership Symposium, 67; National Diversity in Librarianship Conference, 67; newsletter, 200; Office of Diversity Programs, 109; Residency and Internship Programs database, 51, 54; Residency Working Group (RWG), 199

Baby boomers, xvii, xix, 32–33, 95. *See also* Retirement
Ball, Lucille, 195
Banks, Jeff, 194, 196
Beard, Megan, 161, 163
Beecroft, Pauline, 101
Beginning Librarian's Salary (BLS), 121, 129, 130
Beginning Professional Salaries (BPS), 121, 129, 130

Blake, Kristen, 141
Bland, Les, 118–19
Boston College, 190
Boyer, Susan A., 101, 109
Brewer, Julie, xi, 24, 32–34, 36, 103, 107–8, 166, 198–200
Bright, Kawanna, 88
Bureau of Labor Statistics, xvii
Burris, Sidney, 198
Byke, Suzanne, 9

C&RL News, 15, 200
Campbell, Damon, 85, 88, 117
Canadian Association of College and Research Libraries (CARL), 124
Canadian Health Libraries Association, 124
Canadian Library Association, 36, 124
Cantor, Nancy, 62
Caribbean Court of Justice, 175
Cawthorne, Edythe O., 150
Cawthorne, Jon E., xi
Cawthorne, Micah, 151
Census Bureau, xvi, 115, 181
Chenault, John, 49–50
Chesapeake Information and Research Library Alliance, 7
Chinese American Librarians Association, 18, 54, 67, 125
Chronicle of Higher Education, 183
Chung, Hyun-Duck, 138–41
Civilian Complaint Review Board (CCRB), 189–90, 197
Cogell, Raquel, 200
Collins, Shantrie, 85, 117
Communities of practice, 138–42, 207
Conference of Newer Law Librarians (CONELL), 174
Cornell University, 122, 130, 190, 192–93; Libraries Fellows Program, 193; Olin Library, 190
Coustaut, Carmen, 197
Cricket in the Court of Akbar, 197, 201
Cunningham, William D., 150

Dahl, David, 13
Daniels, Carrie, 51
Davis, Denise M., 92–93

Dawes, Trevor, 200
Dawson, Patrick José, xi
Diversity in Libraries: Academic Residency Programs, xi, xii, xvi, 8, 56, 157, 201, 205
De Long, Kathleen, xi
Delaware Library Association, 166
Delaware Water Gap, 190
DeLong, David, xviii
Detroit Public Library, 150
Disclafani, Carrie Bertling, 13
Diversity Librarians' Network (website), 85
Dorjee, Geshe Thupten, 198
Dreyfus model of skills acquisition, 101
Duke University Libraries, 192

E-learning, 7, 138–39
EAD. *See* Encoded Archival Description
Easun, Sue, 201
Edward Bennett Williams Law Library, 171, 174. *See also* Georgetown University
Emerging Leaders program. *See* American Library Association
Employment Report, 116, 132
Encoded Archival Description, 64
Equal Employment Opportunity law, 196
Ethnic and Multicultural Information Exchange Round Table (EMIERT), 125
Eugene Garfield Residency in Science Librarianship (University of Pennsylvania), 3
Experiential Learning, 97–98. *See also* Preceptor, models

Facebook, 117
Federal Depository Library Program (FDLP), 195
Ferris, Kathlene, 160
Foreign, Comparative and International Law Special Interest Section, 175

Gay, Lesbian, Bisexual, and Transgendered Round Table (GLBTRT), 125
Georgetown University, 107, 174; Law Center, 174; Law Library, 171–78; Law Library Resident Program, 3, 171–73, 177–78; Law Library Scholarly Writing Committee, 177

Gherman, Paul, xv
Global Experience Specialists (GES), 191
Goode, Colleen J., 94
Government Documents Round Table (GODORT), 124
Gray, LaVerne, 86
Gruwell, Cindy, xi, xii, xvi, 15, 201

Hall, Tracy D., 92–93
Hall-Ellis, Sylvia, 200
Haring, Marilyn J., 7, 68
Harris, Fred, 160
Harris Interactive, 18
Harris, Ladonna, 160
Henderson, Cynthia L., 34, 36
Henderson, Martha, 183–86
Hepburn, Peter, 31
Higher Education Act Title II-B, 182, 187
Holt, Rachel, 93
Hurricane Katrina, 191
Hurricane Rita, 191

In Our Own Voices: The Changing Face of Librarianship, 172
Intellectual Freedom Round Table (IFRT), 124
International Federation of Library Associations (IFLA), 124
International Relations Round Table (IRRT), 124
International Society of Philosophical Inquiry, 125
Intersection Book Fund, 58
Institute for Museum and Library Services (IMLS), 7
Institutional Review Board (IRB), 36, 103, 117
IRDW. *See* Association of Research Libraries

Jackson, Marguerite, 108
Jackson, Miles, 150
John Wolff International and Comparative Law Library, 171, 174. *See also* Georgetown University
Johnson & Johnson, 182
Johnson, Katherine Burger, 53
Johnson, Lyndon B., 195
Joint Conference of Librarians of Color, 67, 166–67

Josey, E. J., 8, 147, 150, 205

Keally, Jill, 206
Kelly, Michael, 160
Kent State University, 55, 183
Kertis, Margo, 94, 97
KHSL. *See* University of Louisville Kornhauser Health Sciences Library
Knowledge River, 5, 182
Knowles, Malcolm, 96, 109
Kresk, Cathleen A., 93
Kress Fellowship in Art Librarianship (Yale University), 8
Krozek, Charles, 101
Kunzman, Lucy, 101

Lanier, Dan, 34, 36
Laning, Melissa, 51
Lave, Jean, 138
Law Librarians Society of Washington, D.C. (LLSDC), 174
Law Library Journal, 175
Leadership and Self-Deception, 148
Libraries Unlimited, 201
Library and Information Technology Association (LITA), 124
Library Association of Alberta, 124
Library Instruction Round Table (LIRT), 124
Library Journal, 182
Library Leadership and Management Association (LLAMA), 124; Diversity Officers Discussion Group, 18, 199; Leadership Development Committee, 199
Library of Congress, xv, 34, 175, 191
Littletree, Sandy, 138–39, 141
Love Guru, 198
Lowe-Wincentsen, Dawn, 9
Luckenbill, Laurence, 195

MacDonald, Patty, 13
Mack, Thura, 85
Mandala, 197–99, 201
Map and Geography Round Table (MAGERT), 124
Margaret Ellen Kalp Fellowship (UNC), 190
Marquette University, 3

Mary P. Key Diversity Residency (Ohio State University Libraries), 4, 205
Maxwell, Margaret, 183
MENSA Education and Research Foundation Scholarship, 190
Mazure, Emily, 141
Mendelson, Andrew, 197–98
Mentoring, xvii, 2, 4, 6, 7–9, 13, 15, 32, 52–53, 63, 65–66, 68–71, 84–85, 88, 106, 108, 127, 151, 182, 186–87
Miami University (OH), 122–23, 130
Minnesota Institute, xvii, 84, 109, 167, 168, 201
Minnesota Institute for Early Career Librarians from Traditionally Underrepresented Groups, xvii, 84, 109, 139, 167, 168, 201. *See also* Minnesota Institute
MNIECL. *See* Minnesota Institute for Early Career Librarians from Traditionally Underrepresented Groups
Modic, Mary Beth, 102
Moffitt-Wolf, Ann, 94
Morning News, 198
Murray, Marilyn Kettering, 92, 101
My SA News, 181

National Archives and Records Administration, 191
National Center for Education Statistics, 181
National Center for Science Education, xvi, 115
National Conference on Diversity in Academic Libraries (Conference), 62
National Diversity in Libraries Conference (Conference), 200–1
National Diversity in Libraries' Post-Conference on Residency Programs (Conference), 117, 200
National Historical Publications and Records Commission, 160
National Library of Medicine, xv, 1, 5, 26, 34, 107
National Public Radio, 191
Neely, Teresa, 158, 160, 182
Neumann, Julie A., 108
New Orleans Metropolitan Convention Bureau, 191

New Members Round Table. *See* American Library Association
New York City Department of Public Safety, 189
New Yorker, 157
Nicol, Pam, 97–98, 108
Nolan, Deborah A., 12, 200
North Carolina State University, 6, 193; Libraries, 88; Libraries Fellows Program, 3, 130, 138
Northeastern University, 186
Northern Illinois University, 182, 186
Northwest Arkansas Times, 198
Notre Dame, 3, 122
NRP. *See* Nursing residencies
Nursing residencies, 34, 91, 92, 104. *See also* Nursing Residency Program (NRP)
Nursing Residency Program (NRP), 91, 96, 106

Oates, Evangela, 157–58, 161, 163
Oermann, Marilyn H., 94
Offord, Jerome, 172, 199–200
Ohio State University, xv, 3, 55, 147; Libraries, 4, 146
One-Minute Preceptor (OMP), 96–97, 108. *See also* Preceptors, models
Orleans Parish Medical Society Library, xv
Party Girl, 156
Pauline A. Young Residency (University of Delaware Library), 4, 165
Perez, Megan, xi, xii, 7, 33, 34, 117
Perry, Stephen, 191
Peterson, Lorna, 182
Poche, Gene, 191
Porter, Toccara, 54–55, 58–59
Posey, Parker, 156
Preceptors, xi, xvi, 207; and burnout, 92, 94, 97–99, 101–2; and experiential learning, 97–98, 108; and recruitment and retention, 91, 99, 103; definition of, xvi, 91; demand for, 95; development of, 95, 97–98, 100–1, 103; evaluation of, 98; history of, 92, 94, 107; learning needs of, 94, 96; models, 92, 94, 95–103, 107; recognition of, 99; role of, 94, 97–98, 100–2; selection of, 94–95, 97–98, 102; support of, 95, 99–101, 103; teaching tools, 95; use of, 92, 94, 100

Preceptor Incentive Program (PIP), 95–96. *See also* Preceptors, models
Prince Georges' County public Library, 150
Proposition 209, 186
Puente, Mark, 86, 88
Purdue University, xi, 68, 130, 191; Black Caucus of faculty and staff, 62; Center for Instructional Excellence, 67; Copyright Office, 64; Libraries, 62, 63, 66, 68, 69, 172; Libraries Advancement Office, 64; Libraries Diversity Fellowship, 7, 61, 62, 63, 66, 68, 71, 72; mentoring program, 68
PUL. *See* Purdue University, Libraries

Rader, Hannelore, 48
Raftus, Deborah, 190
Raisch, Marylin, 175
Recruitment, 3, 6–7, 15, 18, 34–36, 44, 51, 54, 82, 85, 87, 129, 131, 169, 177, 182, 184, 187, 195; and diversity, 18, 132; and minorities, 3–4, 166; and retention, xv, xvi, 2, 4–5, 34, 92–93, 101, 132, 182, 191; challenges, xviii, xix; for libraries, xii, 32–35, 40, 42–43, 93, 132; for residency programs, 5, 15–16; initiatives, xix, 5; processes, 8, 26, 51; programs, xvii, xviii; strategies, xv, 33, 87;
Reference & User Services Association (RUSA), 124
Reference Services Review, 85
Reflective practice, 96, 99, 102, 109, 137
REFORMA, 67, 124, 182
Regents of the University of California v. Bakke, 186
Residency Working Group (RWG). *See* Association of Research Libraries
Retirement, xvii, xviii, xix, 32, 55, 92, 150, 194; and baby boomers, xvii, xix, 32–33, 95. *See also* Baby boomers
Reynolds, Latisha, 51–52, 54
Robinson, Charles, 199
Roosevelt, Theodore, 195
Rutgers University Libraries Internship/Residency Program, 3

Sampson, Sara, 177
Samuel H. Kress Foundation, 8
San Diego Film Festival, 198
San Diego State University, 149
Sawyer, Raymond, 185
Schloesser, Mary, 102
Schön, Donald, 96, 109
Schopenhauer, Arthur, 146
Scottish Legal History, 176
Seminar on the Acquisition of Latin American Library Materials (SALALM), 125
Simmons College, 36, 148, 169; Managerial Leadership in Information Professions program, 148
Smithsonian Institute, 191
Social Responsibilities Round Table (SRRT), 124, 200
Society of American Archivists (SAA), 167
Society of Photographic Education, 125
South Asian Film Festival, 198
Southwestern University, 189
Special Libraries Association (SLA), 124
Spectrum. *See* American Library Association
Spectrum of the Future (Conference), 57
Speers, Alice T., 91, 94, 108–9
Sprinkle-Hamlin, Sylvia, 150
Sri Mahendra Bhatt Music and Dance Competition, 197
St. Cloud State University, 201
Star Trek V: The Final Frontier, 195
State University of New York (SUNY) at Buffalo, 130
Statistical Report (ALISE), xvi, 93, 115–16, 132
Stohr, Sarah, 206
Strock, Adrienne L., 93
Strzyzewski, Nancy, 91, 94, 108–9
Sullivan, Peggy, 150

Temple University, 186
Tennessee Valley Authority libraries, xv
Texas A&M University, 186
Time Warner Trade Publishing, 190
Toccara Porter Library Scholarship, 57
Tomlinson, Carissa, 13
Toossi, Mitra, xviii

Towson University, xi, 11–13, 15–16, 20, 24–27, 200; Albert S. Cook Library, 11, 13–14, 18, 24; Diversity Action Committee, 25; Reflective Process for Diversity initiative, 12
Trejo, Arnulfo, 182
Trumpeter, Margo, xv
Tyson, John C., 150

U.S. Department of Education, 181
United Kingdom Privy Council, 175
United Nations Development Program, 172
University of Alberta, 32, 120, 122; internship program, 32, 35, 37; Libraries, 32
University of Arizona, 182–84; Graduate Library Institute for Spanish-Speaking Americans, 182; Graduate Library School, 182
University of Arkansas, 103, 107, 117, 194–95, 197–98, 200–1, 203; David Pryor Center, 194; Diversity Collection Enhancement Grant, 197; Fulbright College of Arts and Sciences, 198; Librarian-In-Residence program, 193–94, 203, 205; Libraries, 193; Libraries Diversity Officer, 196–99; Students for a Free Tibet, 198
University of Buffalo, 182
University of Denver, Morgridge College of Education, 200
University of Calgary, 173
University of California at Irvine, 185
University of California at Los Angeles, Library Science Program, 184
University of California at San Diego Medical Center, 95
University of California at Santa Barbara (UCSB), 3, 183–87, 205
University of California at Santa Cruz, 185
University of Delaware, 3, 26, 198; Library, 4, 166; residency program, 6, 165
University of Illinois at Chicago, 3, 31, 34
University of Iowa, 3, 16, 86
University of Kentucky, 47, 49–50, 156, 159; School of Library and Information Science, 48–50
University of Louisville, xi, 47, 48, 50, 55, 56, 57, 58, 59; Archives and Records Center, 48, 57; diversity program and initiatives, 50; Ekstrom Library, 48, 50; Kornhauser Health Sciences Library, 49–50; librarians, 48, 53; Libraries 48–49, 52, 55, 58–59; Libraries internship program, 49–50; Office of Lesbian, Gay, Bisexual, and Transgender Services, 58; Pan African Studies Department, 50
University of Maryland, xii
University of Michigan Research Library Residency Program, 3, 7, 86
University of Michigan School of Information, xvi, 116
University of Minnesota, 3, 122, 201; libraries, 109
University of New Brunswick, 32, 35, 37
University of New Mexico, 3, 156, 158, 173, 183–84; Center for Southwest Research, 160; Latin American and Iberian Studies Program, 184; Zimmerman Library, 157–62, 182–83
University of North Carolina at Chapel Hill, Carolina Academic Library Associate, 190; School of Information Science, 190
University of Oregon, 149
University of Pennsylvania, Eugene Garfield Residency in Science Librarianship, 3
University of Pittsburgh, 120
University of Tennessee, Knoxville, xi, 81, 177, 206; Council for Diversity and Interculturalism, 88; Cultural Development Grant, 85; Diversity Librarians' Network, 85; Diversity Resident Librarian Program, 85, 205; librarians, 84; Libraries, 5, 81, 82, 88; Minority Librarian Residency Program, 82
University of the District of Columbia, David A. Clarke School of Law Library, 178
University of Toronto, 172
University of Washington, 85, 190
University of Winnipeg, 32, 35, 37
University System of Maryland, 11

Vanderbilt University, Eskind Biomedical Library, 3, 107
Versed, 86
Vermont Nurse Internship Program (VNIP), 100–1, 109. *See also* Preceptors, models

Walter, Scott, 85
Wedgeworth, Robert, 150
Wenger, Etienne, 138, 142
Wheatley, Meg, 148

Wheeler, Maurice, 150
Winston, Mark, 33, 103, 107
William Beaumont Hospital, 108
Williams, Carolyn J., 94

Yale University, Haas Family Arts Library, 8
Yonge, Olive, 99–100, 109
Young, Courtney L., xii
Young, Melisa, 97–98, 108

Ziolkowski, Linda D., 91, 94, 108–9

About the Editors and Contributors

JULIE BREWER is Coordinator, Personnel and Staff Development, University of Delaware Library. She participated in the 1987–1989 residency program at the University of Colorado—Denver Auraria Library and currently serves as coordinator of the Pauline A. Young Residency Program at the University of Delaware Library.

DAMON CAMPBELL is the Acquisitions Librarian for the Florida Coastal School of Law Library. He participated in the University of Tennessee Libraries' Diversity Residency program from 2007 to 2009 and was a participant in the 2008 Minnesota Institute for Early Career Librarians from Traditionally Underrepresented Groups.

JON E. CAWTHORNE is the Interim Dean of Library and Information Access at San Diego State University. Active in the American Library Association, he chaired the Spectrum Advisory Committee and regularly participates in their leadership programs. He attended the UCLA Senior Fellows and the Frye Leadership Institutes and currently is pursuing a graduate degree in Managerial Leadership in the Information Professions at Simmons University. Jon was the Minority Library Intern at Ohio State University, 1993–1995.

JOHN CHENAULT is an Assistant Professor at the Kornhauser Health Sciences Library on the University of Louisville Medical Campus and a lecturer in the Department of Pan African Studies in the College of Arts and Sciences. He participated in the University of Louisville Library Internship Program, 2003–2006.

HYUN-DUCK CHUNG is the Librarian for Management and Entrepreneurship at North Carolina State University (NCSU) Libraries in Raleigh, North Carolina. She was a part of the 2007–2009 class of NCSU Libraries Fellows, a participant in the 2008 Minnesota Institute for Early Career Librarians from Traditionally Underrepresented Groups, and a Diversity Scholar in the Association of Research Libraries' Initiative to Recruit a Diverse Workforce from 2006–2008. Hyun-Duck also received an ACRL National Conference Librarian Scholarship to attend ACRL's 14th National Conference in Seattle, Washington, and a $5,000 Emerald Research Grant from the Business Reference & Services Section of the American Library Association.

RAQUEL VON COGELL was Yale University Library's first Librarian-in-Residence from 1995 through 1997. She was a participant in the 1998 Minnesota Institute for Early Career Librarians from Traditionally Underrepresented Groups, and she coedited *Diversity in Libraries: Academic Residency Programs*, published in 2001.

SHANTRIE COLLINS is the Systems Librarian for the Maxwell-Gunter Air Force Base Library. Ms. Collins manages day-to-day operations for two branch libraries and participated in the University of Tennessee Libraries Diversity Residency Program from 2007 through 2009. She also received a Spectrum Scholarship in 2006, participated in the 2008 Minnesota Institute for Early Career Librarians from Traditionally Underrepresented Groups, and, also in 2006, was awarded an Academic Librarians for Tomorrow's Academic Researchers (ALSTARS) Fellowship from the University of South Florida.

CAROLINE DANIELS is the Acting Director of the University of Louisville Archives and Records Center. She participated in the redesign of the University of Louisville Libraries' Diversity Residency Program.

PATRICK JOSÉ DAWSON is Dean of Libraries at Northern Illinois University. He participated in the University of California at Santa Barbara Minority Internship Program in 1985–1986.

KATHLEEN DE LONG is Associate University Librarian at the University of Alberta Libraries and coordinates the Academic Library Internship Program. She is currently a doctoral candidate at Simmons University Graduate School of Library and Information Science.

CARRIE BERTLING DISCLAFANI is a Reference and Instruction Librarian for Emerging Technologies at Towson University and the library liaison to Towson's Visual Arts and Women's Studies departments. She serves as mentor to Towson's first residency librarian.

CINDY ANN GRUWELL is Associate Professor, Information Literacy Librarian, and Coordinator of Instruction, St. Cloud State University, Minnesota. She participated in the University of Minnesota Libraries' Affirmative Action Residency Program, 1995–1997, and is currently a member of the organizing committee for the Minnesota Institute for Early Career Librarians from Traditionally Underrepresented Groups.

ASHER JACKSON received a B.A. from the University of California, Berkeley, and an M.S. in Library and Information Science from Simmons College. He was chosen as the 2006–2008 Pauline A. Young Resident at the University of Delaware, where he worked in both the special collections and cataloging departments. During his time there, he was also selected to attend the Minnesota Institute for Early Career Librarians from Traditionally Underrepresented Groups. In 2008, he was awarded an ALA Spectrum Doctoral Fellowship. He is currently a Ph.D. student at the Graduate School of Library and Information Science at Simmons College.

JILL KEALLY is Executive Associate Dean at the University of Tennessee Libraries in Knoxville. She participated in the design of the diversity librarian residency program at Tennessee and served as program coordinator for the 2003–2005 and 2005–2007 resident groups.

SANDRA LITTLETREE is the Program Manager for Knowledge River at the School of Information Resources and Library Science, University of Arizona. She was a Fellow at North Carolina State University Libraries, 2007–2009; a Spectrum Scholar in 2005–2006; and a participant in the 2008 Minnesota Institute for Early Career Librarians from Traditionally Underrepresented Groups.

PATRICIA A. MACDONALD is the Associate University Librarian for Administrative Services at Towson University and coordinates the Towson Residency Librarian Program.

About the Editors and Contributors

SCOTT MANDERNACK is Head of Research and Instructional Services in the Raynor Memorial Libraries at Marquette University where he coordinates reference and research services, information literacy instruction, library diversity services, and the libraries' Residency Program. He formerly served as Head of the Undergraduate Library and Codirector of the Libraries' Diversity Fellowship Program at Purdue University.

YASMIN MORAIS is Cataloging Librarian in the Charles N. & Hilda H. M. Mason Law Library, University of the District of Columbia. She was Resident Librarian at the Georgetown Law Library, 2007–2009, and a participant in the 2005–2007 ARL Initiative to Recruit a Diverse Workforce program. She also received an E. J. Josey Scholarship in 2005 and an ACRL Student Scholarship to attend ACRL's 13th National Conference in Baltimore, Maryland.

DEBORAH A. NOLAN is the University Librarian at Towson University. She established the Towson University Residency Librarian Program.

MEGAN ZOE PEREZ is a visiting assistant professor at the University of Arkansas Libraries. He was the first Librarian-In-Residence at the University Libraries from 2007 through 2010, and participated in the 2008 Minnesota Institute for Early Career Librarians from Traditionally Underrepresented Groups. Megan was also a Spectrum Scholar in 2005–2006, a participant in the 2005–2007 ARL Initiative to Recruit a Diverse Workforce program, and a recipient of the Margaret Ellen Kalp Fellowship award from the University of North Carolina at Chapel Hill.

TOCCARA PORTER is the 2008–2010 Diversity Residency Librarian at the University of Louisville. She received her MLIS from Kent State University in 2007.

LATISHA REYNOLDS is the Humanities and Social Sciences Librarian at the University of Louisville's Ekstrom Library, and she participated in the redesign of the Libraries' Diversity Residency Program. Latisha was also a participant in the 2008 Minnesota Institute for Early Career Librarians from Traditionally Underrepresented Groups, and the University of Louisville Library Internship Program from 2003 to 2006.

REBECCA A. RICHARDSON is the Digital Resources Librarian for Purdue University Libraries. She codirected the 2006–2008 Purdue University Libraries Diversity Fellowship Program.

SARAH STOHR is the Distance Services Librarian at the University of New Mexico and Western Governors University. She participated in the Residency Program at the University of New Mexico from 2006 to 2008 and was a member of the 2008 American Library Association Emerging Leaders cohort.

CARISSA TOMLINSON is a Reference and Instruction Librarian for Emerging Technologies at Towson University and a library liaison to Towson's College of Health Professions. She served on the search committee for the first residency librarian at Towson.